Comments on the original The

As a music teacher, I have all my child[...]
little book. The basics of music theory [...]
clearly, with accompanying short exerc[...]

Dr T J Worrall

I'm a music teacher, and can honestly say this series of books is by far the most concise and fun to work with when helping kids. Adults also enjoy them.

C J Gascoine

Very thorough and approachable theory practice book for young students age 7 upwards.

Susan A. Harris

Theory can be a barrier for some young students but this book is set out well, it's easy to read and understand, and has logical progression. Highly recommended.

Steve Riches

I might at last be able to learn my theory and I am an old age pensioner learning to play the piano.

Violet

Very good book that puts things very simply. I was recommended this by my piano teacher even though I am an adult learner as it covers all the technical points very progressively.

Amazon Customer

Music Theory is Fun Book 1
978-1-987926-09-5
Treble clef, bass clef, notes and letter names. Time names and values. Dotted notes, tied notes and rests. Accidentals, tones and semitones. Key signatures and scales (C, G, D & F major). Degrees of the scale, intervals and tonic triads. Time signatures and bar-lines. Writing music and answering rhythms. Puzzles, quizzes and ten one-page tests. Musical terms dictionary and list of signs.

Music Theory is Fun Book 2
978-1-987926-10-1

Major key signatures to 3 sharps & flats. Minor keys to 1 sharp & flat. Degrees of the scale and intervals. Tonic triads. Keyboard, tones and semitones. Time signatures. Grouping notes and rests, triplets. Two ledger lines below and above the staves. Writing four-bar rhythms. Puzzles, quizzes and ten one-page tests. Musical terms and signs.

Music Theory is Fun Book 3
978-1-987926-11-8
Major & minor key signatures 4 sharps or flats. Harmonic and melodic minor scales. Degrees of the scale, intervals, tonic triads. Simple and compound time signatures. Grouping notes & rests. Transposition at the octave. More than two ledger lines. Writing four-bar rhythms, anacrusis. Phrases. Puzzles, quizzes and ten one-page tests. Musical terms & signs.

Music Theory is Fun Book 4
978-1-987926-12-5
Key signatures to 5 sharps or flats. Alto clef. Chromatic scale, double sharps & flats. Technical names of notes in the diatonic scale. Simple & compound time, duple, triple, quadruple. Primary triads, tonic, subdominant & dominant. Diatonic intervals up to an octave. Ornaments. Four-bar rhythms and rhythms to words. Orchestral instruments and their clefs. Puzzles, quizzes and ten one-page tests. Musical terms & signs including French.

Music Theory is Fun Book 5
978-1-987926-13-2
Key signatures to 7 sharps or flats. Tenor clef and scales. Compound intervals: major, minor, perfect, diminished & augmented. Irregular time signatures, quintuple & septuple. Tonic, super-tonic, subdominant & dominant chords. Writing at concert pitch. Short & open score. Orchestral instruments. Composing a melody. Perfect, imperfect & plagal cadences. Puzzles, quizzes and ten one-page tests. Musical terms and signs including French and German.

Music Theory is Fun – A Handy Reference
978-1-987926-10-1
A concise reference to all the rudiments of music covered by the above five Music Theory is Fun books.

MUSIC THEORY IS FUN
Books 1 to 5
OMNIBUS

Maureen Cox

Copyright © Mimast Inc 2018

All rights reserved.

No part of this publication may be reproduced, stored in a retrieval system, or transmitted in any form or by any means, electronic, mechanical, photocopying, recording or otherwise, without the prior written permission of the Publishers.

Canadian ISBN 978-1-987926-15-6

The rights of Maureen Cox to be identified as the author of this Work have been asserted by her in accordance with the Copyright, Designs and Patents Act 1988.

All enquiries regarding this paperback omnibus edition to:

Mimast Inc
email: mimast.inc@gmail.com

If you want to play an instrument, sing well or just improve your listening, you need to read music and understand theory.

These five books take you through the theory of music in a simple, straightforward way. There are plenty of fun illustrations and a variety of activities to help you along.

At the back of each book there are puzzles, quizzes and ten one-page tests composed of questions you could meet in an exam. At the end of this omnibus edition there is a dictionary of musical terms, a collection of common alternative terms and a list of signs and symbols for easy reference.

With my help you can master and enjoy the theory of music. With this book you can discover that Theory is Fun.

Maureen Cox

Acknowledgements

I am grateful to the many Professional Private Music Teachers and Members of the Incorporated Society of Musicians who used Theory is Fun with their pupils and to Christina Bourne, Brenda Harris, Alison Hogg, Judith Holmes, Ann Leggett and Marion Martin for their helpful suggestions. I am especially grateful to Alison Hounsome for her insightful comments and helpful recommendations in the preparation of this revised edition.

A word about this omnibus edition

Using the previous editions of my Theory is Fun books, more than a half million people, young and not so young, mostly in the UK, had fun learning music theory. This omnibus edition contains the five Music Theory is Fun books that have been revised and extended to include students in other countries such as America and Canada where, for example, a bar is a measure, a minim is a half note and a tone is a whole step. Common alternatives terms and a full dictionary of musical terms and signs are listed at the back of the book.

These books cover the basic rudiments of theory required by the various Boards and Colleges including the Associated Board of the Royal Schools of Music, Trinity College London, the Music Examinations Boards of Australia and New Zealand and the Royal Conservatory of Canada.

Any errors are entirely my responsibility. Should there be any in this edition, I would be most grateful for them to be drawn to my attention so that they may be corrected in a future edition.

Maureen Cox

CONTENTS
Book 1

Topic	page
Treble Clef & Letter Names	6
Bass Clef & Letter Names	12
Time Names & Note Values	20
The note pyramid	22
Dotted Notes	26
Tied Notes	30
Rests	32
Accidentals	34
sharp	34
flat	35
natural	36
Tones & Semitones	37
Key Signatures and Scales	39
Degrees of the Scale	45
Intervals	46
melodic	47
harmonic	48
Tonic Triads	49
Time Signatures	52
Writing Your Own Music	56
Answering Rhythms	58
Puzzles, Quizzes and Tests	60
Musical Terms and Signs	79

THE TREBLE CLEF

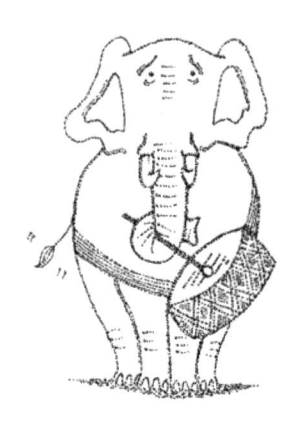

This is a treble clef.

Can you finish these treble clefs?

Now you draw four treble clefs.

Book 1 page 6

LETTER NAMES

The notes **E G B D F** sit on the lines.

E G B D F

Elephant **G**eorge **B**eats **D**rum **F**ast

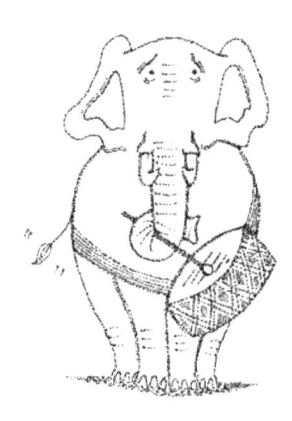

The notes **F A C E** sit in the spaces.

F A C E

Think of a happy face and you will remember the notes **F A C E**

Book 1 page 7

Test yourself

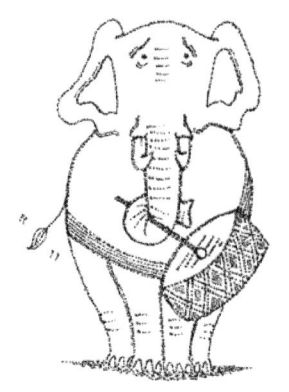

Show Elephant George how well you know the notes in the treble clef.

Write the letter name on the line under the note. Remember the happy face.

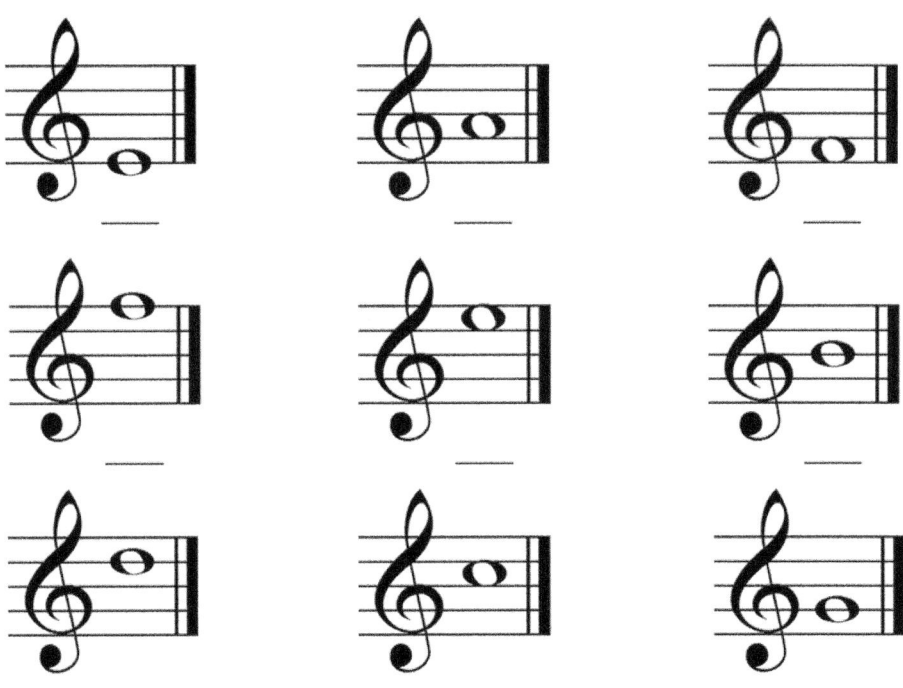

Count how many you had right. Put the number in the box.

Book 1 page 8

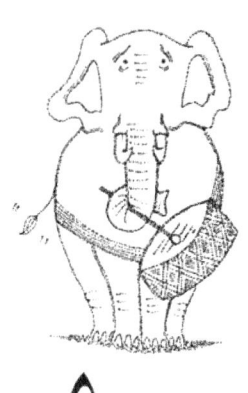

Draw the note 𝅝 on a line or in a space to match the letter name.

Each of these nine notes is in a different place on the stave.

F	B	D
F	G	E
A	C	E

Count how many you had right. Put the number in the box. □/9

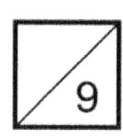

Book 1 page 9

The lost puppy

Fill in the letter names of the notes.

Tom looked into the water.

He saw his ___ ___ ___
looking back at him.

Suddenly he saw another ___ ___ ___ ___
next to his.

It was a puppy.
It looked lost.

"I wonder what ___ ___ ___ it is?" thought Tom.

Book 1 page 10

The puppy looked hungry.

Tom had a biscuit in his pocket.

Should he ___ ___ ___ ___ it?

Then Tom saw a boy. He was calling,

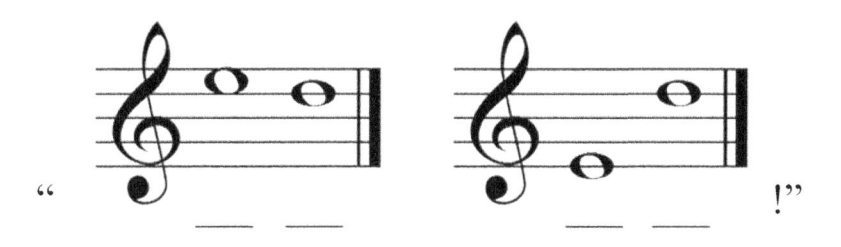

" ___ ___   ___ ___ !"

Tom was happy. The puppy was not lost any more.

THE BASS CLEF

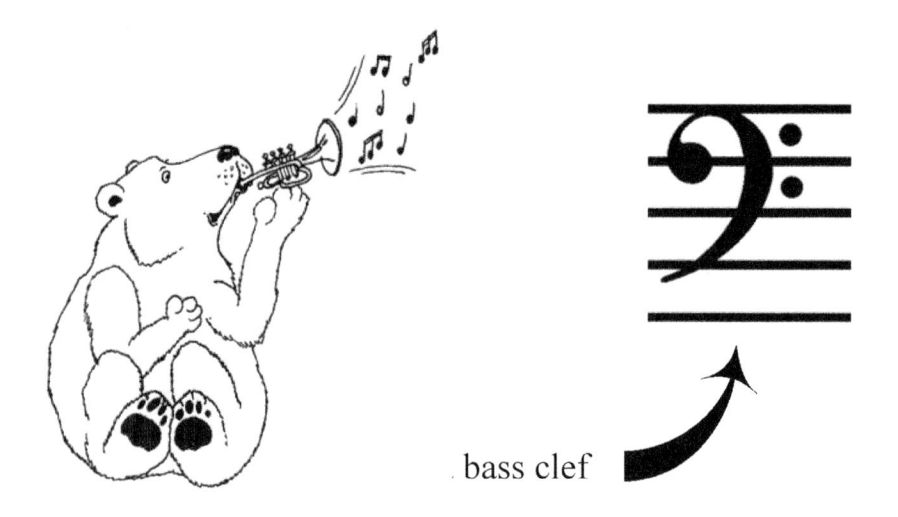

bass clef

Draw a bass clef in each space.

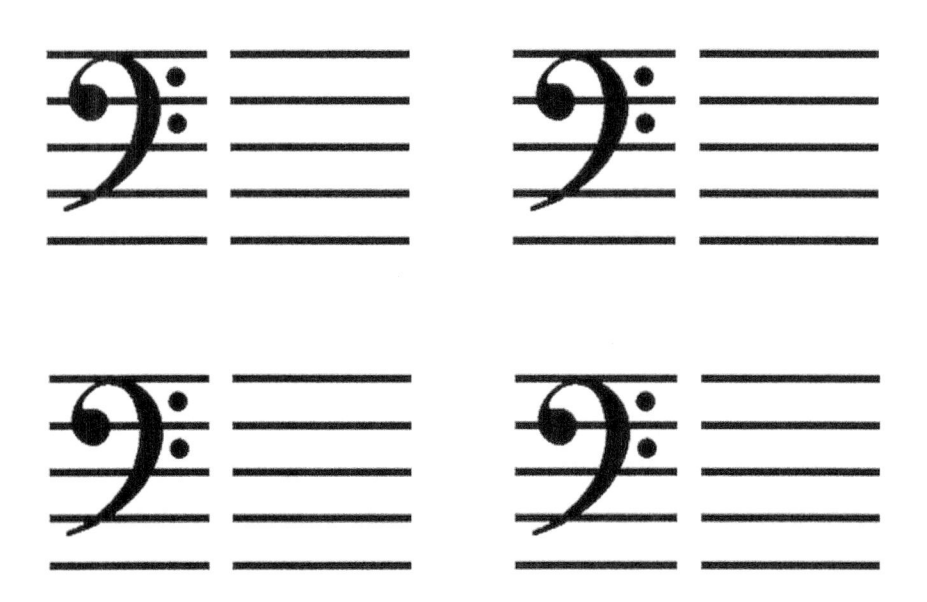

Book 1 page 12

LETTER NAMES

The notes **G B D F A** sit on the lines.

Georgina **B**ear **D**eserves **F**ood **A**lways.

The notes **A C E G** sit in the spaces.

All **C**ats **E**njoy **G**rieg

Book 1 page 13

Test yourself

Show Georgina Bear how well you know the bass clef notes. Name each of the nine notes.

Put the number in the box to show how many you had right.

Book 1 page 14

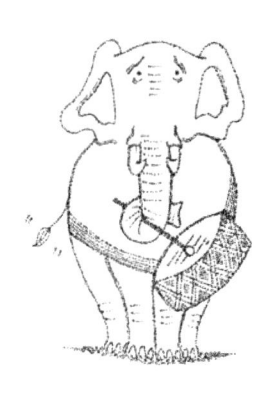

Draw the note 𝐨 on a line or in a space to match the letter name.

Each of these nine notes is in a different place on the stave.

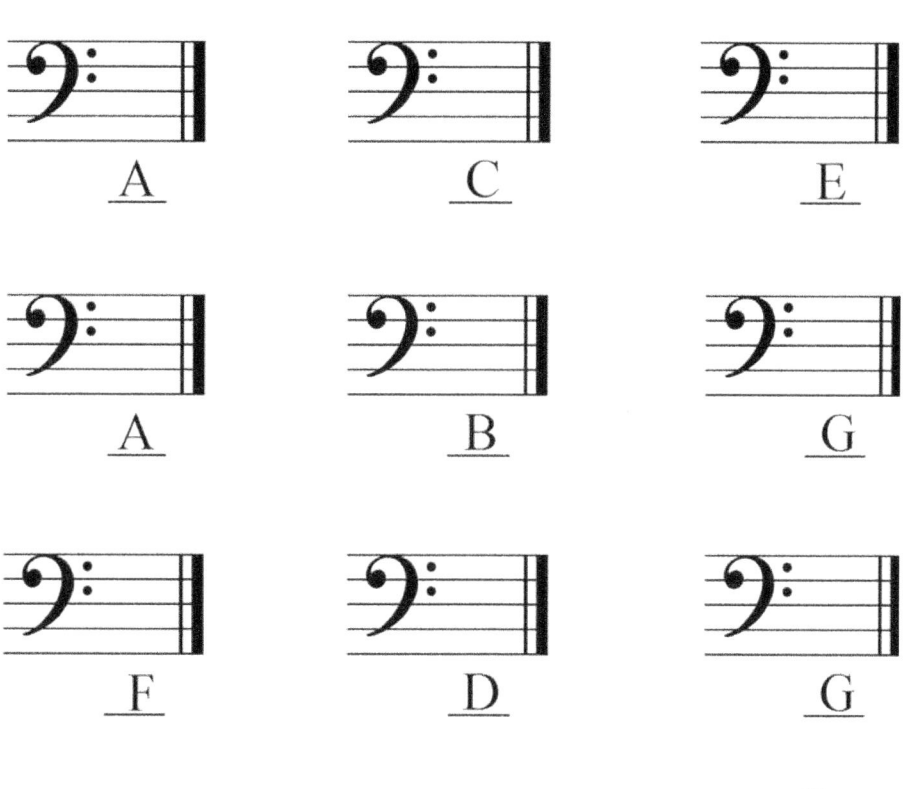

A   C   E

A   B   G

F   D   G

Count how many you had right.
Put the number in the box. /9

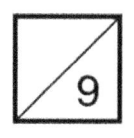

Book 1 page 15

Life on the farm

Fill in the letter names of the notes.

Early one morning a farmer took a __ __ __ of corn

and set out to

__ __ __ __ the chickens.

They were pleased to see him.

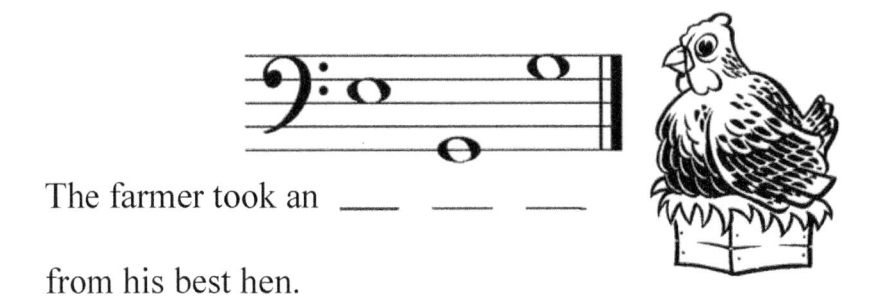

The farmer took an __ __ __

from his best hen.

Book 1 page 16

He showed it to his son ___ ___ ___

who was in the cowshed milking the cows.

"What a fine ___ ___ ___ ,"

said ___ ___ ___ .

Then the farmer went to the field to

look at a ___ ___ ___ ___ ___ ___ ___

to see if it was ready to cut for dinner.

Book 1 page 17

More notes

There are notes on the lines and in the spaces of the **stave** or **staff**. There are other notes that sit on top and underneath.

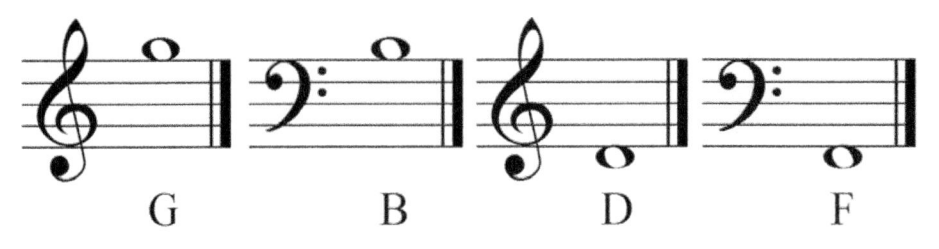

G   B   D   F

Ledger lines

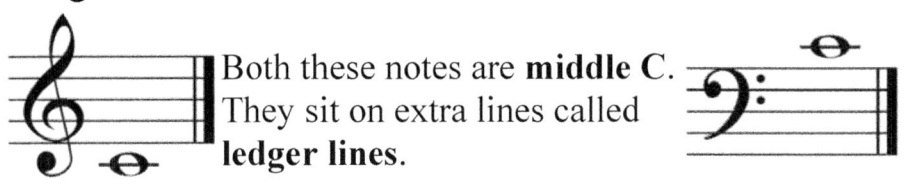

Both these notes are **middle C**. They sit on extra lines called **ledger lines**.

Test yourself

Put a treble clef or a bass clef in front of each note to make it say its correct name.

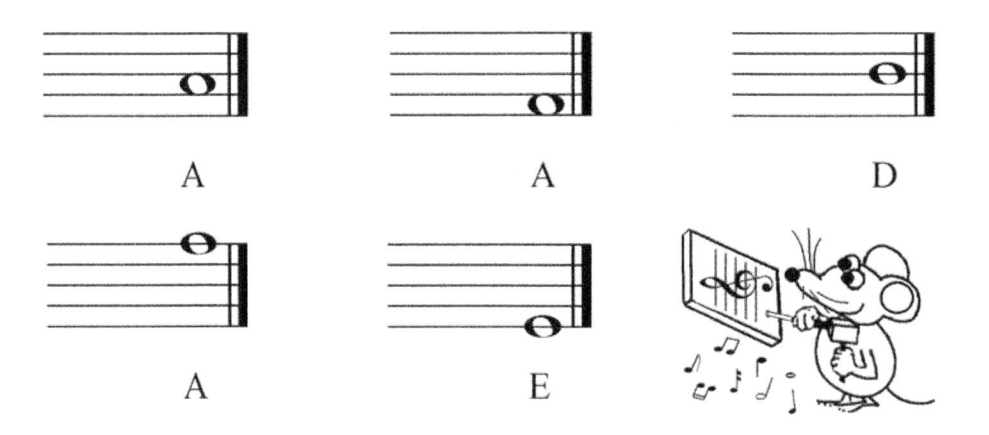

A   A   D

A   E

Book 1 page 18

C   D   B

F   G

B   C   F

C   G

Count how many you had right.
Put the number in the box. /15

Book 1 page 19

TIME NAMES & NOTE VALUES

You now know the names of all the notes and where they are on the **stave** or **staff**.

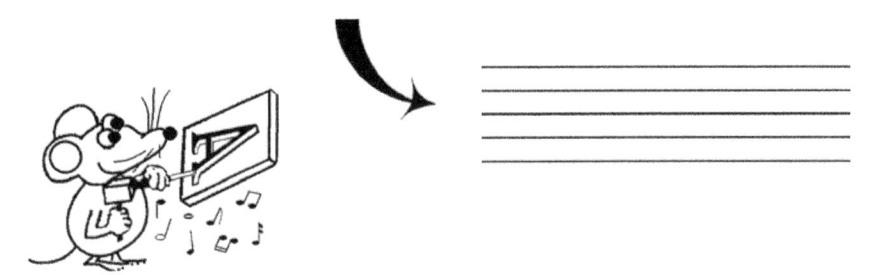

So far you have met only the **letter** names of the notes.

Notes also have **time** names.

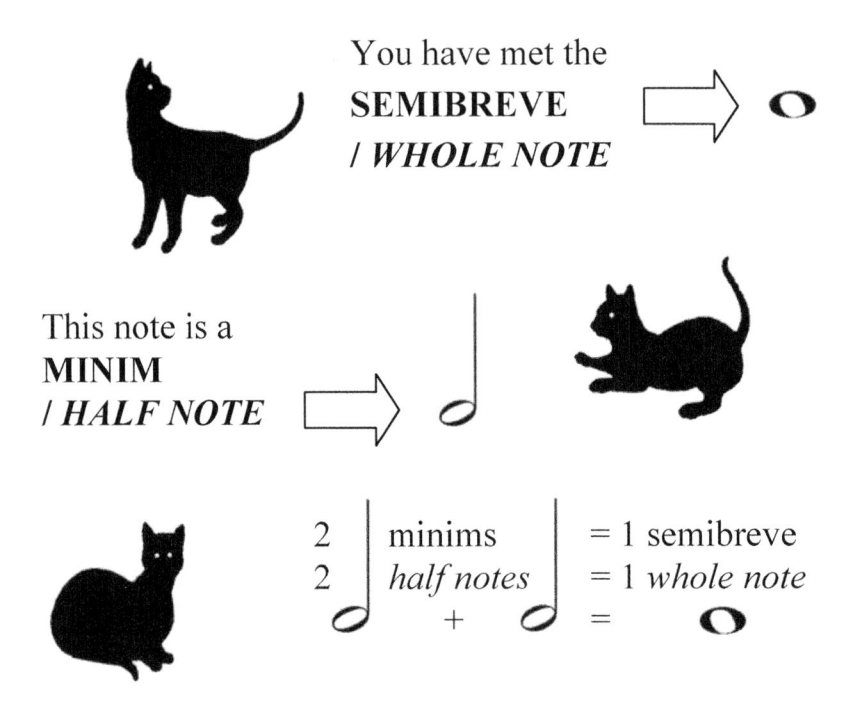

You have met the
SEMIBREVE
/ WHOLE NOTE

This note is a
MINIM
/ HALF NOTE

| 2 | minims | = 1 semibreve |
| 2 | half notes | = 1 whole note |

Book 1 page 20

This note is a
CROTCHET
/ *QUARTER NOTE* ⇒ ♩

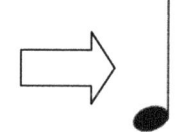

2 crotchets = 1 minim
2 *quarter notes* = 1 *half note*
♩ + ♩ = 𝅗𝅥

This note is a
QUAVER
/ *EIGHTH NOTE* ⇒ ♪

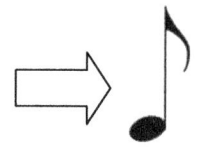

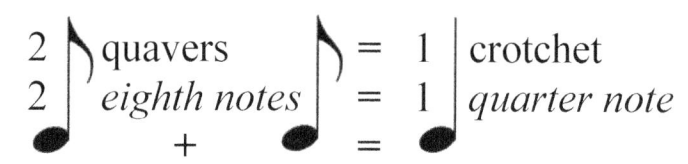

2 quavers = 1 crotchet
2 *eighth notes* = 1 *quarter note*
♪ + ♪ = ♩

This note is a
SEMIQUAVER
/ *SIXTEENTH NOTE* ⇒

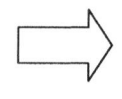

2 semiquavers = 1 quaver
2 *sixteenth notes* = 1 *eighth note*
𝅘𝅥𝅯 + 𝅘𝅥𝅯 = ♪

Notes worth less than a crotchet / *quarter note* can be joined together or **beamed**.

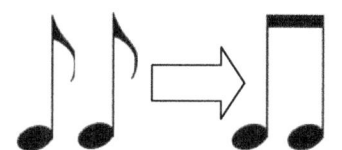

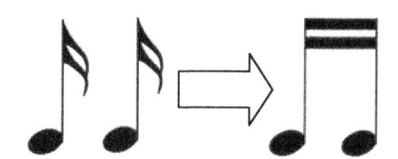

♪ ♪ ⇒ ♫   𝅘𝅥𝅯 𝅘𝅥𝅯 ⇒ 𝅘𝅥𝅰𝅘𝅥𝅰

The note pyramid

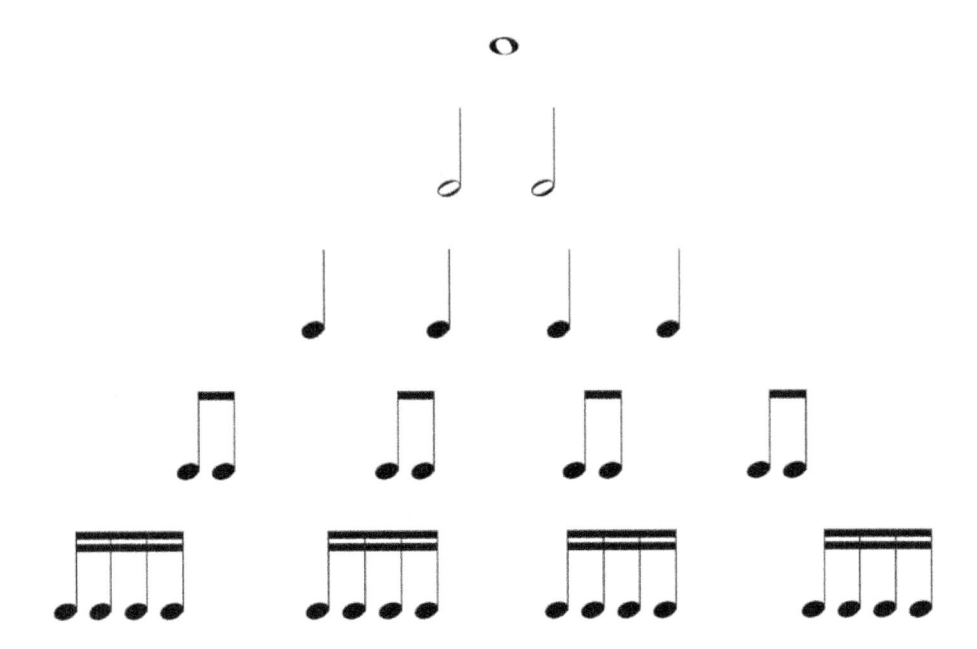

The note pyramid is very useful. You can see at a glance the values of the notes.

For example, you can see that a semibreve / *whole note* is worth two minims / *half notes* or sixteen semiquavers / *sixteenth notes*.

Book 1 page 22

Use the **note pyramid** to find the correct number.

A semibreve / *whole note* equals

☐   minims / *half notes*

☐   crotchets / *quarter notes*

☐   quavers / *eighth notes*

☐   semiquavers / *sixteenth notes*

A minim / *half note* equals

☐   crotchets / *quarter notes*

☐   quavers / *eighth notes*

☐   semiquavers / *sixteenth notes*

A crotchet / *quarter note* equals

☐   quavers / *eighth notes*

☐   semiquavers / *sixteenth notes*

A quaver / *eighth note* equals

☐   semiquavers / *sixteenth notes*

Book 1 page 23

Test your note values

How many

crotchets / *quarter notes* in a semibreve / *whole note*? ☐

semiquavers / *sixteenth notes* in a quaver / *eighth note*? ☐

quavers / *eighth notes* or in a crotchet / *quarter note*? ☐

minims / *half notes* in a semibreve / *whole note*? ☐

semiquavers / *sixteenth notes* in a crotchet / *quarter note*? ☐

quavers / *eighth notes* in a minim / *half note*? ☐

crotchets / *quarter notes* in a minim / *half note*? ☐

quavers / *eighth notes* in a semibreve / *whole note*? ☐

semiquavers / *sixteenth notes* in a minim / *half note*? ☐

semiquavers / *sixteenth notes* in a semibreve / *whole note*? ☐

How many did you get right?
Put the number in the box. ☐/10

Book 1 page 24

Where shall I put the stem?

The stems of notes are on the **left** when they go **down**.

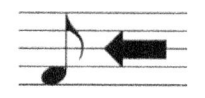

The stems are on the **right** when they go **up**.

If a note is written **above** the **middle line**, its stem goes **down**.

When a note is written **below** the **middle line**, its stem goes **up**.

If a note is written **on** the **middle line**, its stem can go **up** but often it goes **down**.

Draw stems for **crotchets** / *quarter notes* in the treble clef.

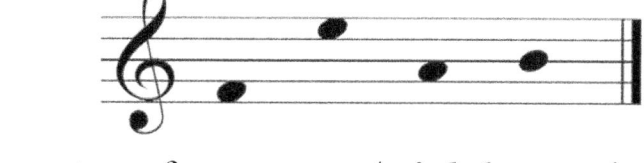

Draw stems for **quavers** / *eighth notes* in the bass clef..

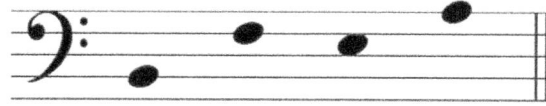

Book 1 page 25

DOTTED NOTES

A dot after a note is worth **half** the value of the note.

A dot is placed in the **same space** if a dotted note is **in a space**.

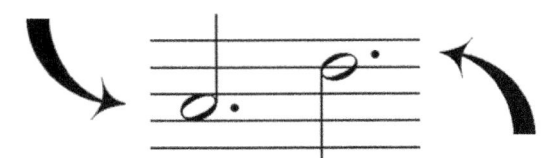

A dot is placed in the **space above** if a dotted note is **on a line**.

Book 1 page 26

Test yourself

Fill in the missing numbers.

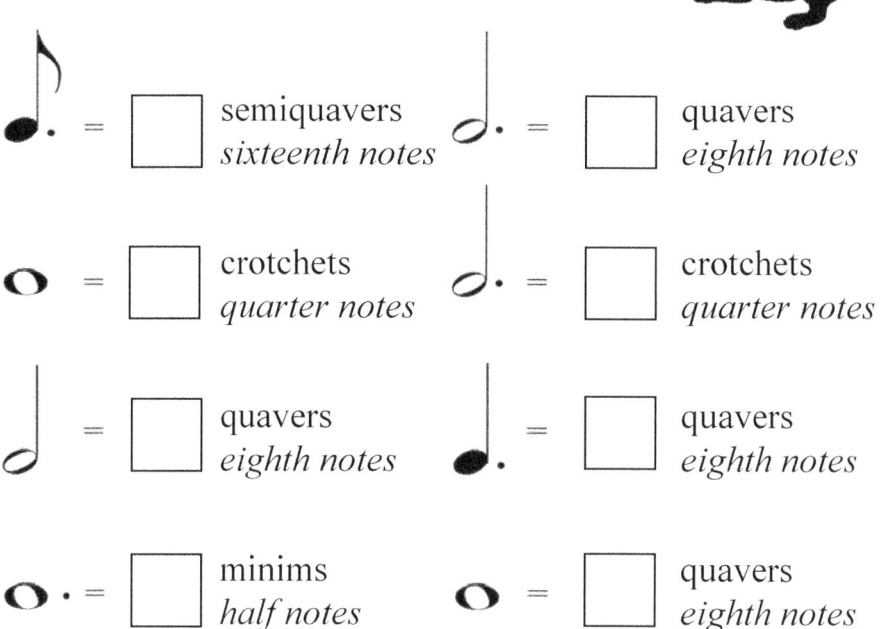

♪. = ☐ semiquavers / *sixteenth notes*   𝅗𝅥. = ☐ quavers / *eighth notes*

o = ☐ crotchets / *quarter notes*   𝅗𝅥. = ☐ crotchets / *quarter notes*

𝅗𝅥 = ☐ quavers / *eighth notes*   ♩. = ☐ quavers / *eighth notes*

o. = ☐ minims / *half notes*   o = ☐ quavers / *eighth notes*

Draw one note for your answer.

𝅗𝅥. ♪ _____   𝅗𝅥 𝅗𝅥 𝅗𝅥 = _____

How many did you get right?
Put the number in the box.

☐/10

Book 1 page 27

Test yourself

Draw

(1) a semibreve / *whole note* in each space of the stave.

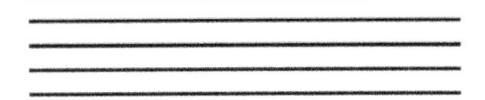

(2) a crotchet / *quarter note* on each line of the stave.

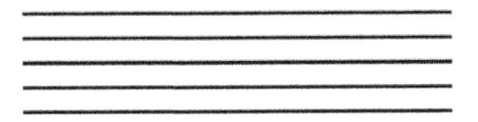

(3) a minim / *half note* in each space of the stave.

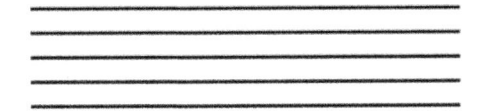

(4) a quaver / *eighth note* on each line of the stave. The 'tail' is on the right-hand side of the stem.

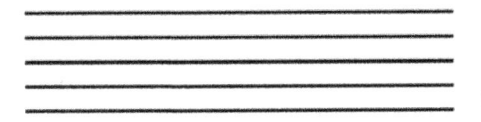

(5) a minim / *half note* on middle C.

Book 1 page 28

(6) a semiquaver / *sixteenth note* in each space of the stave.

(7) two quavers / *eighth notes* joined together
    in the C space.

(8) two semiquavers / *sixteenth notes* joined together
    on the G line.

(9) a dotted minim / *dotted half note* in each space.

(10) a dotted crotchet / *dotted quarter note* on each line.

TIED NOTES

A tie joins notes which are **at the same pitch**. The notes sound the same.

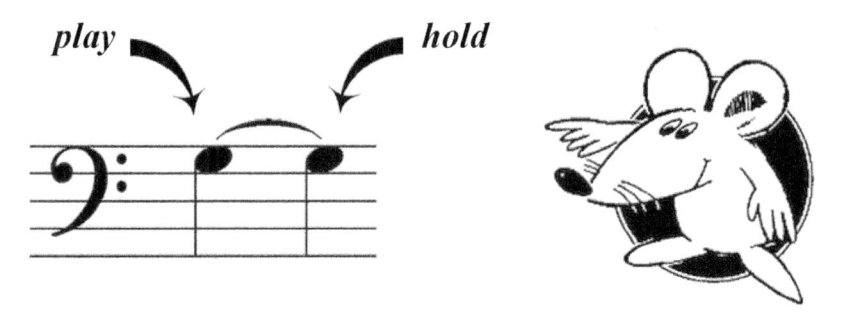

Tied notes are joined together **at the heads** (not the stems) and **from the outside** (not the inside) of each head.

You can join more than two notes with ties as long as they are the **same notes** and are **next to each other**.

Count the beats

How many crotchets / *quarter notes* is each tie worth?

How many answers did you have right?
Put the number in the box.

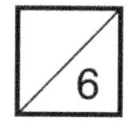

/6

Book 1 page 31

RESTS

There are times in music when we need to be absolutely quiet. In order to do this, we use **rests** instead of notes.

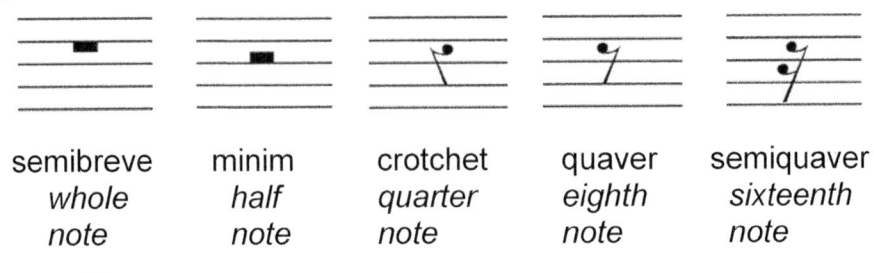

semibreve	minim	crotchet	quaver	semiquaver
whole note	*half note*	*quarter note*	*eighth note*	*sixteenth note*

If you want to rest for the length of a **dotted** note, put a **dot** after the rest in the **second space from the top** of the stave.

Now put the correct **rest** to match each note:-

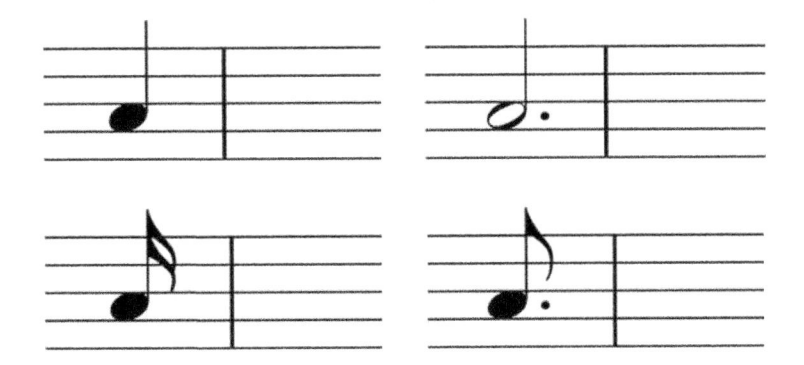

Book 1 page 32

There are two ways to write a **crotchet / *quarter note*** rest. The one you have met so far is the easiest, but the one below is very impressive if you can copy it accurately.

It looks like a **c** with a **z** on top.

snooZe for a Crotchet

Mr **Crotchet's** rest

Try to match the rests

with these notes **without** looking back at the last page:-

How many were correct?
Put the number in the box.

Book 1 page 33

ACCIDENTALS

I expect you have noticed in your music that there are sometimes signs in front of notes. These signs are called **accidentals**. There are three accidentals - the sharp, the flat and the natural.

The sharp

It looks like this.

It is written **in front** of a note and makes that note **higher**.

Write a sharp **in front** of each crotchet / *quarter note*.

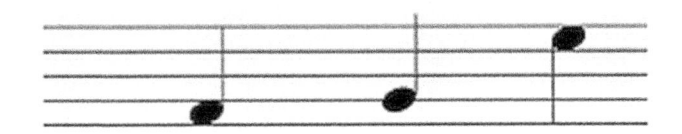

Book 1 page 34

The flat

It looks like a small letter b.

It is written **in front** of a note and makes that note **lower**.

Write a flat ♭ **in front** of each minim / *half note*.

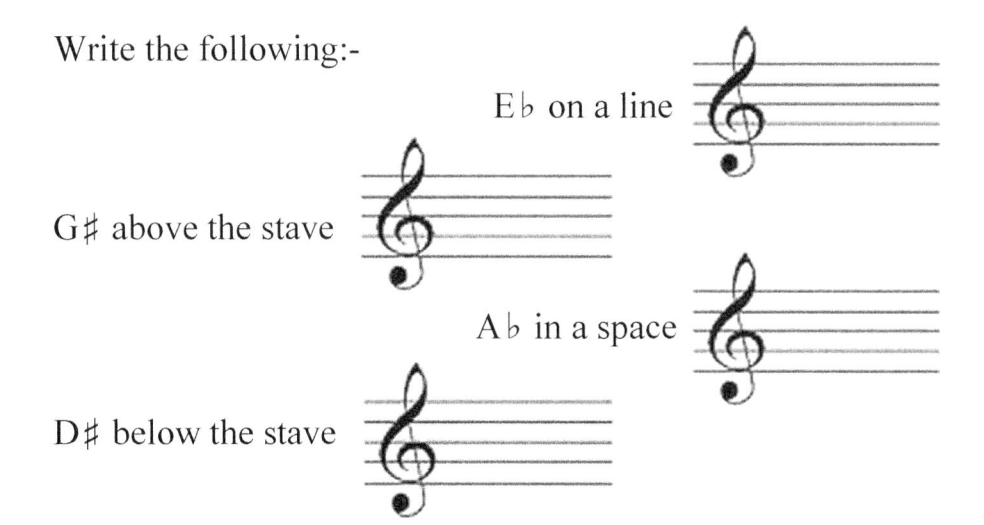

Write the following:-

E♭ on a line

G♯ above the stave

A♭ in a space

D♯ below the stave

The Natural

It looks like this.

It is written **in front** of a note that has been raised or lowered and it changes the note back to its normal pitch.

This means it can make a note **higher** or **lower**.

If you have an accidental in a bar / *measure* of music, it changes all other notes in the bar / *measure* which are at the same pitch.

If a note is an octave higher or lower, you will need another accidental if you want to raise or lower it.

Important
Accidentals are written **in front** of notes.

Book 1 page 36

TONES AND SEMITONES

The easiest way to learn about tones / *steps* and semitones / *half steps* is to study closely a piano keyboard.

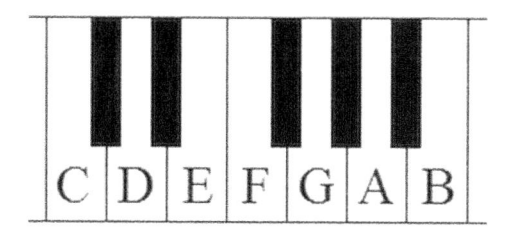

First of all, learn the names of the **white** keys. There are only seven: **ABCDEFG**. Then look at the **black** keys: they come between some of the white keys.

When you move **up the keyboard** the black keys are called **sharps**.

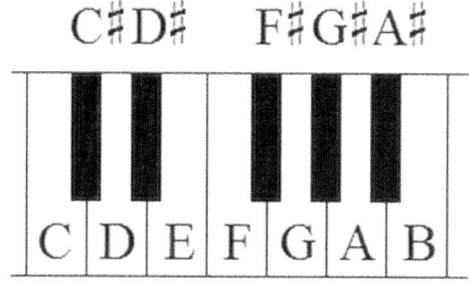

When you move **down the keyboard** the black keys are called **flats**.

Book 1 page 37

B & C and E & F have no black key between them. This means that there is a **semitone** / *half step* between B & C and E & F.

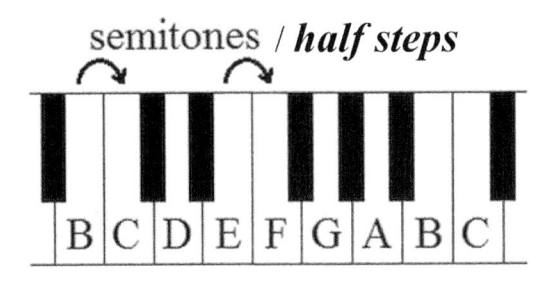

Every step you take between a **black** key and a **white** key is a **semitone** / *half step*. You take **two semitones** / *half steps* for a **tone** / *whole step*.

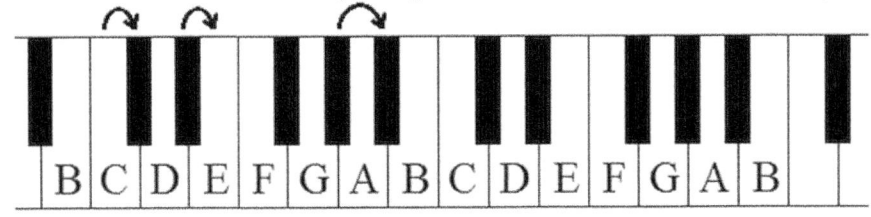

Black keys can be sharps or flats.

Fill in the missing letter names:

D raised one semitone / *half step* = ____

B lowered one semitone / *half step* = ____

C raised one tone / *whole step* = ____

F lowered one tone / *whole step* = ____

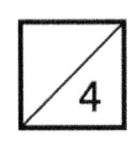

Book 1 page 38

KEY SIGNATURES AND SCALES

Here are four important key signatures. They tell you which accidentals are in the scale.

C major   G major   D major   F major

Important

Notice where the accidentals are written on the stave. They are **always** on these lines and spaces when they are written as key signatures.

C Major has no sharps and no flats.

G Major has one sharp – F

D Major has two sharps - F and C.

Think of **F**ather **C**hristmas and you will always remember the order of sharps.

F Major has one flat - B.

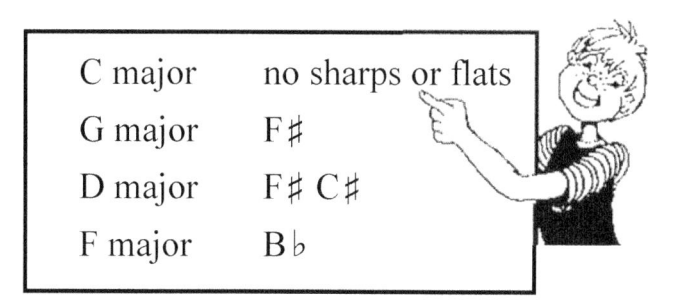

C major	no sharps or flats
G major	F♯
D major	F♯ C♯
F major	B♭

Book 1 page 39

Now you have met four key signatures, you are ready to learn about their scales. A **scale** is a group of notes arranged in order. For example, in C major, the order is **C D E F G A B C**.

C Major

There are no accidentals in C major which makes it very easy.

Here is the scale in semibreves / *whole notes* **ascending** – going up. Write the names of the eight notes.

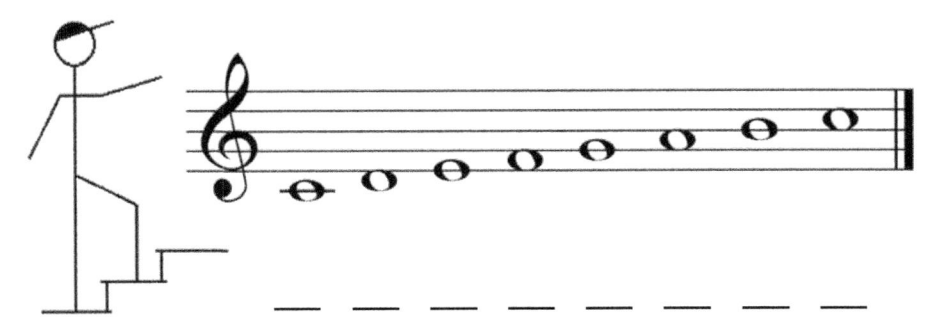

Here is the scale in semibreves / *whole notes* **descending** – going down. Write the names of the eight notes.

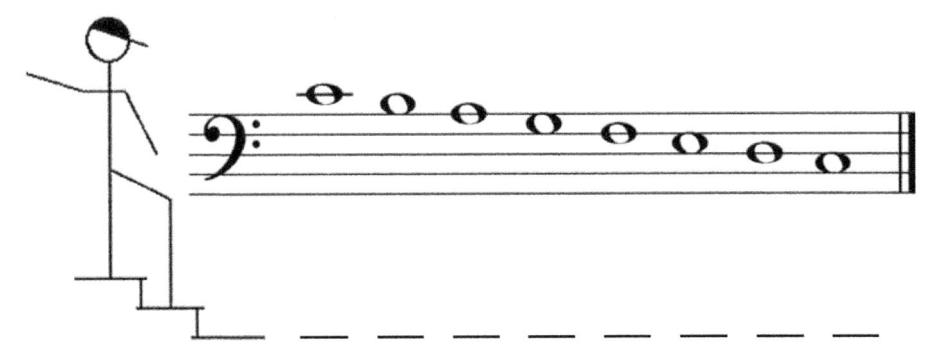

Book 1 page 40

In **all major** scales there is a **semitone** / *half step* between notes 3-4 and 7-8.

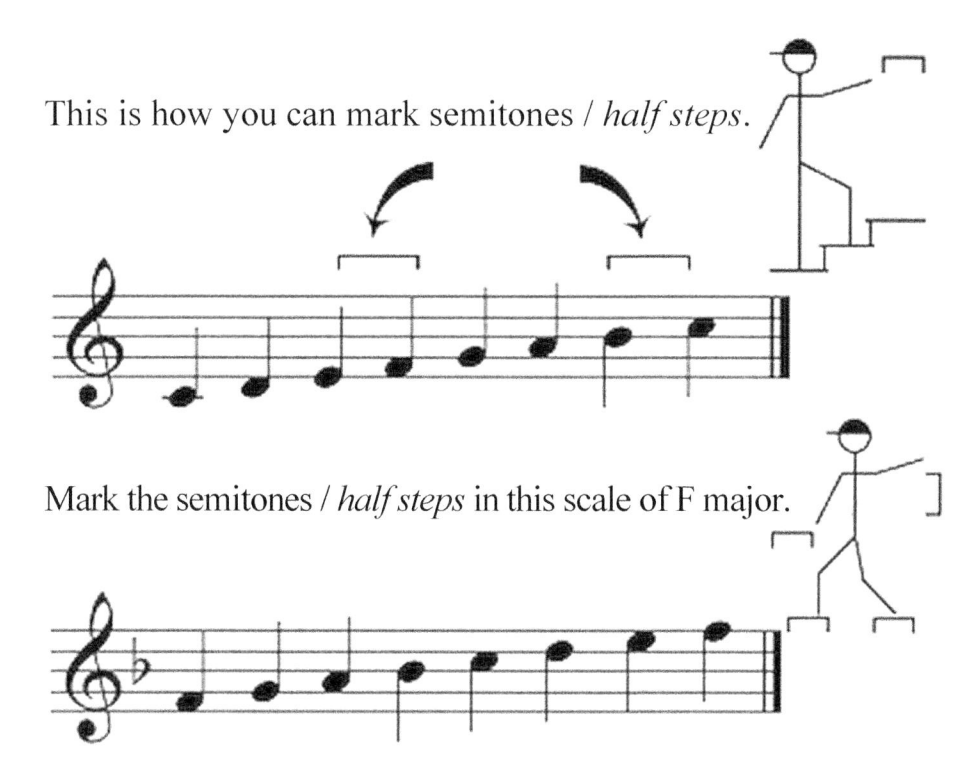

This is how you can mark semitones / *half steps*.

Mark the semitones / *half steps* in this scale of F major.

Important
When descending, you can find the semitones / *half steps* by counting from the bottom of the scale.

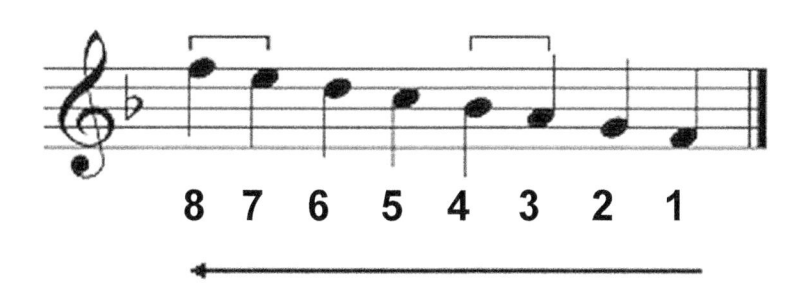

8 7 6 5 4 3 2 1

Book 1 page 41

G Major

Write the key signatures in the correct places in the treble and bass clefs.

When, for example, you are asked to write the scale of G Major ascending, without key signature, in crotchets / quarter notes in the treble clef, marking the semitones / half steps, it is a good idea to **underline all the important instructions first**.

I did this one for you. ☺

Write the scale of G Major ascending, in crotchets / *quarter notes*, with key signature, in the bass clef.

Mark the semitones / *half steps* with ⌐⌐.

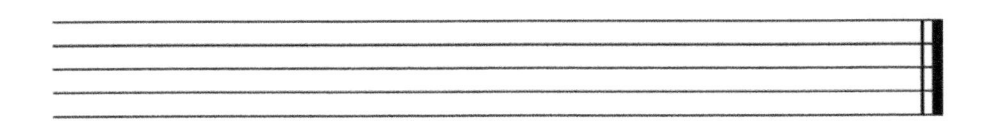

Book 1 page 42

D Major

Write the key signatures in the correct places in the treble and bass clefs. Clue:- **F**ather **C**hristmas.

Write the scale of D Major descending, in crotchets / *quarter notes*, with key signature, in the treble clef.

Mark the semitones / *half steps* like this ⌐¬. ☺

☺ I did this one for you as well.

Write the scale of D Major ascending, in crotchets / *quarter notes*, without key signature, in the treble clef.

Draw ⌐¬ over each semitone / *half step*.

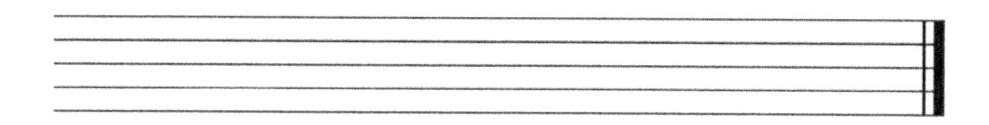

Book 1 page 43

F Major

Write the key signatures in the correct places in the treble and bass clefs.

Underline the important words in this question:

> Write the scale of F Major ascending, without key signature, in minims / *half notes*, in the bass clef. Mark the semitones / *half steps*.

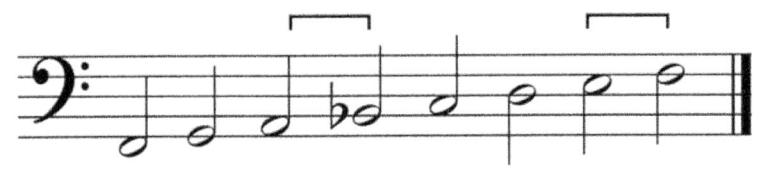

Underline the important words in this question. Remember to use ⌐¬ to mark the semitones / *half steps*.

Write the scale of F Major descending, in minims / *half notes*, with key signature, in the treble clef.

Mark the semitones / *half steps*.

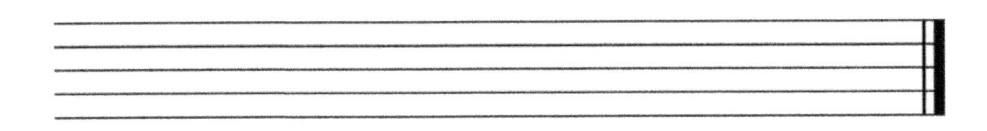

Book 1 page 44

DEGREES OF THE SCALE

The first note of the scale is called the keynote or the **first degree**. Therefore the second note is the **2nd degree**, the third, the **3rd degree** and so on, until you reach the **8th degree** or **octave** - written as **8ve**.

Write the degree of the scale which is asked for.

I have written the first answer for you. ☺

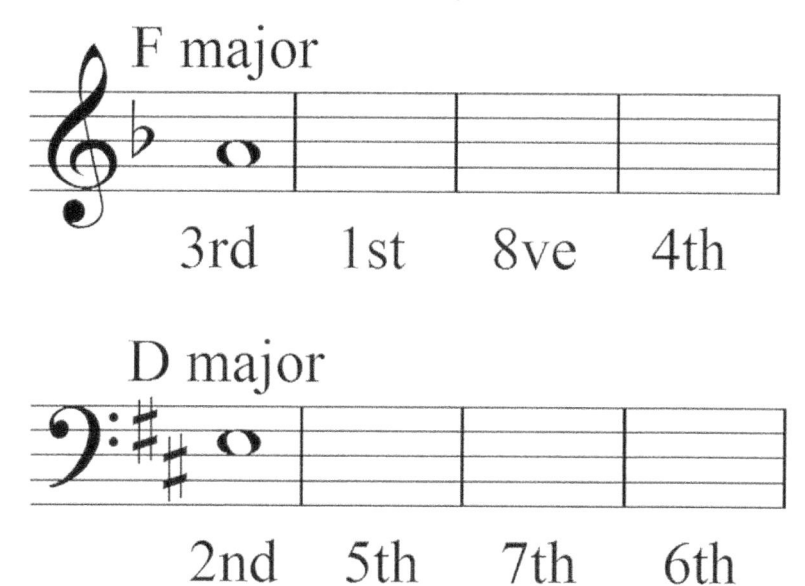

F major

3rd   1st   8ve   4th

D major

2nd   5th   7th   6th

How many did you get right?
Put the number in the box.

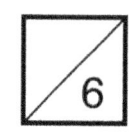

6

Book 1 page 45

INTERVALS

An interval is the **distance** or **difference in pitch between two notes**.

For example, in D major there is an interval of a 3rd (third) between notes D and F♯.

I have written the scale of D major to show you each interval.

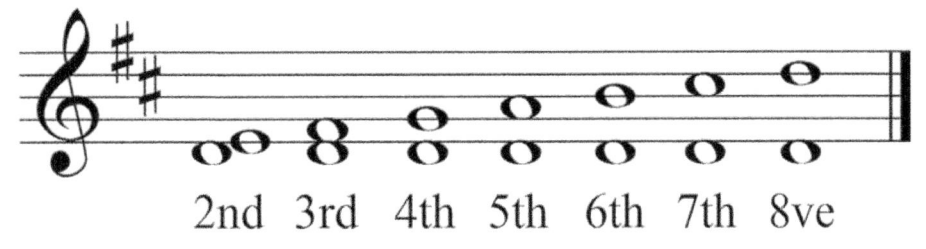

2nd 3rd 4th 5th 6th 7th 8ve

Write the intervals for G major in the same way.

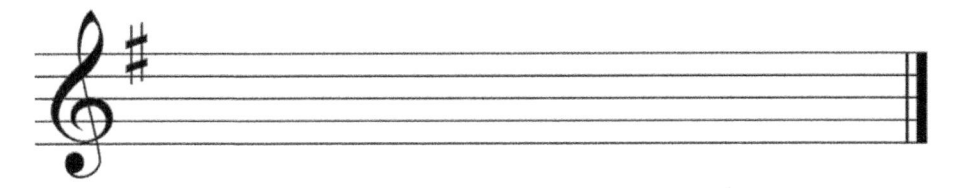

Write the key signature and the intervals for F major.

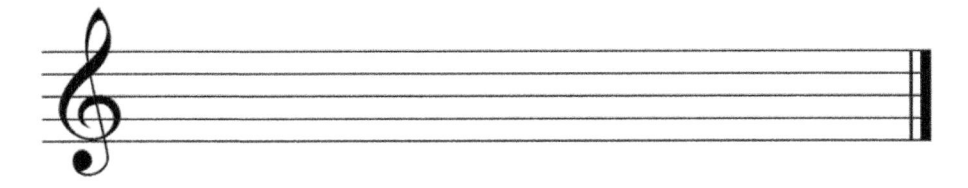

Book 1 page 46

The melodic interval

This is a melodic interval.

When the two notes are written **one after the other** they are **played separately**.

Put a number below the stave to show which melodic interval has been written. I have answered the first one for you. ☺

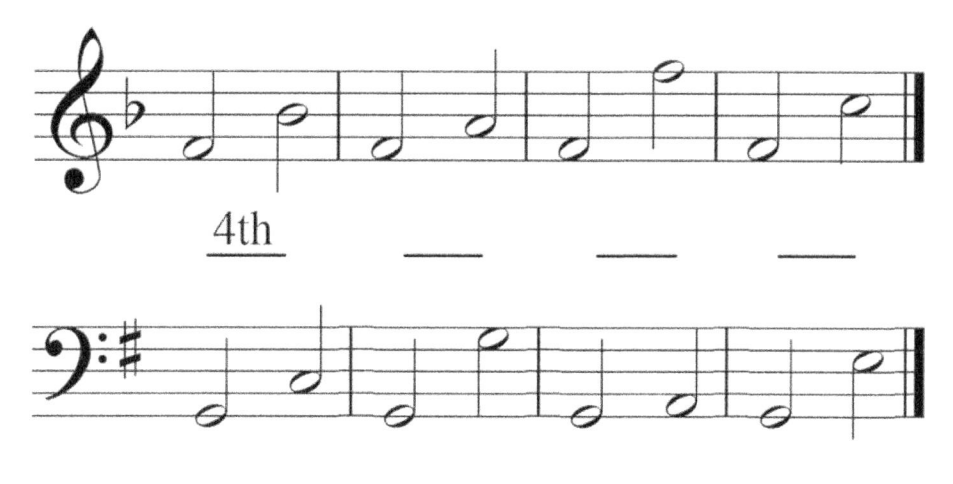

4th

How many did you get right?
Put the number in the box

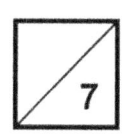

/ 7

Book 1 page 47

The harmonic interval

This interval is a harmonic interval.

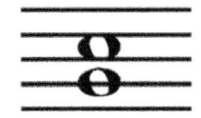

When the two notes are written **one above the other** they are **played at the same time**.

Write a note above each of the keynotes to make the harmonic interval. I have written the first one for you.

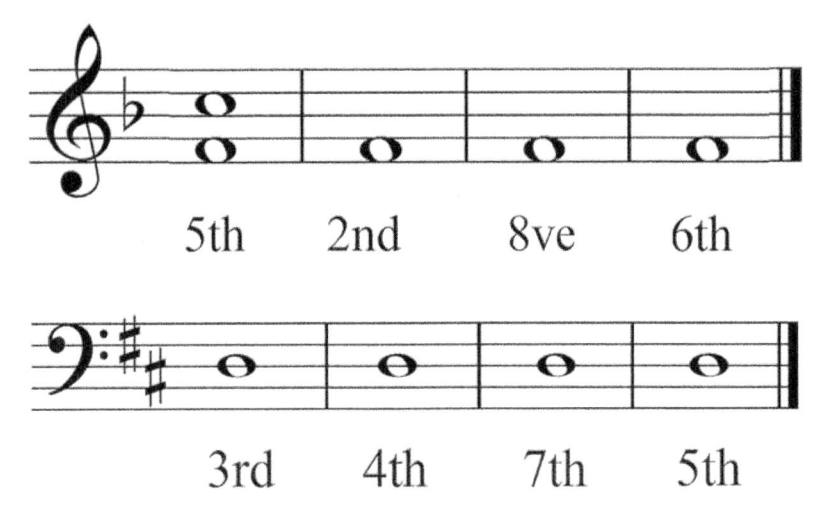

5th   2nd   8ve   6th

3rd   4th   7th   5th

How many did you get right? Put the number in the box.

7

Important
Remember, we always count from the keynote.

Book 1 page 48

TONIC TRIADS

The first note of a scale is called the **keynote** or the **tonic**. A tonic triad is made up of **three** notes:-

1. The keynote or tonic.

2. The 3rd degree (note) of the scale.

3. The 5th degree (note) of the scale.

Sometimes you will be asked to write a tonic triad **with** key signature.

Sometimes you will be asked to write a tonic triad **without** key signature. This will only be a problem in D Major where the 3rd note is F sharp.

Book 1 page 49

Test yourself

Write these tonic triads **with** key signature

G major

F major

Write these tonic triads **without** key signature

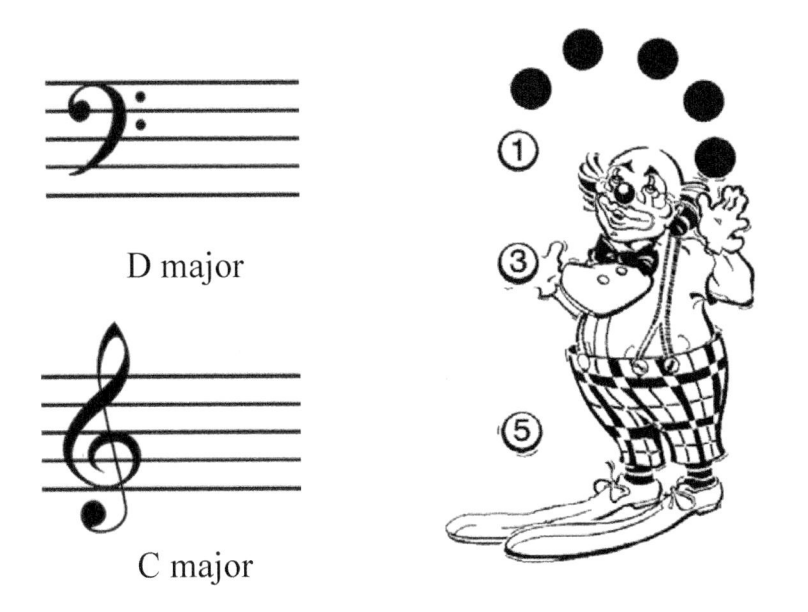

D major

C major

Book 1 page 50

Draw the **treble clef** and these tonic triads **with** key signature.

F major	G major	D major

Draw the **bass clef** and these tonic triads **with** key signature.

G major	D major	F major

Draw the **treble clef** and these tonic triads **without** key signature.

F major	D major	G major

Draw the **bass clef** and these tonic triads **without** key signature.

G major	D major	C major

How many were correct? Put the number in the box. /16

Book 1 page 51

TIME SIGNATURES

At the beginning of a piece of music you will find a **Clef**, a **K**ey signature of sharps or flats (but not for C major) and **two numbers** we call a **T**ime signature.

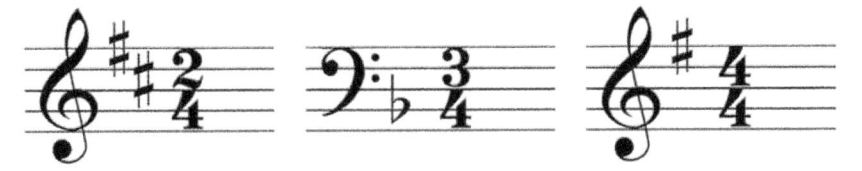

The order is always the same and you can remember it because the words are in alphabetical order:-

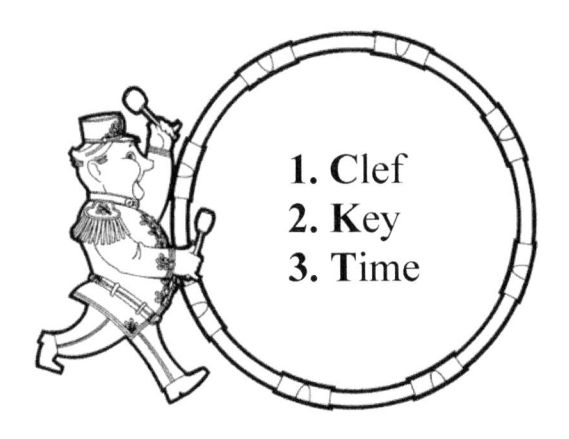

1. Clef
2. Key
3. Time

The **top number** of the time signature tells you **how many** beats there are in a bar / *measure*.

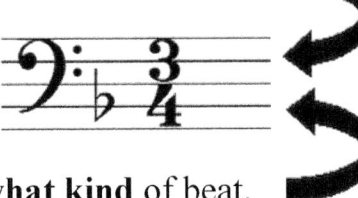

The **bottom number** tells you **what kind** of beat.

Book 1 page 52

Simple duple time

In this book you will meet only one simple **duple** time signature. Duple means two.

Duple time is $\frac{2}{4}$.

The top number [**2**] tells us there are two beats in a bar / *measure*.
The bottom number [**4**] tells us the beats are crotchets / *quarter notes*.

Bar lines divide music into **bars /** *measures.*

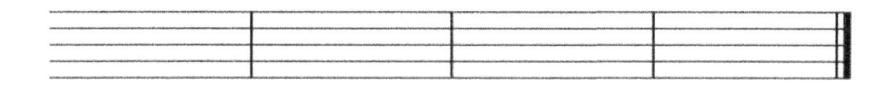

A double bar line comes at the end of a piece of music. It is written as a thin line followed by a thicker line.

Here is a passage of music in $\frac{2}{4}$ time.

I have left out **two bar lines**. Put them in for me.

What is the name of the key of the passage? ___ major.

Book 1 page 53

Simple triple time

In this book you will only meet one simple **triple** time signature. Triple means three.

Triple time is $\frac{3}{4}$.

The top number [**3**] tells us there are
_____.

The bottom number [**4**] tells us
_____.

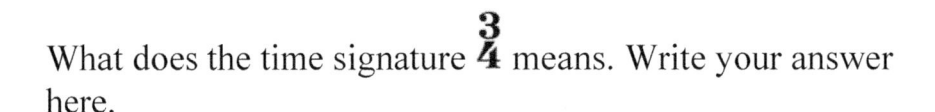

What does the time signature $\frac{3}{4}$ means. Write your answer here.

_____

Simple quadruple time

In this book you will only meet one simple **quadruple** time signature. Quadruple means four.

Quadruple time is $\frac{4}{4}$.

$\frac{4}{4}$ is sometimes written as **C**.

Write down what $\frac{4}{4}$ or **C** means here.

_____

Book 1 page 54

Test yourself on time signatures

Add **one note** to each bar / *measure* (under the ∗) so that the time signature is correct.

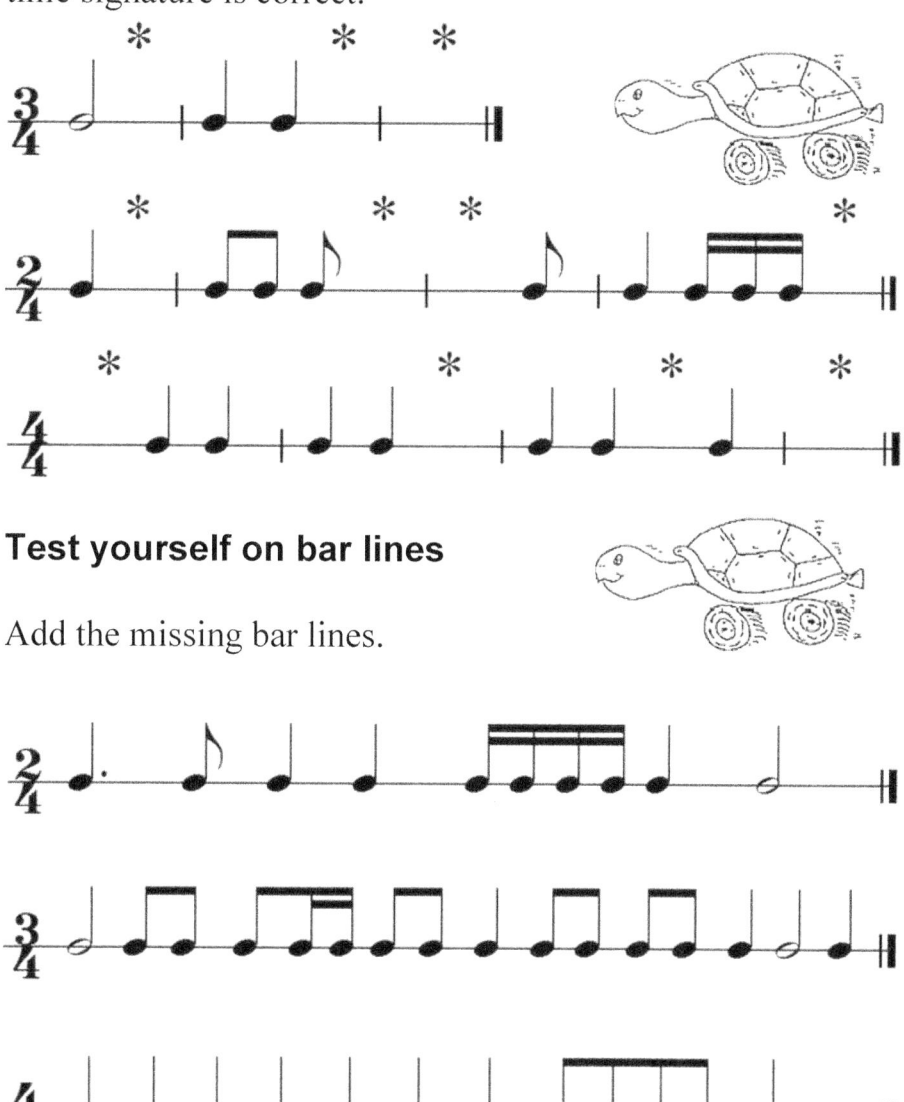

Test yourself on bar lines

Add the missing bar lines.

WRITING RHYTHMS

In $\frac{2}{4}$ time.

If there are semiquavers / *sixteenth notes* beam them together in crotchet / *quarter note* beats. Join the tails or flags. Do this with any group that has a semiquaver / *sixteenth note*.

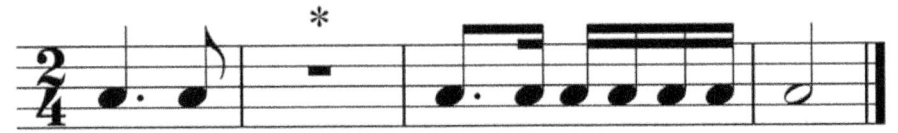

Notice we use a **semibreve / *whole note* rest** (*) for a whole bar or measure.

In $\frac{3}{4}$ time.

You can beam together a whole bar of quavers / *eighth notes*.

In $\frac{4}{4}$ time.

You can join beats 1 and 2 or 3 and 4.

You **cannot** join beats 2 and 3 using **beamed** notes.

Book 1 page 56

You know all the notes and rests. You have seen examples of rhythms in simple time. You know all the rules. Well, now it's your turn!

In the space for the note A, write **four** bars / *measures* of rhythms, with time signature, in each of these given times.

simple **duple** time:

simple **triple** time:

simple **quadruple** time

simple **triple** time:

ANSWERING RHYTHMS

In an exam you could be given a two-bar rhythm with a time signature and asked to write another two bars.

Hints

Tap the rhythm to yourself and feel how it should continue and how it should end. It would not feel right to end on a very short note such as a semiquaver / *sixteenth note*.

Here is a two-bar rhythm:

    bar 1   bar 2   bar 3   bar 4

You may want to use one of the rhythms given in bars one or two. That is fine as long as you put some rhythms of your own to show that you understand how to write music.

There is not one correct answer but many. Bars 1 and 3 could have the same rhythm:

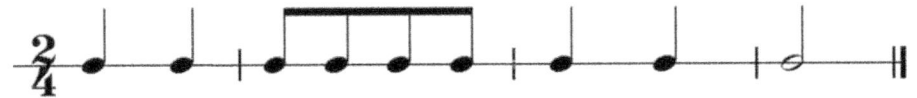

or bars 2 and 3 could have the same rhythm:

Book 1 page 58

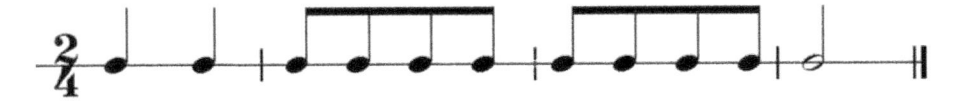

Write two-bar answering rhythms for the following:

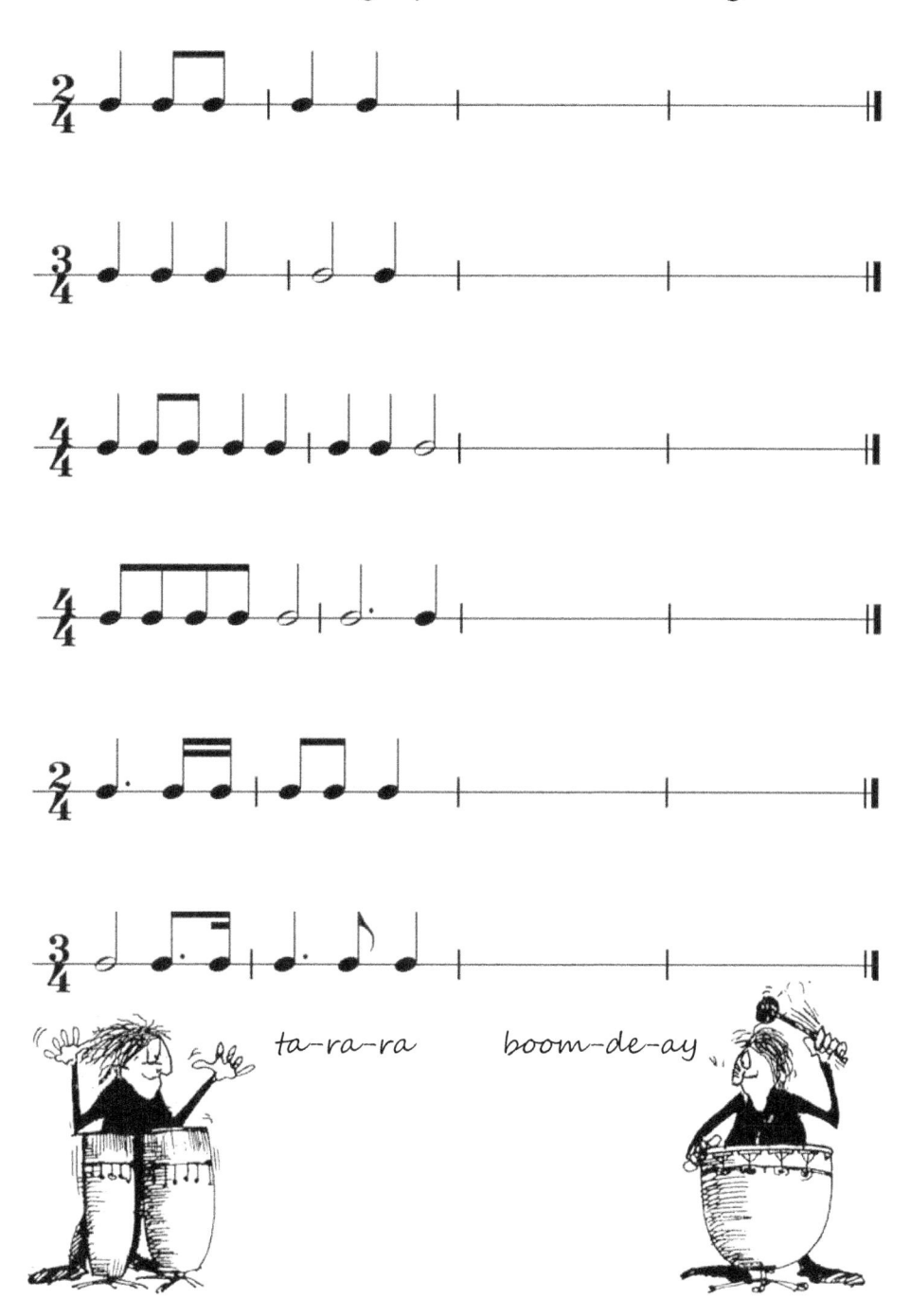

ta-ra-ra   boom-de-ay

PUZZLES

QUIZZES

TESTS

Book 1 page 60

Fun page

Connect the note to the rest of the same length.

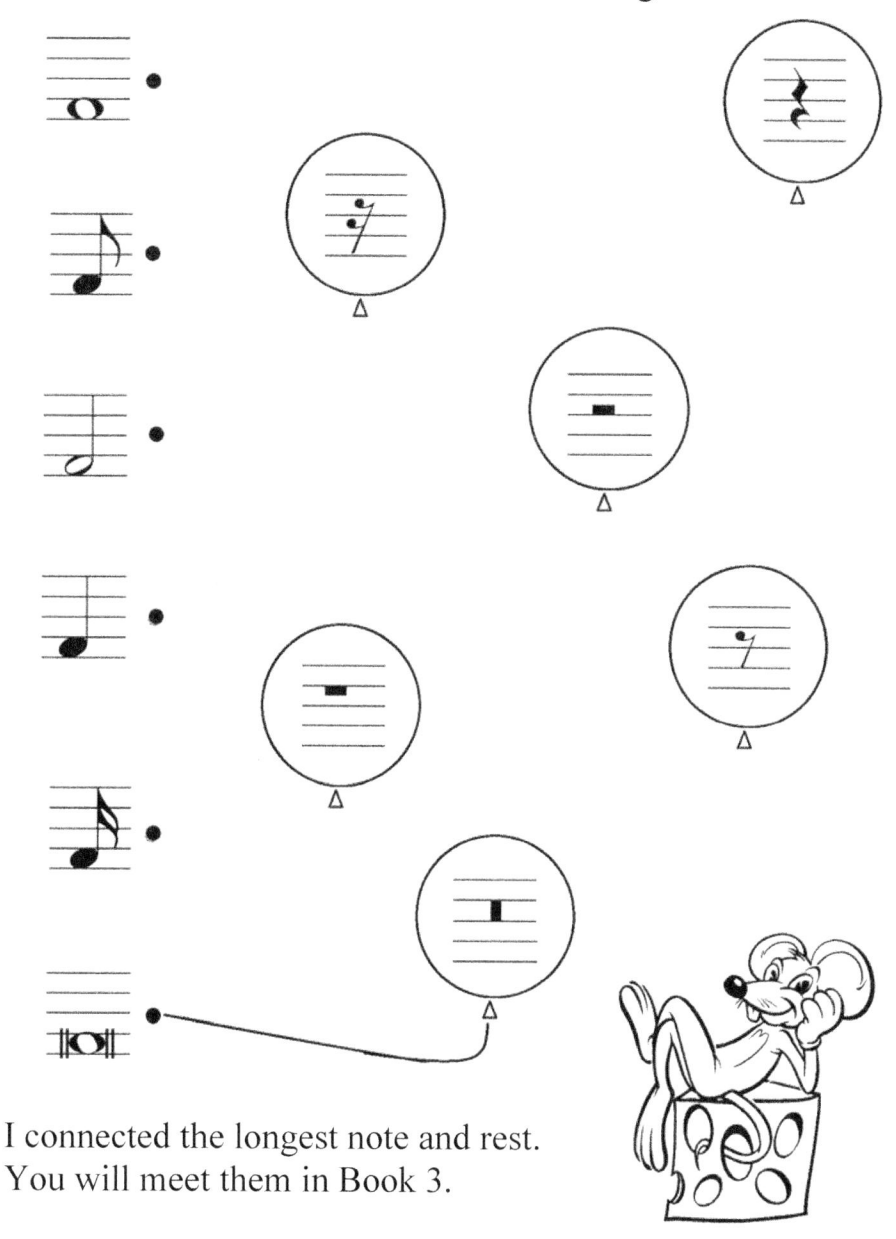

I connected the longest note and rest.
You will meet them in Book 3.

Book 1 page 61

Merry-go-round

The last letter or the last two letters of one word will be the start of the next word. Go around the shell to find the answers to the questions below.

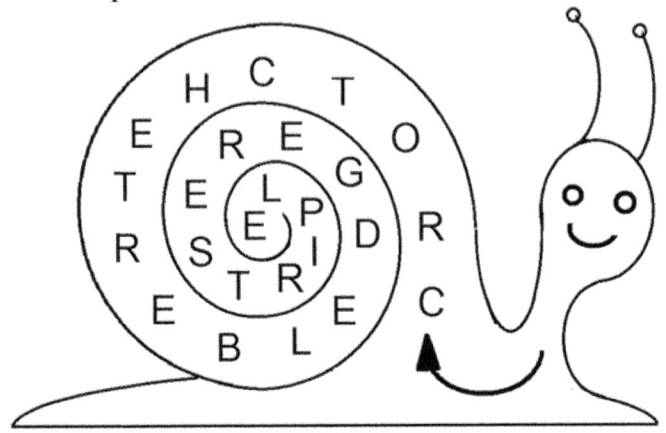

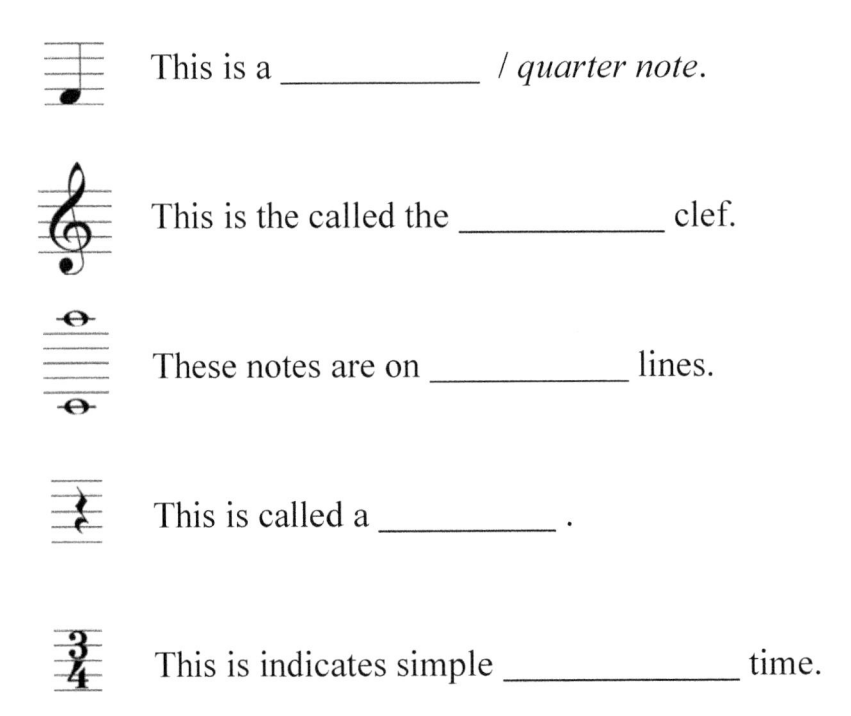

This is a _____ / quarter note.

This is the called the _____ clef.

These notes are on _____ lines.

This is called a _____ .

This is indicates simple _____ time.

Book 1 page 62

Word search

E	B	A	N	D	A	N	T	E	D
O	L	O	D	E	N	I	F	E	O
A	E	L	P	A	N	V	E	L	T
O	G	C	K	L	G	V	C	O	A
C	A	N	T	A	B	I	L	E	C
P	T	M	A	R	L	V	O	X	C
T	O	B	H	G	I	A	D	O	A
P	I	A	N	O	U	C	E	T	T
N	A	S	O	I	J	E	M	I	S
D	R	A	X	P	O	C	O	S	S

Meaning	Musical term
A little	poco
At a walking pace	
Slow, stately, broad	
Soft	
The end	
Smoothly	
In a singing style	
Slow, leisurely	
Lively, quick	
Sweetly	
Short, detached	

Book 1 page 63

Crossword

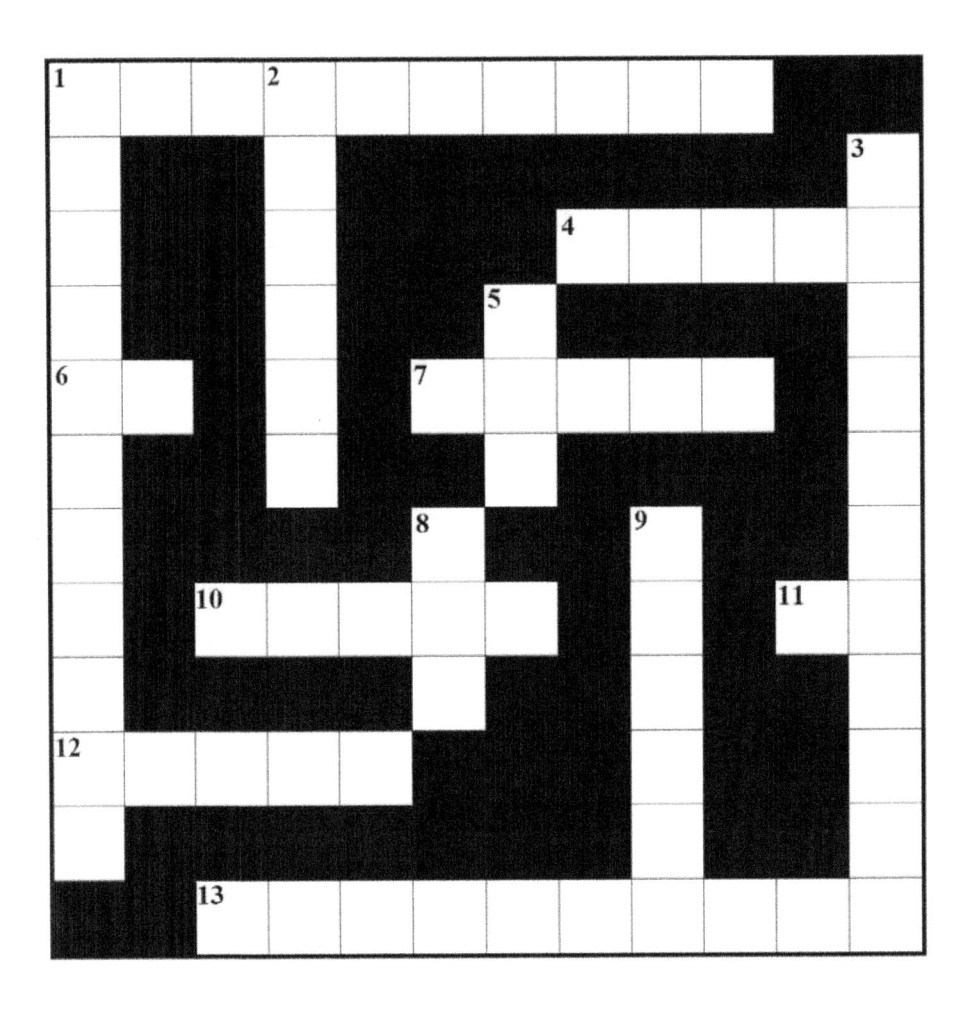

Book 1 page 64

Clues

Across

1 gradually slower
4 loud
6 3rd and 4th degree of C major
7 speed, time
10 slow and stately, broad
11 6th and 7th degrees of D major
12 sweetly
13 gradually softer

Down

1 becoming gradually slower
2 slow, leisurely
3 gradually softer
5 tonic triad
8 1st, 2nd and 3rd degrees in the scale of F major
9 lively, quick

Book 1 page 65

Quiz 1

Put a tick / *check mark* (✓) in the correct box.

1. adagio

☐ at a walking pace

☐ slow, leisurely

☐ lively, reasonably fast

☐ slightly slower than allegro

2. staccato

☐ suddenly

☐ smoothly

☐ very quick

☐ short, detached

3. sweetly

☐ cantabile

☐ dolce

☐ maestoso

☐ pesante

4. quietly

☐ forte

☐ leggiero

☐ piano

☐ tranquillo

5. scherzo

☐ a joke

☐ lightly

☐ heavily

☐ playfully

6. gradually softer

☐ decresc.

☐ rall.

☐ rit.

☐ *sfz*

Check your answers.
Put a number in the box.   ▢/6

Book 1 page 66

Quiz 2

Put a tick / *check mark* (✓) in the correct box.

1. >

☐ becoming louder
☐ becoming softer
☐ accent the note
☐ slur

2. >

☐ becoming softer
☐ accent the note
☐ pause on the note
☐ short, detached

3. <

☐ becoming softer
☐ becoming louder
☐ becoming slower
☐ short, detached

4.

☐ short, detached
☐ accent the note
☐ play an octave higher
☐ pause on the note

5. **play notes smoothly**

☐ 8va
☐ <
☐ ⌒
☐

6. **gradually louder**

☐ *sfz*
☐ **cresc.**
☐ **rall.**
☐ **rit**

Check your answers. Put a number in the box.

Book 1 page 67

Handy hints for tests

This section is for you to practise the different types of questions you could have in a test or an exam.

The questions could be on any topic covered in this book.

Revise each topic in this book thoroughly.

Don't forget to study musical terms and signs – they are **always** included.

Practice makes perfect!

Practice makes perfect!

If you have worked through this book carefully and understood each topic, this will be an easy task for you.

Before you begin any test, write out your key signature chart from page 39. Always refer to the chart when tackling questions that require you to know a key signature.

Book 1 page 68

Test 1

Put a tick / *check mark* (✓) in the correct box.

1. Name this note:

    A ☐   D ☐   B ☐

2. Name this note:

    B natural ☐   G flat ☐   B flat ☐

3. Name the notes to find the hidden word:

    CAFE ☐   CAGE ☐   FACE ☐

4. How many quavers / *eighth notes* are there in a minim / *half note*?

    2 ☐   4 ☐   8 ☐

5. For how many crotchets / *quarter notes* does this rest last?

    3 ☐   2 ☐   4 ☐

6. Which is the correct time signature?

    3/4 ☐   4/4 ☐   2/4 ☐

Book 1 page 69

Test 2

1. Which pair of notes has a distance / *step* of a semitone / *half step* between them?

   A and B ☐   F and G ☐   B and C ☐

2. Here is the scale of F major. Where are the semitones / *half steps*?

   Between 1st and 2nd and 7th and 8th degrees ☐
   Between 3rd and 4th and 7th and 8th degrees ☐
   Between 5th and 6th and 7th and 8th degrees ☐

3. Which is the correct key signature of D major?

4. Choose the key note for this tonic triad.

   F ☐   G ☐   C ☐

5. Which note needs to be added to complete this tonic triad in G major?

   C ☐   B ☐   A ☐

6. Name this interval.

   5th ☐   7th ☐   6th ☐

Book 1 page 70

Test 3

Write the words.

1. 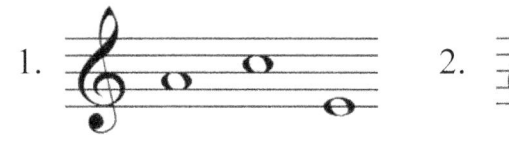
2. 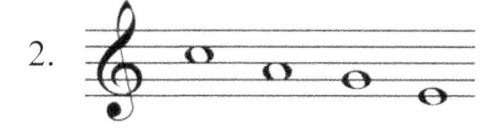
3. 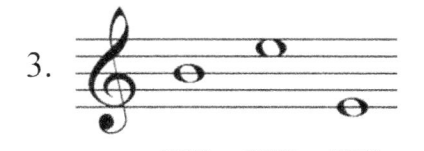
4. 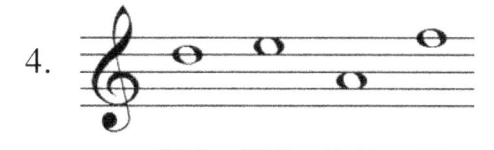
5. 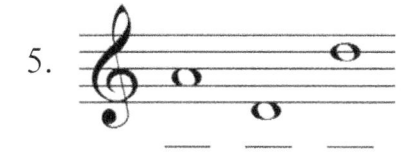
6. 
7. 
8. 
9. 
10. 
11. 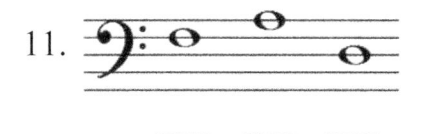
12.

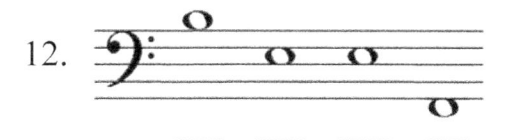

Book 1 page 71

Test 4

Write the notes.

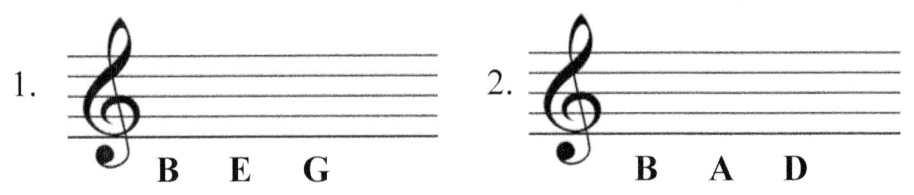

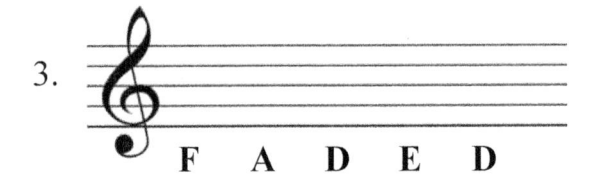

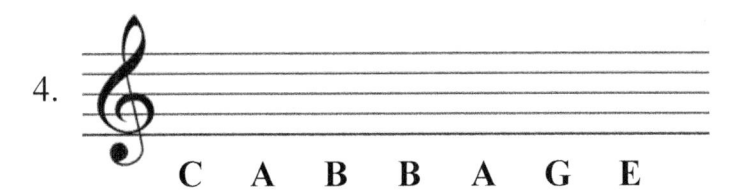

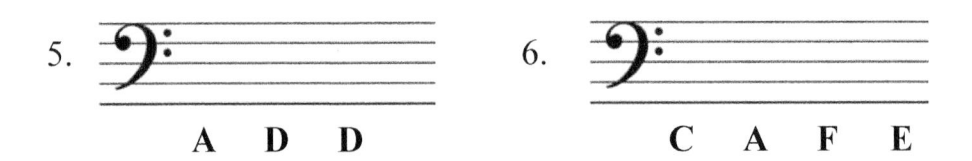

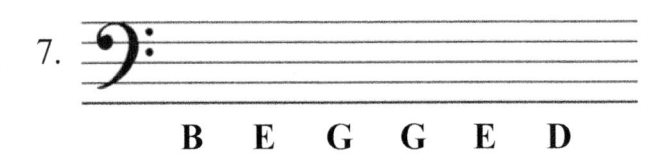

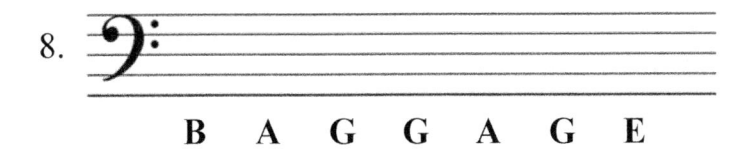

1.   B   E   G

2.   B   A   D

3.   F   A   D   E   D

4.   C   A   B   B   A   G   E

5.   A   D   D

6.   C   A   F   E

7.   B   E   G   G   E   D

8.   B   A   G   G   A   G   E

Book 1 page 72

Test 5

1. 2 crotchets / *quarter notes* = 1 _____ / _____

2. 2 semiquavers / *sixteenth notes* = 1 _____ / _____

3. 2 quavers / *eighth notes* = 1 _____ / _____

4. 1 minim / *half note* = ___ quavers / *eighth notes*.

5. 1 semibreve / *whole note* = ___ minims / *half notes*.

6. 1 crotchet / *quarter note* = ___ semiquavers / *sixteenth notes*.

7. In $\frac{4}{4}$ time you can beam together beats __&__ and __&__

8. In $\frac{4}{4}$ time you cannot beam together beats __&__ and __&__

9. $\frac{3}{4}$ is simple _____ time.

10. $\frac{2}{4}$ is simple _____ time.

11. Write a whole bar of quavers / *eighth notes*.

$\frac{3}{4}$ —————————————————||

12. Write a whole bar of quavers / *eighth notes*.

$\frac{4}{4}$ —————————————————||

Test 6

1. Write the scale of F major ascending, one octave only. Use semibreves / *whole notes*. Put in the key signature. Mark the semitones / *half steps* with a bracket ⌐¬ or ⌐¬.

2. There are mistakes in the following music. Write it out correctly.

3. Answer the following rhythm.

4. Name the notes in the tonic triad of G major.

    GBD ☐   GBC ☐   GAD ☐

5. Name these intervals.

    (a) _____   (b) _____   (c) _____

    (d) _____   (e) _____   (f) _____

Book 1 page 74

Test 7

1. Write a higher note above each given note to make the named harmonic interval. The first one has been done for you. The key is C major.

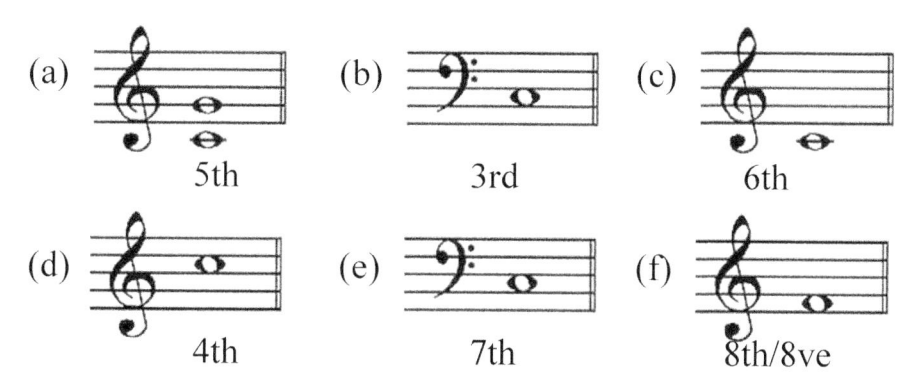

   (a) 5th   (b) 3rd   (c) 6th

   (d) 4th   (e) 7th   (f) 8th/8ve

2. Name the key of each scale. Draw a bracket over the notes that make a semitone / *half step*. The first one is done for you.

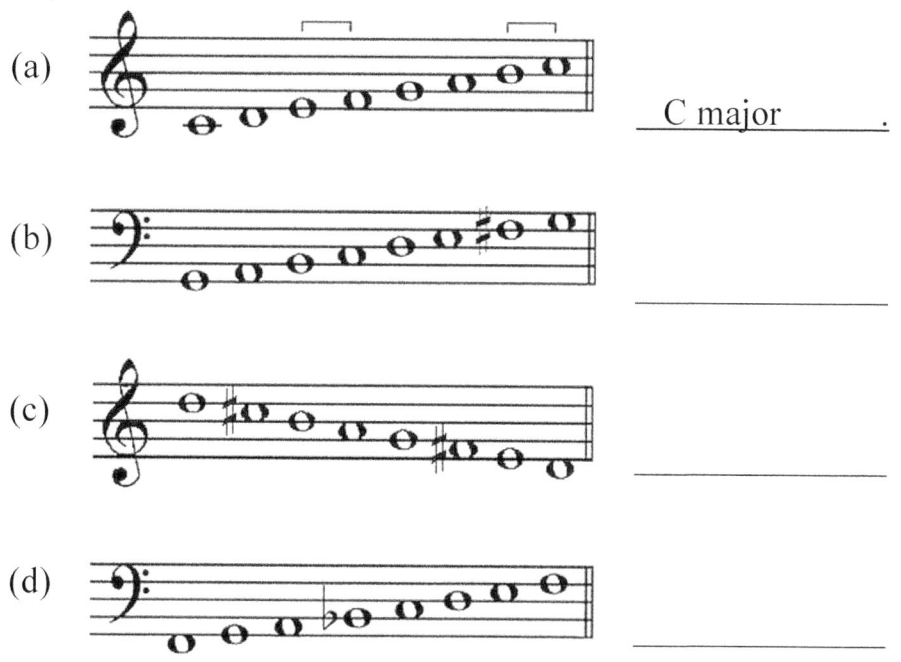

   (a) __C major__.

   (b) _____

   (c) _____

   (d) _____

Book 1 page 75

Test 8

1. Name the degree of the scale of the notes marked * . The key is C major.

   5th   ___   ___   ___   ___   ___   ___

2. Name the key of each tonic triad.

3. Write tonic triads with key signature for the following:

   F major   G major   D major

4. Write these dynamics in the correct order from the quietest to the loudest.

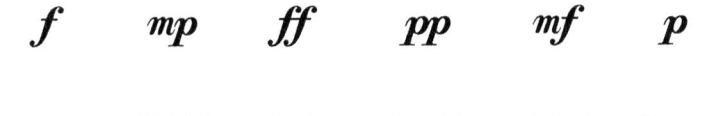

   f   *mp*   *ff*   *pp*   *mf*   *p*

   ___   ___   ___   ___   ___   ___

5. Name the key of this scale _____
   Mark the semitones / *half steps* with ⌐⌐.

Book 1 page 76

Test 9

Answer the questions on these eight bars / *measures*.

1. What is the major key of this music?

   _____

2. How many crotchets / *quarter notes* are in a bar / *measure*?

   _____

3. In which bar / *measure* is the rhythm the same as bar / *measure* 5?

   _____

4. Write the meaning of

   Presto _____

   mf _____

5. Which bars have only staccato notes?

   _____

6. Write the highest and lowest notes as crotchets / *quarter notes*.

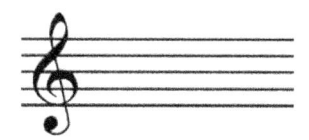

Book 1 page 77

Test 10

1. Copy the piece of music above. Include the clef, key signature, time signature and all other details shown.

   In this F major melody

2. What is the letter name of the highest note?_____

3. Name the degree of the scale in bar 2._____

4. Which bar / *measure* has all the notes of the tonic triad?___

5. How many staccato notes are there?_____

6. Answer true or false to this statement.
   The notes in bar / *measure* 5 are the quietest._____

7. Write the meaning of

   pp _____

   < _____

8. What is the meaning of Andante?

   _____

9. Which bar / *measure* has a dotted crotchet / *dotted quarter note*? _____

Book 1 page 78

CONTENTS
Book 2

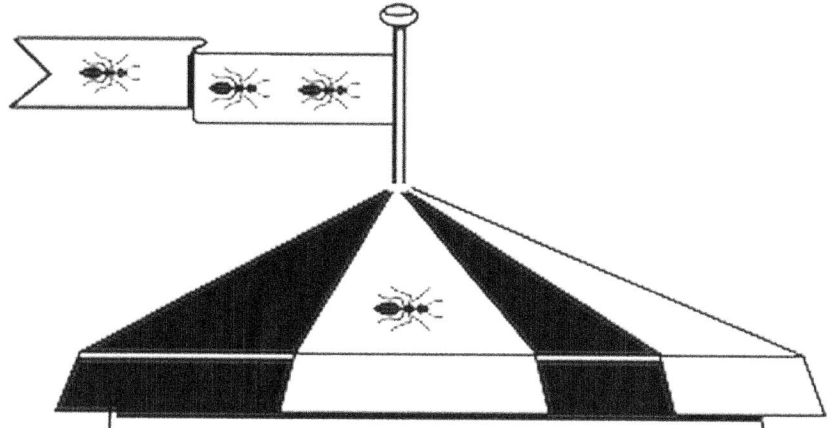

Topic	page
Major Key Signatures	6
tones and semitones	9
semitones in major scales	11
Minor Key Signatures	14
harmonic minor scales	17
melodic minor scales	19
Intervals	23
melodic	24
harmonic	24
Tonic Triads	26
Time Signatures	28
The Grouping of Notes	31
The Grouping of Rests	34
Triplets	36
Ledger Lines	38
Four-Bar Rhythms	41
Puzzles, Quizzes and Tests	42
Musical Terms and Signs	62

MAJOR KEY SIGNATURES

In Book 1 you met four key signatures.

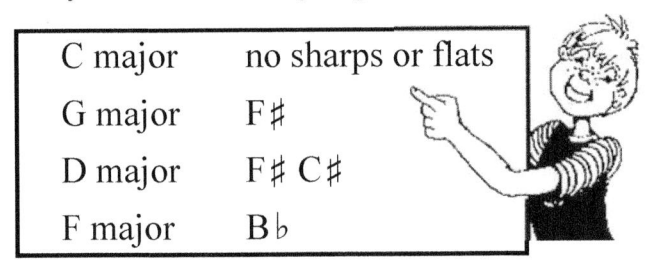

C major	no sharps or flats
G major	F♯
D major	F♯ C♯
F major	B♭

Write letter names of the key signatures for these four keys.

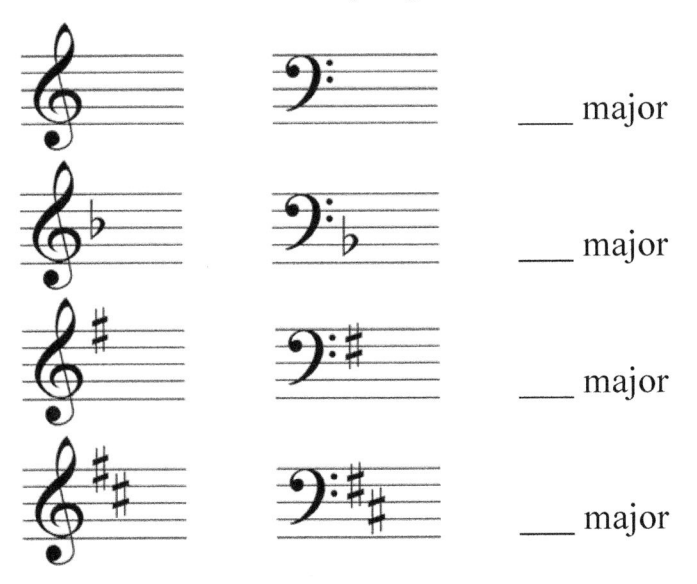

_____ major

_____ major

_____ major

_____ major

The sharps and flats are always on the same lines and in the same spaces for key signatures.

Book 2 page 6

In this Book 2 you meet three new major keys.

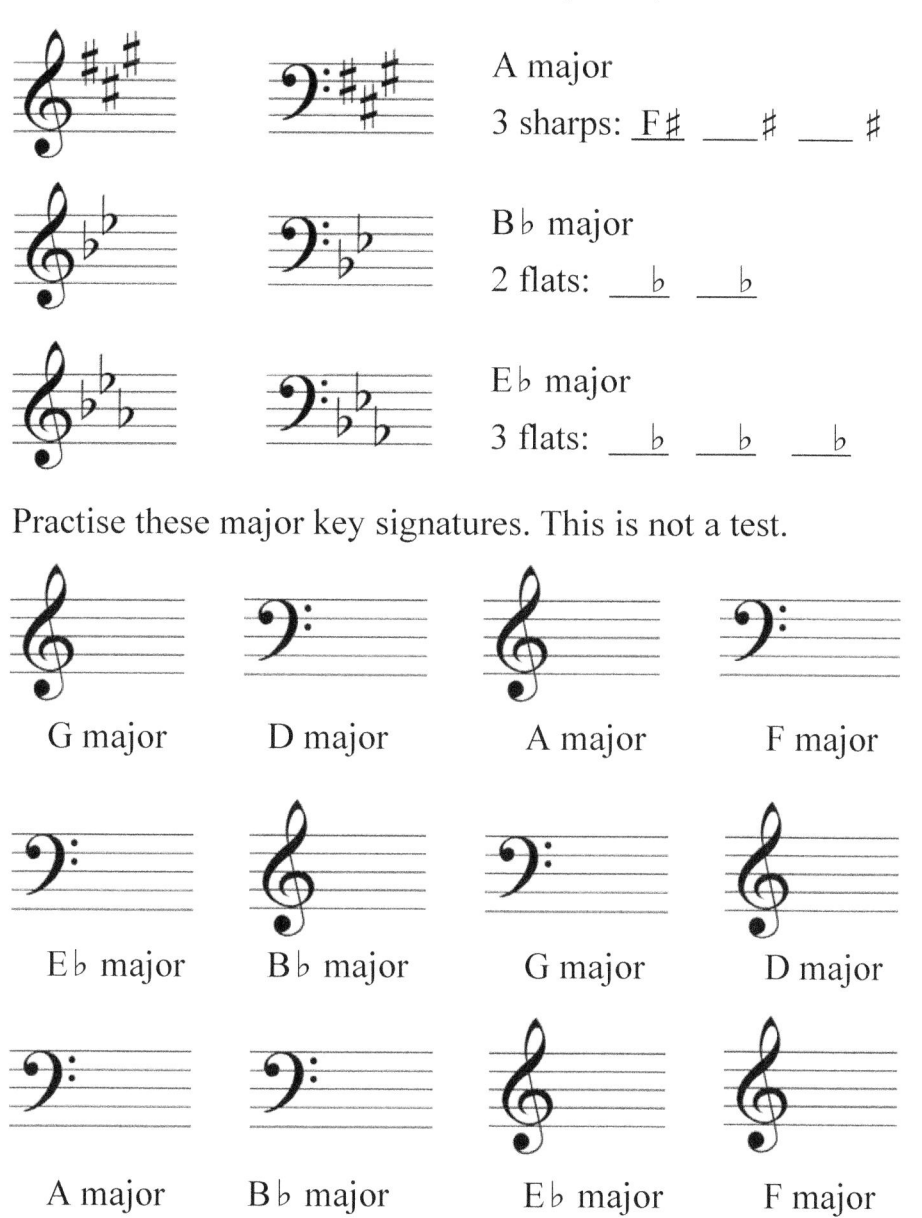

A major
3 sharps: F♯ ___♯ ___♯

B♭ major
2 flats: ___♭ ___♭

E♭ major
3 flats: ___♭ ___♭ ___♭

Practise these major key signatures. This is not a test.

G major   D major   A major   F major

E♭ major   B♭ major   G major   D major

A major   B♭ major   E♭ major   F major

When you are sure of all seven key
signatures, turn the page and test yourself.

Book 2 page 7

Test yourself

You now know the key signatures for seven major scales up to 3 sharps and 3 flats. You need to remember where the sharps and flats sit on the stave and their order. Clue: for the two sharps in D major think **Father Christmas**.

D major   F major

A major   B♭ major

E♭ major   G major

Check your answers. /12

Did you check your answers?

Yes I did. I always do.

Book 2 page 8

Tones and semitones

In Music Theory is Fun Book 1 you learnt about tones / *whole steps* and semitones / *half steps* by using a keyboard.

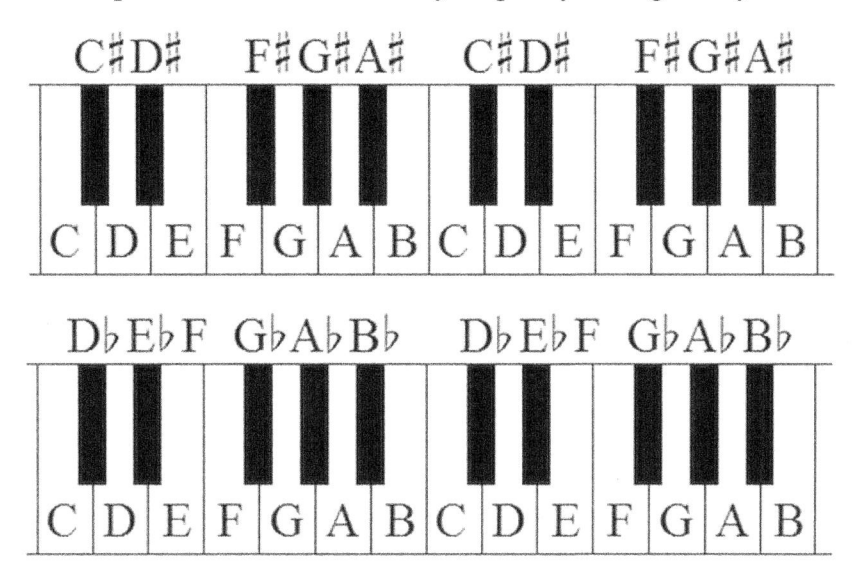

Fill in the missing letter names:

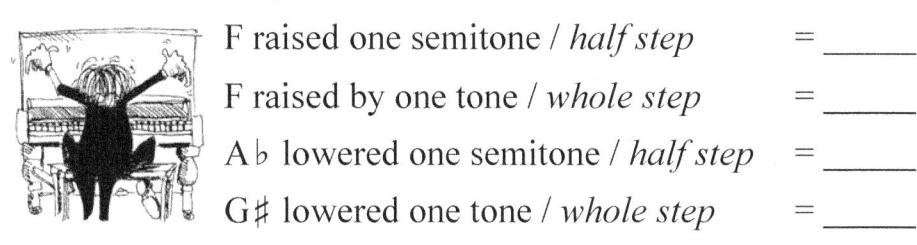

F raised one semitone / *half step* = _____

F raised by one tone / *whole step* = _____

A♭ lowered one semitone / *half step* = _____

G♯ lowered one tone / *whole step* = _____

When you think you can put in all the letter names on a keyboard, turn the page.

Yes you are. Hurry up!

I'm not ready for a test yet!

Book 2 page 9

Test yourself

Write the letter names of the white keys in capital letters on the keyboard below.

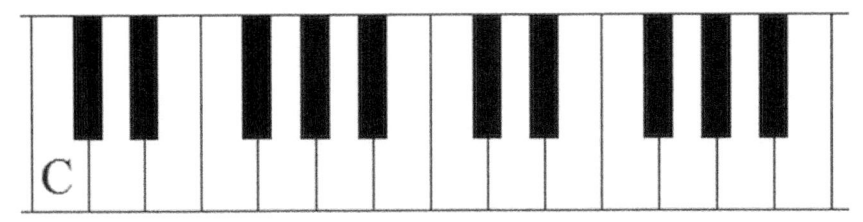

C

Put the letter names of the white keys in capital letters on the keyboard below and write the names of the sharps above the black keys.

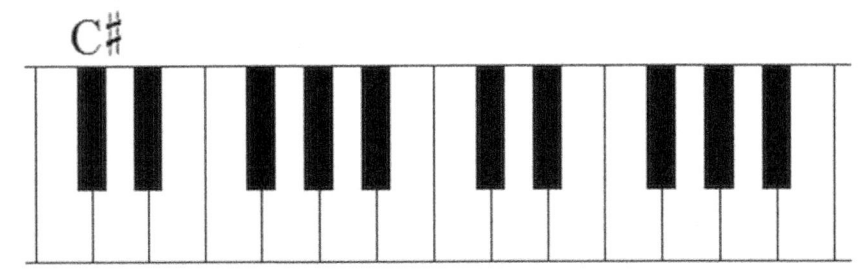

C♯

Put the letter names of the white keys in capital letters on the keyboard below and write the names of the flats above the black keys.

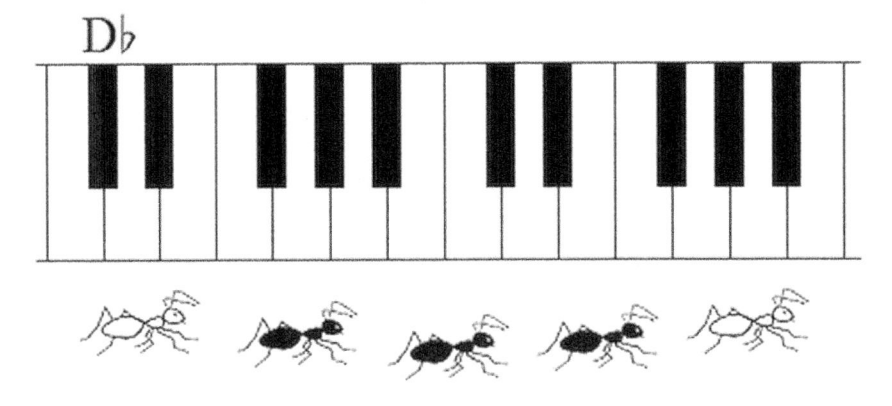

D♭

Book 2 page 10

Semitones / half steps in major scales

In major scales there is a semitone / *half step* between notes 3 and 4 and between notes 7 and 8. Here is one of your new scales – A major – with the semitones / *half steps* marked.

Write with key signature in the treble clef the scale of B♭ major in crotchets / *quarter notes* ascending. Mark the semitones / *half steps* with ⌐¬.

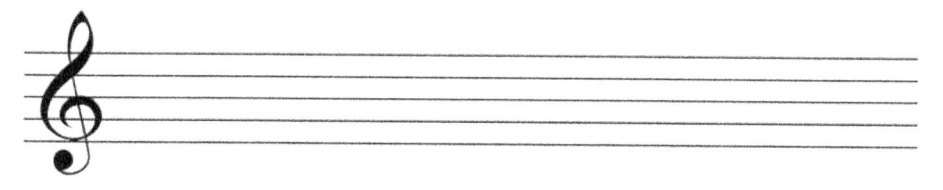

Write with key signature in the bass clef the scale of B♭ major in crotchets / *quarter notes* descending. Mark the semitones / *half steps* with ⌐¬.

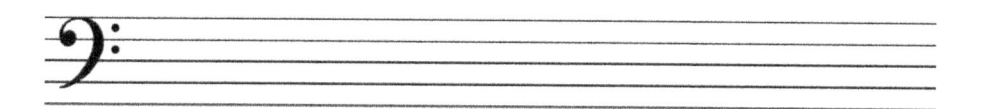

When you are ready to test yourself on the major scales, turn over the page.

I'm ready for a test.

Book 2 page 11

Test yourself

Write with key signature in the treble clef the scale of F major ascending in semibreves / *whole notes*. Mark the semitones / *half steps* with ⌐⌐.

Write with key signature in the bass clef the scale of A major descending in minims / *half notes*. Mark the semitones / *half steps*.

Write without key signature in the bass clef the scale of E♭ major ascending in crotchets / *quarter notes*. Mark the semitones / *half steps*.

Write with key signature in the treble clef the scale of G major ascending in minims / *half notes*. Mark the semitones / *half steps*.

4 more to do...

Book 2 page 12

Write without key signature in the bass clef the scale of D major descending in crotchets / *quarter notes*. Mark the semitones / *half steps*.

Write without key signature in the bass clef the scale of B♭ major ascending in semibreves / *whole notes*. Mark the semitones / *half steps*.

Write without key signature in the treble clef the scale of A major ascending in semibreves / *whole notes*. Mark the semitones / *half steps*.

Write without key signature in the treble clef the scale of E♭ major descending in minims / *half notes*. Mark the semitones / *steps*.

Ready for a new topic?

Yes please. Let's hurry.

Book 2 page 13

MINOR KEY SIGNATURES

Natural minor scales.

A minor: no sharps or flats. A minor is the relative minor of C major. If you count three notes from A you reach C in 3 semitones / *half steps*.

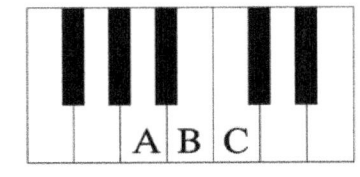

E minor: one sharp F♯. E minor is the relative minor of G major. If you count three notes from E you reach G in 3 semitones / *half steps*.

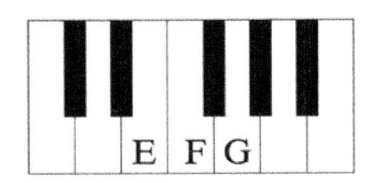

D minor: one flat B♭. D minor is the relative minor of F major. If you count three notes from D you reach F in 3 semitones / *half steps*.

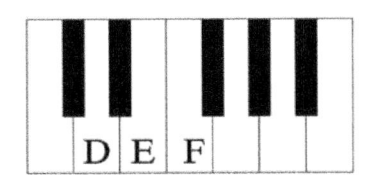

Practise the minor key signatures by writing them in the treble and bass clefs.

E minor   D Minor

Book 2 page 14

Test yourself

How many sharps has

G major?   1 ☐   2 ☐   3 ☐
A major?   1 ☐   2 ☐   3 ☐
D major?   1 ☐   2 ☐   3 ☐

How many flats has

E♭ major?   1 ☐   2 ☐   3 ☐
F major?   1 ☐   2 ☐   3 ☐
B♭ major?   1 ☐   2 ☐   3 ☐

Where are the semitones / *half steps* in major scales?

Between notes 4 & 5 and notes 7 & 8   ☐

3 & 4 and notes 6 & 7   ☐

3 & 4 and notes 7 & 8   ☐

5 & 6 and notes 7 & 8   ☐

On the piano keyboard, if you raise F 3 semitones / *half steps* you go to   G♯ ☐   A ☐   A♯ ☐

On the piano keyboard, if you lower E♭ 3 semitones / *half steps* you go to   B ☐   D♭ ☐   C ☐

Check your answers.   /12

Book 2 page 15

Which minor key signature has one sharp?

    A ☐   D ☐   E ☐

Which minor key signature has one flat?

    E ☐   A ☐   D ☐

Which minor key signature has no sharps or flats?

    E ☐   D ☐   A ☐

What is the relative major of A minor?

    C ☐   F ☐   G ☐

What is the relative minor of G major?

    A ☐   E ☐   D ☐

What is the relative minor of F major?

    A ☐   D ☐   E ☐

Write the key signatures of

    A major   E♭ major   E minor

Check your answers. /9

Book 2 page 16

Harmonic minor scales

Harmonic minor scales sound frightening but they are really very easy. All you do is raise the 7th note one semitone / *half step* ascending and descending.

A minor

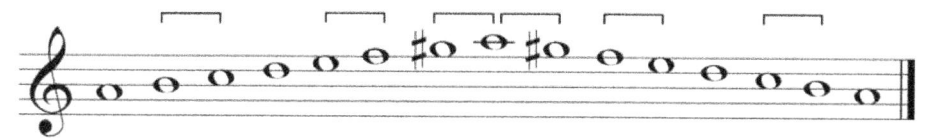

E minor

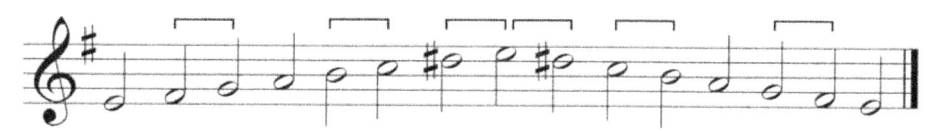

D minor

Important
There are semitones / *half steps* (marked ⌐⌐) between notes 2 & 3, 5 & 6 and 7 & 8 when ascending and descending.

Test yourself

Write without key signature in the treble clef the scale of
A harmonic minor ascending in semibreves / *whole notes*.
Mark the semitones / *half steps* with ⌐─┐.

Write with key signature in the bass clef the scale of
E harmonic minor descending in minims / *half notes*. Mark
the semitones / *half steps*.

Write without key signature in the bass clef the scale of
D harmonic minor ascending in crotchets / *quarter notes*.
Mark the semitones / *half steps*.

Time to check your answers.

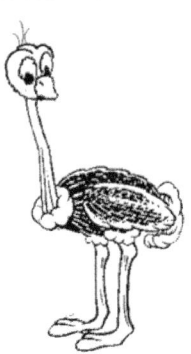

Book 2 page 18

Melodic minor scales

To write these scales you raise the 6th and 7th notes one semitone / *half step* ascending and lower them a semitone / *half step* when descending.

A minor

E minor

D minor

Semitones / *half steps* are between notes 2 & 3 and 7 & 8 when ascending.

Semitones / *half steps* are between notes 2 & 3 and 5 & 6 when descending.

Book 2 page 19

Test yourself

Write with key signature in the treble clef the scale of E melodic minor ascending in minims / *half notes*. Mark the semitones / *half steps*.

Write without key signature in the bass clef the scale of A melodic minor descending in crotchets / *quarter notes*. Mark the semitones / *half steps*.

Write with key signature in the bass clef the scale of D melodic minor descending in semibreves / *whole notes*. Mark the semitones / *half steps*.

Time to check your answers.

Book 2 page 20

Write the notes of the following scales ascending on these keyboards. The first scale has been done for you.

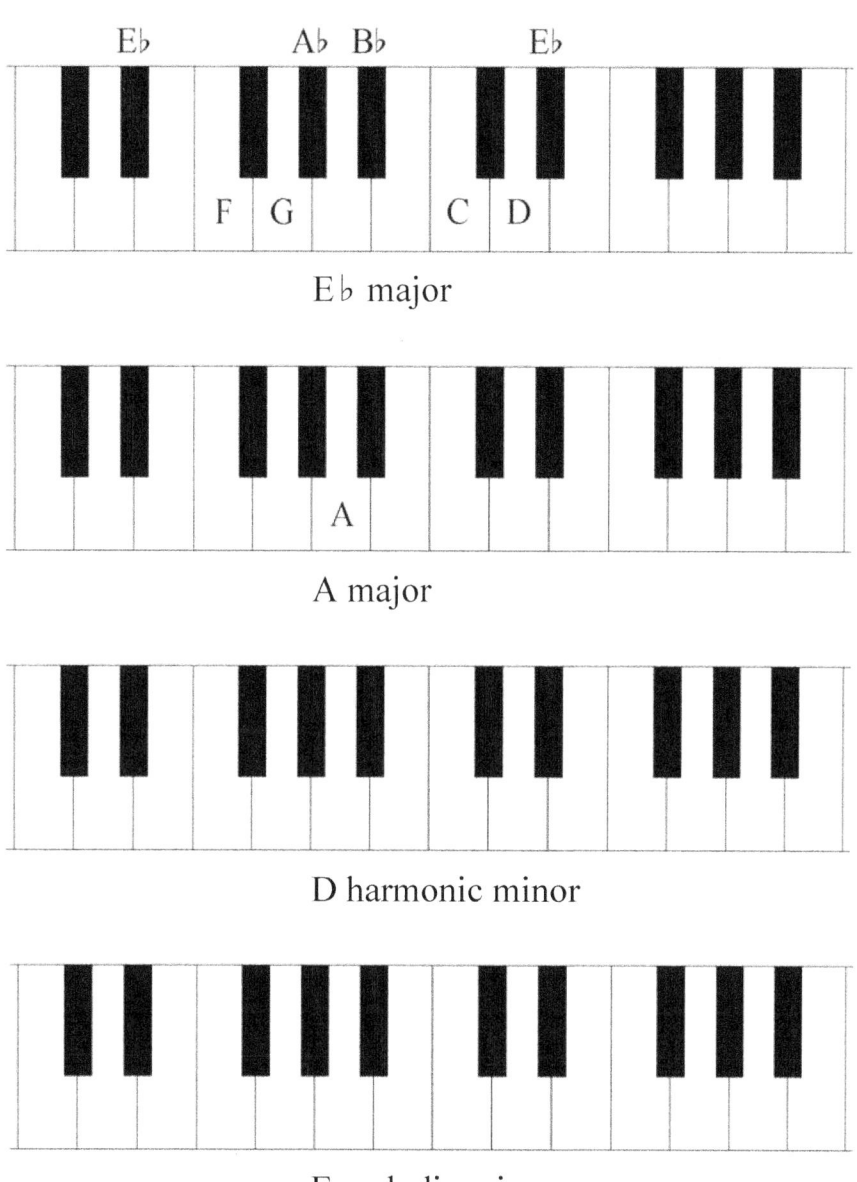

Eb   Ab   Bb   Eb
F   G   C   D

Eb major

A

A major

D harmonic minor

E melodic minor

Book 2 page 21

Key signature chart

You have now met the key signatures of seven major scales and three minor scales. Here they are.

major	key signature	minor
C	no sharps or flats	A
G	F♯	E
D	F♯ C♯	
A	F♯ C♯ G♯	
F	B♭	D
B♭	B♭ E♭	
E♭	B♭ E♭ A♭	

They are important. You will need to know them if, for example, you are going to take a music theory examination.

In this book, you only need to know the minor key signatures up to and including one sharp and one flat.

If you are given a choice between the harmonic and melodic scales, make sure you say which form of minor scale you are using in your answers.

We should learn these key signatures.

Book 2 page 22

INTERVALS

In Music Theory is Fun Book 1 you learnt that the first note of a scale is called the keynote or the 1st degree. The second note is the 2nd degree. The third note is the 3rd degree and so on until you reach the 8th degree or octave 8ve.

Write the degree of the scale (1st, 2nd, 3rd, etc.) under each of the notes marked with * in the following passages.

The key is D major.

The key is E♭ major.

The number of an interval is the number of degrees in the scale, counting always from the keynote.

For example, in A minor the keynote is A. Therefore, you count each interval from A like this:-

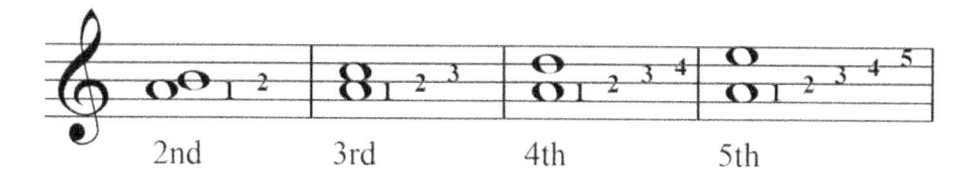

2nd   3rd   4th   5th

Book 2 page 23

Remember that in minor scales the 6th note and 7th notes might be sharpened. This will not alter the number of the interval.

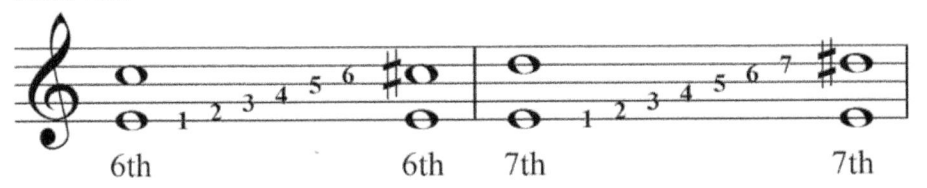

6th   6th   7th   7th

An interval is the difference in pitch between two notes. Let me remind you of melodic and harmonic intervals.

The melodic interval

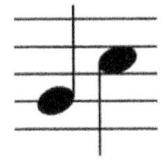

This is a melodic interval. The two notes are written one after the other and are played separately.

The harmonic interval

This interval is called a harmonic interval. The two notes are written one above the other and played at the same time.

Test yourself

In a melodic interval, always count from the lower note, even if the upper note is written first. Both of these are intervals of a 5th.

Give the number of these melodic intervals (2nd, 3rd, etc.).

The key is E minor.

The key is F major.

Give the number of each harmonic interval. The lower note is the keynote.

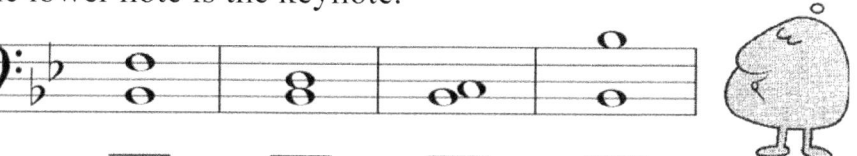

Check your answers.

Book 2 page 25

TONIC TRIADS

The first note of a scale is called the keynote or tonic.

A tonic triad is made up of three notes:-

1. The keynote or tonic.

2. The 3rd degree (note) of the scale.

3. The 5th degree (note) of the scale.

Sometimes you will be asked to write a tonic triad with key signature, sometimes without key signature.

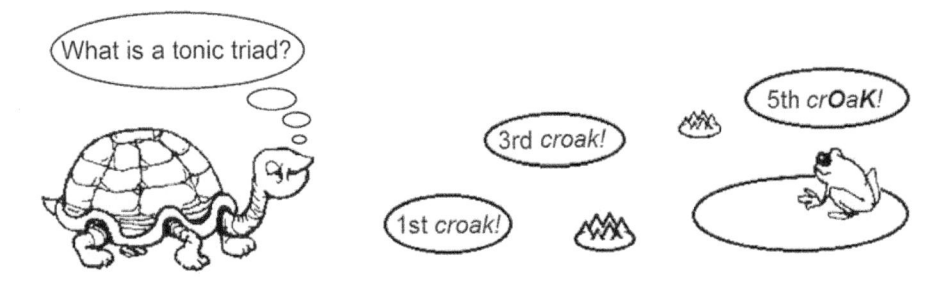

So far you have met the tonic triad of D major with its F♯.

with key signature   without key signature

With the key signatures that have been added in this book, there are other keys where accidentals occur in the first five notes of the scale.

Book 2 page 26

Test yourself

Write these tonic triads with key signatures.

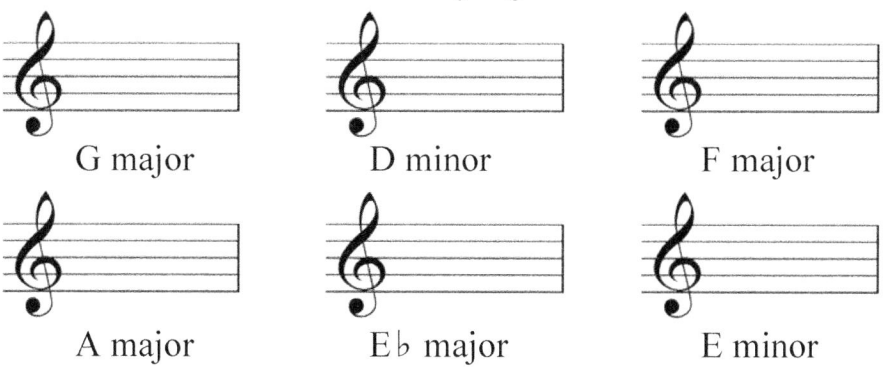

G major D minor F major

A major E♭ major E minor

Write these tonic triads without key signatures.

D major B♭ major

A major E♭ major

G major

E minor What is your score? /12

TIME SIGNATURES

In Music Theory is Fun Book 1 you met three time signatures. $\frac{2}{4}$ $\frac{3}{4}$ $\frac{4}{4}$ or C

The top number tells you how many beats in a bar or measure.

The bottom number tells you what kind of beat.

Simple duple time

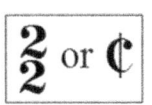

$\frac{2}{2}$ or ₵ is the only new simple duple time in this book. It means two minim / *half note* beats in a bar.

Simple triple time

Here are two new simple triple time signatures. $\frac{3}{2}$ $\frac{3}{8}$

You can easily work out $\frac{3}{2}$ time – 3 minim / *half note* beats in a bar.

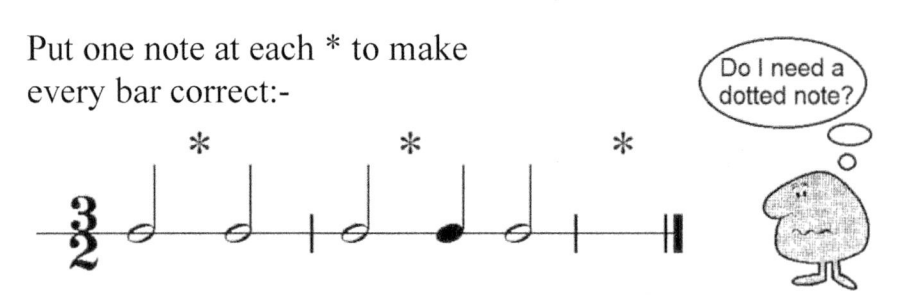

Put one note at each * to make every bar correct:-

Do I need a dotted note?

$\frac{3}{8}$ time is 3 beats in a bar – but what kind of beat?

Book 2 page 28

What is the other name for an eighth note?
Yes, a quaver.

3/8 time means 3 quaver / *eighth note* beats in a bar.

If the top number is 3,
there are three beats in a bar
and it is simple triple time.

Simple quadruple time

4/2 is the only new simple quadruple time. It means 4 minim / *half note* beats in a bar.

Test yourself

Add a time signature to each of the following:-

Book 2 page 29

Test yourself

Rewrite these rhythms, as shown in the first bar, using half the time values.

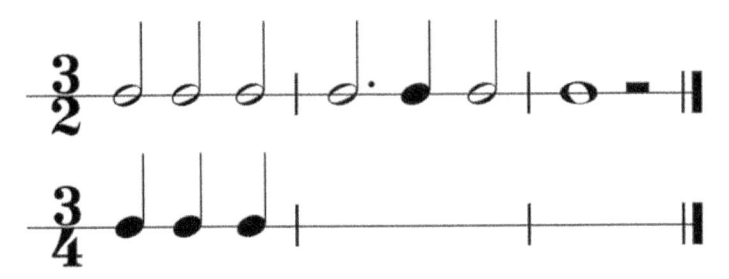

Rewrite these rhythms, as shown in the first bar, using twice the time values.

Rewrite these rhythms, as shown in the first bar, using half the time values.

Check your answers.

Book 2 page 30

THE GROUPING OF NOTES

I shall remind you first of the rules for time signatures you met in my Music Theory is Fun Book 1. Then I shall add the rules for the new time signatures in this book.

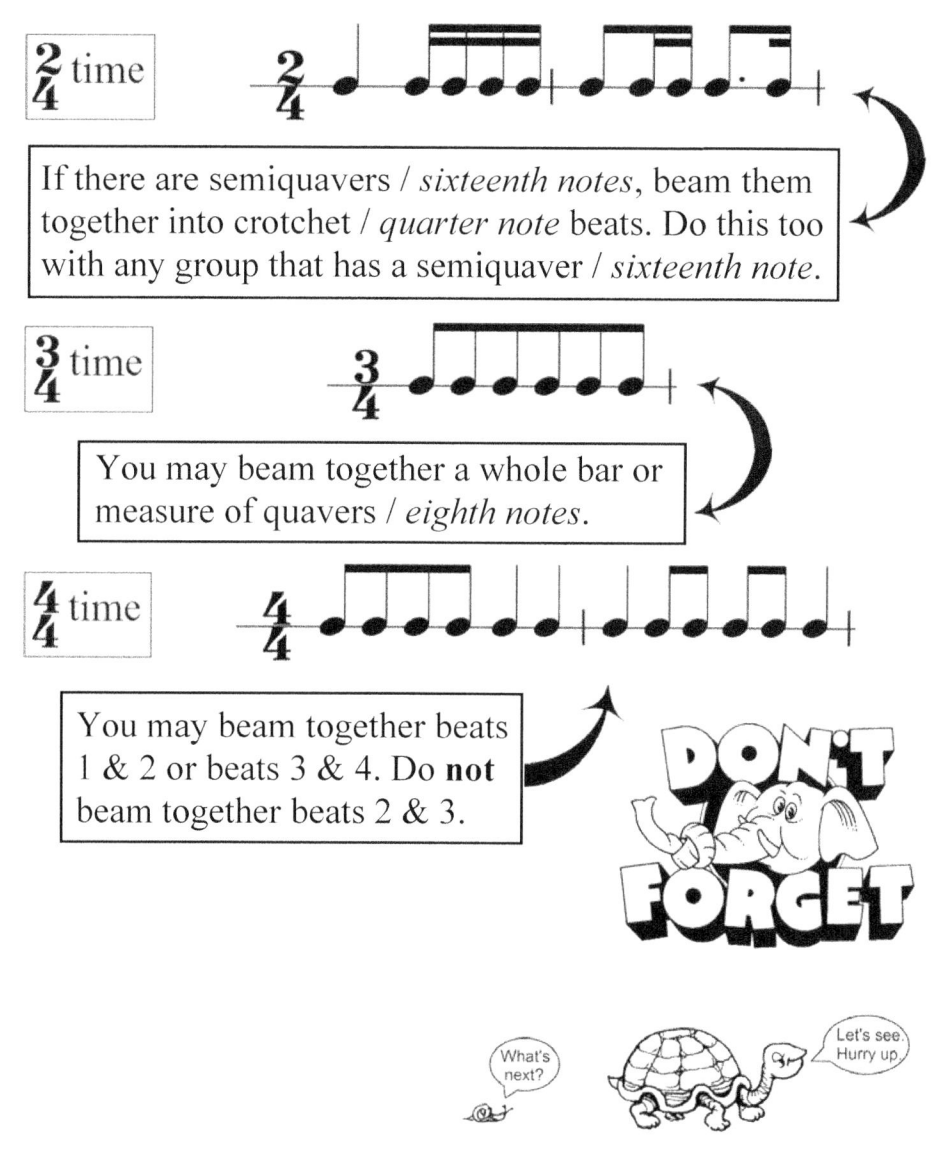

2/4 time

If there are semiquavers / *sixteenth notes*, beam them together into crotchet / *quarter note* beats. Do this too with any group that has a semiquaver / *sixteenth note*.

3/4 time

You may beam together a whole bar or measure of quavers / *eighth notes*.

4/4 time

You may beam together beats 1 & 2 or beats 3 & 4. Do **not** beam together beats 2 & 3.

The new time signatures are $\frac{2}{2}$ or ¢ $\frac{3}{2}$ $\frac{4}{2}$ $\frac{3}{8}$

Here are some rules for grouping the notes.

Beam together a group of 4 quavers / *eighth notes* if they could be replaced by a minim / *half note*.

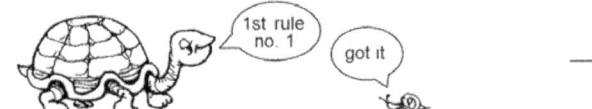

Beam together a group of 4 semiquavers / *sixteenth notes* if they could be replaced by a crotchet / *quarter note*.

If possible, use a semibreve / *whole note* rather than a tied minim / *half note*.

Do not join beats 2 and 3.

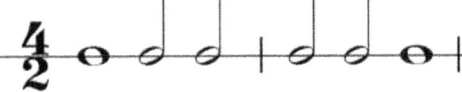

Normally you should not beam together more than 4 semiquavers / *sixteenth notes* but there are exceptions.

You may beam together a group of quavers / *eighth notes* and semiquavers / *sixteenth notes*.

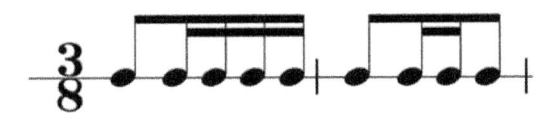

Book 2 page 32

Write a whole bar of quavers / *eighth notes* in the times given.

$\frac{3}{4}$ |————————————|

$\frac{4}{4}$ |————————————————|

Write a whole bar of semiquavers / *sixteenth notes* in the times given.

$\frac{2}{4}$ |————————————|

$\frac{3}{8}$ |————————————————|

When a group of notes is beamed together all the stems in the group go either up or down.

If there are two notes beamed together, the note that is further from the middle line has the correct stem. The other note has to follow.

Beam together each group of quavers / *eighth notes*.

Check your answers.

Book 2 page 33

THE GROUPING OF RESTS

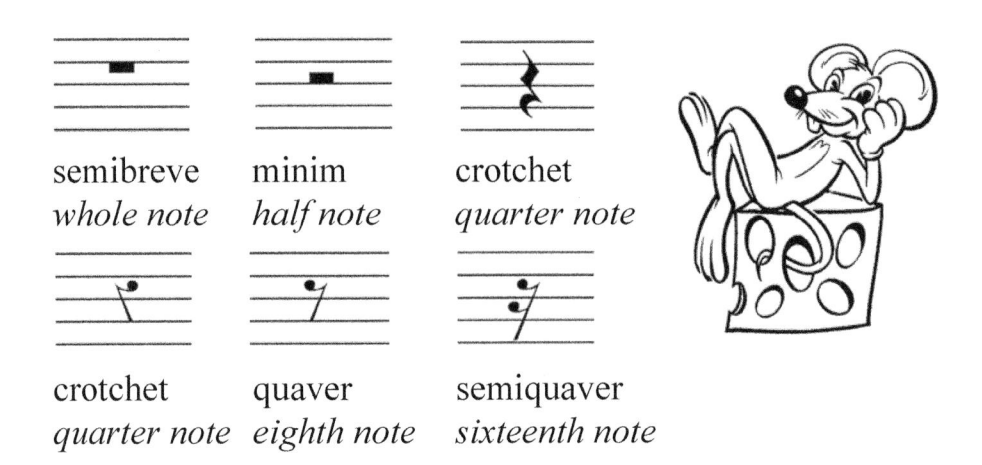

semibreve / *whole note*

minim / *half note*

crotchet / *quarter note*

crotchet / *quarter note*

quaver / *eighth note*

semiquaver / *sixteenth note*

Whole bar / *measure*

A semibreve rest / *whole note* rest is used for a whole bar with these time signatures. You will not need the 4/2 whole bar rest until Book 4.

Part of a bar / *measure*

In quadruple time you can join beats 1 and 2 or 3 and 4.

In triple time rests for beats 2 and 3 must be separate but rests for beats 1 and 2 may be joined.

In duple time each beat needs a separate rest.

Book 2 page 34

Always finish one beat before you start another.

Put the correct rest or rests where you see ✱

Check your answers.

Book 2 page 35

TRIPLETS

A triplet is a group of three notes, or three notes and rests, played in the time of two.

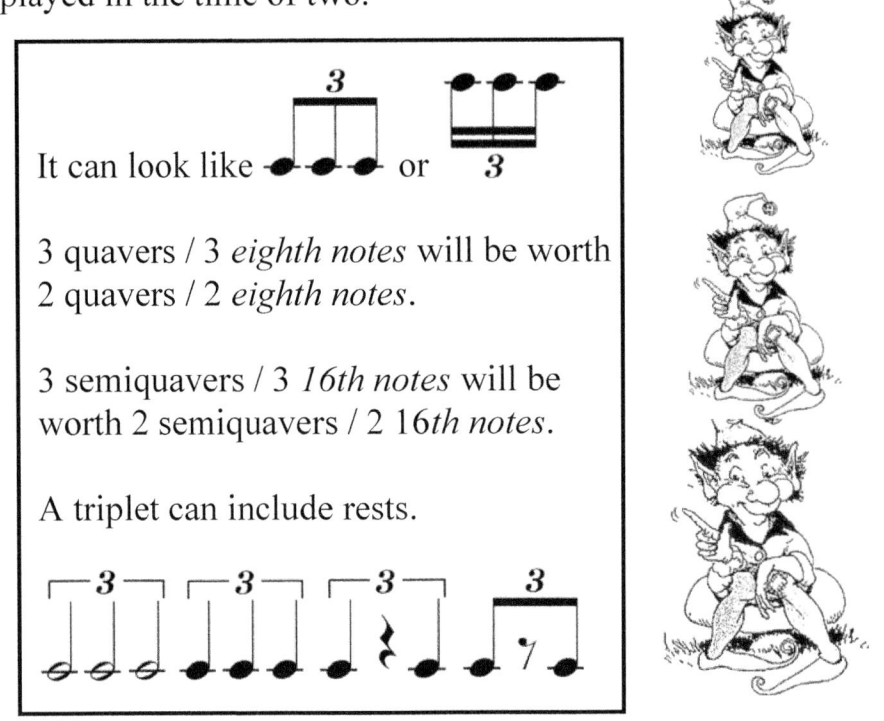

It can look like [♪♪♪] or [♬♬♬]

3 quavers / 3 *eighth notes* will be worth 2 quavers / 2 *eighth notes*.

3 semiquavers / 3 *16th notes* will be worth 2 semiquavers / 2 *16th notes*.

A triplet can include rests.

Try these. The first one is done for you:-

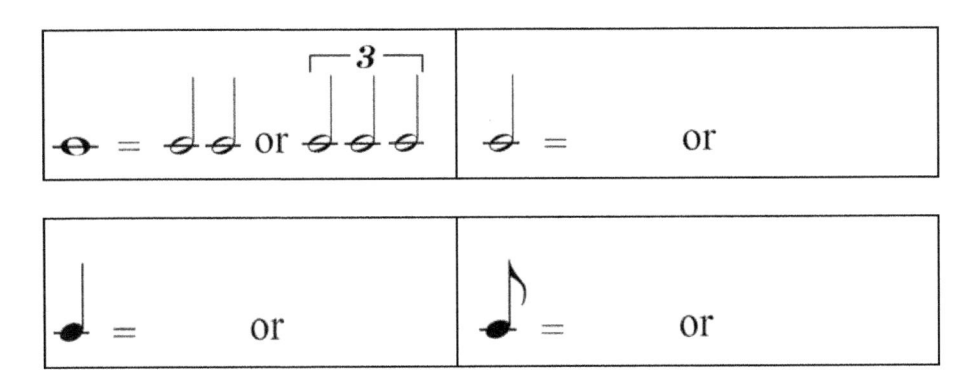

𝅝 = 𝅗𝅥 𝅗𝅥 or 𝅗𝅥 𝅗𝅥 𝅗𝅥 (triplet)   𝅗𝅥 = _____ or _____

♩ = _____ or _____   ♪ = _____ or _____

Book 2 page 36

Here are two examples of triplets written for you.

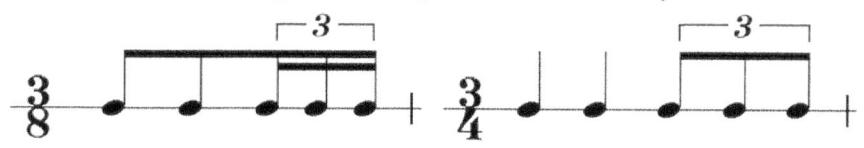

Put a triplet sign [⌐3⌐] where you think it is needed to make the time signature correct.

Write a triplet of 3 quavers / 3 *eighth notes* or 3 semiquavers / 3 *sixteenth notes* where you see the *

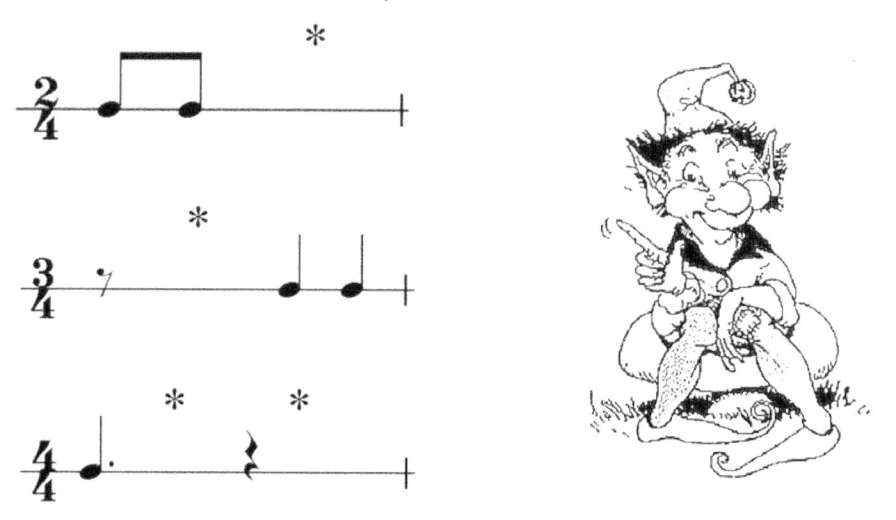

Book 2 page 37

LEDGER LINES

In Music Theory is Fun Book 1 you learnt the letter names of notes written one ledger line below the stave in the treble clef and one ledger line above the stave in the bass clef.

Now you will meet notes on more ledger lines above and below the stave in both clefs.

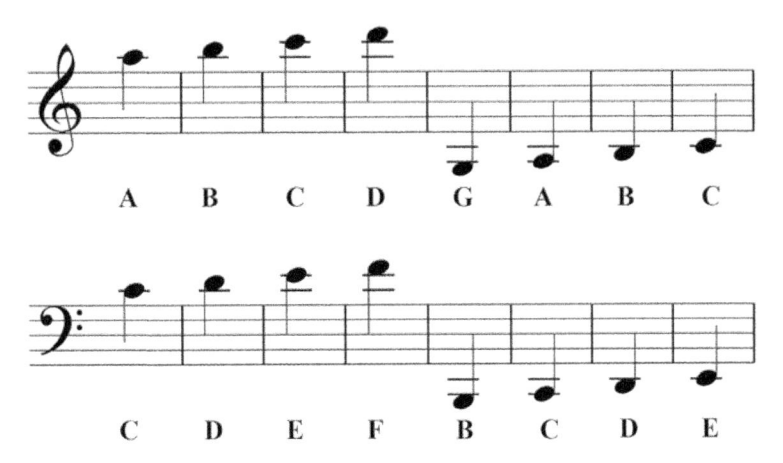

A   B   C   D   G   A   B   C

C   D   E   F   B   C   D   E

Friends forever

Sasha was lonely.
She had no-one to play with.

She lived next door to a ___ ___ ___ ___

Each day Sasha hoped that a friend would come.

Book 2 page 38

One day, she saw
a dog with a friendly — — — —
at the café.

His name was __ __ __

She __ __ __ __ __ __ her master
to let her out of the house.

Dab was the same __ __ __ as Sasha.

He often came back to the __ __ __ __

Sasha was not lonely any more.

She and Dab stayed friends forever.

Writing at the same pitch

Here you see a note written in the treble clef. Next to it is the same note written in the bass clef. We say the two notes are at the same pitch.

Write in the treble clef at the same pitch the same note as the one shown in the bass clef.

Write the bass clef notes at the same pitch as the treble clef notes:-

Take care to draw the ledger lines the same width apart as the stave lines.

FOUR-BAR THYTHMS

In Music Theory is Fun Book 1 you were given a two-bar rhythm with a time signature and asked to write another two bars. In this book I shall give you the first bar of a rhythm and ask you to continue writing until you have completed a four-bar rhythm.

Handy hints

1. Notice the time signature. Take care to follow the rules for grouping notes and rests in that time signature.
2. Experiment with different rhythms. Tap each one. Which one seems best?
3. Write your rhythms on paper first.
4. End on a strong beat.

Complete each line to make a four-bar rhythm. Try to make each bar different in some of your answers. If you want the rhythm to be especially fast (or slow) put Presto (or Lento) at the beginning.

Book 2 page 41

PUZZLES

QUIZZES

TESTS

Book 2 page 42

Fun page

Draw a string for each balloon. I drew the first for you.

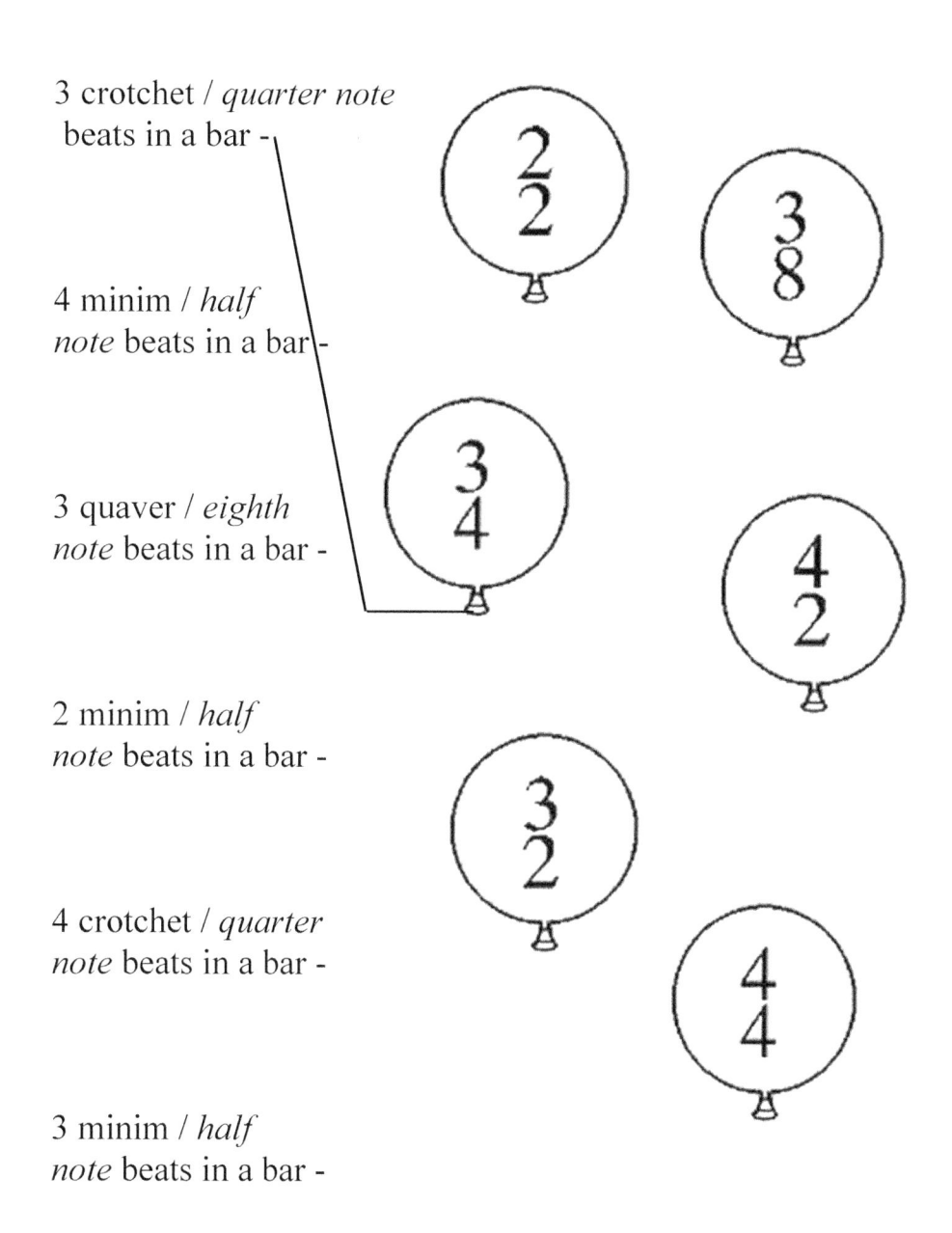

3 crotchet / *quarter note* beats in a bar -

4 minim / *half note* beats in a bar -

3 quaver / *eighth note* beats in a bar -

2 minim / *half note* beats in a bar -

4 crotchet / *quarter note* beats in a bar -

3 minim / *half note* beats in a bar -

Book 2 page 43

Musical Matchword

Can you join the boxes to make ten musical words? I have joined the first one for you.

DEG	ENTAL	_____
TRIP	ADS	_____
LED	VALS	_____
INTER	REES	_____
ACCID	TONE	_____
MIN	JOR	_____
SEMI	LETS	_____
MA	ALES	_____
SC	GER	_____
TRI	OR	_____

Book 2 page 44

Musical Anagrams

techcrot / *traquer eton* _____

Clue: A note worth 4 semiquavers / *4 sixteenth notes.*

dregle sinle _____

Clue: These are above and below the stave.

charmion _____

Clue: For this interval play the notes together.

comidel _____

Clue: For this interval play the notes separately.

veremibes / *weloh tone* _____

Clue: A whole bar's rest hangs from the line.

vertinal _____

Clue: Count from the keynote to find its number.

icont dratis _____

Clue: These use the 1st, 3rd and 5th notes of a scale.

plaquedur _____

Clue: The time with four beats in a bar.

pliter _____

Clue: The time with three beats in a bar.

pudle _____

Clue: The time with two beats in a bar.

Crossword

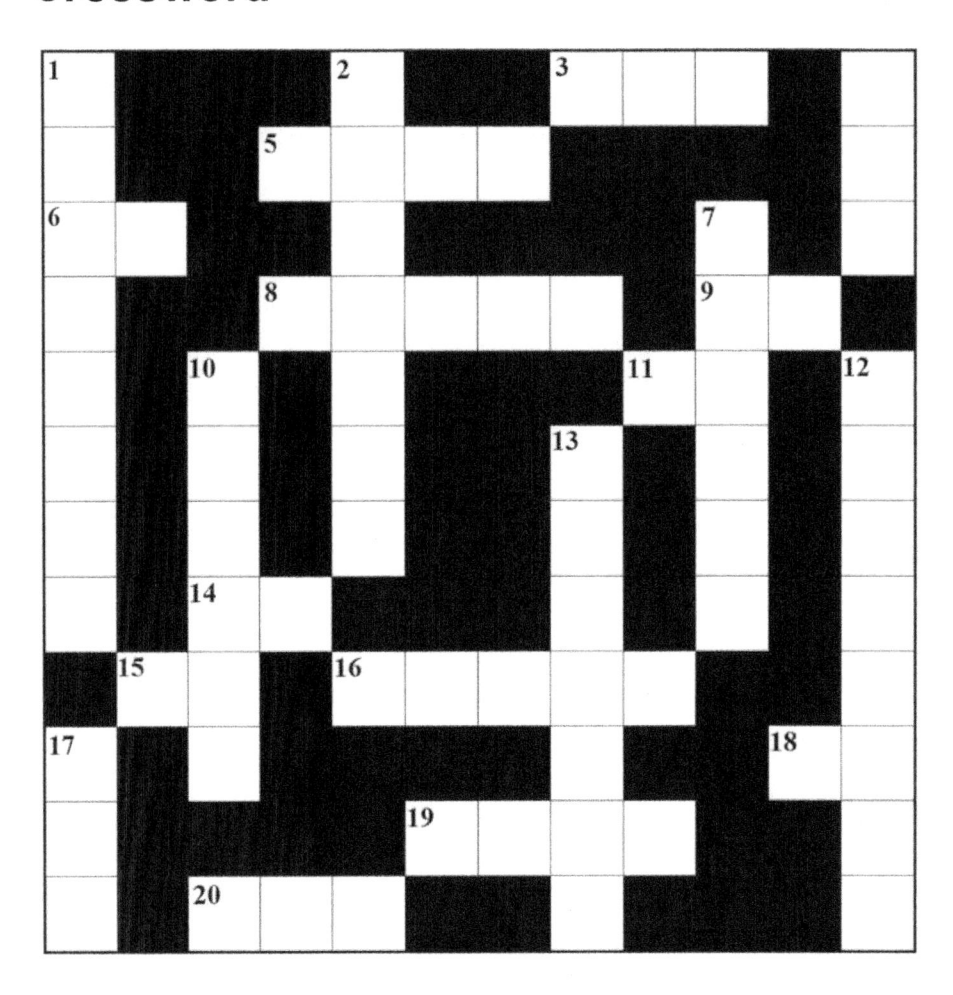

Clues

Across

3 hold back, slower at once
5 musical term meaning less
6 short for moderately loud
8 musical term meaning much

Book 2 page 46

9 two notes a semitone / *half step* apart
11 an interval of a 5th in C major
14 an interval of a 2nd in G major
15 two notes a tone / *whole step* apart
16 the 1st, 3rd and 5th notes of a scale
18 an interval of a 3rd in F major
19 musical term meaning movement
20 musical term meaning with

Down

1 the distance between two notes
2 you raise the 6th and 7th notes in this scale
4 musical term meaning more
7 play a group of notes smoothly
10 extra lines above or below the stave
12 short, detached
13 at a walking pace
17 musical term meaning not

Book 2 page 47

Musical terms word search

S	A	M	E	N	O	A	C	T	E
O	S	A	G	M	S	T	O	S	T
S	S	J	I	X	O	Z	E	P	E
T	A	S	O	F	I	N	G	H	O
E	I	L	C	R	Z	T	E	N	M
N	H	O	O	A	A	T	D	Y	A
U	J	D	S	T	R	O	P	P	O
T	L	O	O	O	G	R	A	V	E
O	M	E	F	M	O	T	O	G	T
H	M	A	E	S	T	O	S	O	U

Meaning	Musical term
movement	moto
majestically	_____
gracefully	_____
sustained	_____
very slow	_____
too much	_____
without	_____
less	_____
merry	_____
loud	_____
very	_____

Book 2 page 48

Quiz 1

Put a tick / *check mark* (✓) in the correct box.

1. **allargando**
   - ☐ at a walking pace
   - ☐ slow, leisurely
   - ☐ broadening out
   - ☐ very quick

2. **larghetto**
   - ☐ faster than largo
   - ☐ slow and stately
   - ☐ very slow
   - ☐ at a walking pace

3. **sustained**
   - ☐ subito
   - ☐ sostenuto
   - ☐ maestoso
   - ☐ ritenuto

4. **held on**
   - ☐ marcato
   - ☐ staccato
   - ☐ subito
   - ☐ tenuto

5. **mosso**
   - ☐ less
   - ☐ more
   - ☐ movement
   - ☐ much

6. **semi-staccato**

Check your answers.

Book 2 page 49

Quiz 2

True (**T**) or False (**F**)?

1. The key of C major has no sharps or flats.   T ☐   F ☐

2. The key of B♭ major has two flats.   T ☐   F ☐

3. The key of A major has three sharps.   T ☐   F ☐

4. The key of E minor has three flats.   T ☐   F ☐

5. The 7th note in a harmonic minor scale is raised one semitone / *one half step* ascending and descending.   T ☐   F ☐

6. In E♭ major the 6th degree is B♭.   T ☐   F ☐

7. The two notes in a melodic interval are written one above the other and played at the same time.   T ☐   F ☐

8. The tonic triad of D minor is D F♯ A.   T ☐   F ☐

9. The symbol ¢ means 2 minim / *2 half note* beats in the bar.   T ☐   F ☐

10. A minim rest / *half note rest* is used for a whole bar's rest in 4/4 time.   T ☐   F ☐

Check your answers.   /10

Book 2 page 50

Handy hints for tests

This section is for you to practise the different types of questions you could have in a test or an exam.

The questions could be on any topic covered in this book and in Music Theory is Fun Book 1.

Revise each topic in this book thoroughly.

Don't forget to study musical terms and signs – they are **always** included.

Practice makes perfect!

Practice makes perfect!

If you have worked through this book carefully and understood each topic, this will be an easy task for you.

> Before you begin any test, write out your key signature chart from memory (see page 22). Always refer to the chart when tackling questions that require you to know a key signature.

Book 2 page 51

Test 1

Put a tick / *check mark* (✓) in the box next to the correct answer.

1. Name this note:

   C sharp ☐   A sharp ☐   G natural ☐

2. How many crotchet / *quarter note* beats are in a bar with this time signature?

   2 ☐   3 ☐   4 ☐

3. For how many quaver / *eighth note* beats does this rest last?

   2 ☐   3 ☐   4 ☐

4. Add the total number of crotchet / *quarter note* beats of silence in these rests.

   6 ☐   5 ☐   4 ☐

5. The relative minor of F major is:

   D minor ☐   A minor ☐   E minor ☐

6. Name this scale.

   G melodic minor ☐
   A melodic minor ☐
   E harmonic minor ☐

Book 2 page 52

Test 2

1. Write a triplet of 3 quavers / *3 eighth notes* or
   3 semiquavers / *3 sixteenth notes* where you see *.

   (a)

   (b)

   (c)

2. Name the key of this tonic triad.

3. Complete each line to make a 4-bar rhythm.

   (a)

   (b)

   (c)

   (d)

Book 2 page 53

Test 3

1. Write a one-octave E♭ major scale with key signature in semibreves / *whole notes* descending.
   Mark the semitones / *half steps*.

2. Write a one-octave A major scale without key signature in crotchets / *quarter notes* ascending. Put in accidentals where needed and mark the semitones / *half steps*.

3. Write a one-octave E harmonic minor scale without key signature in minims / *half notes* descending. Put in accidentals where needed and mark the semitones / *half steps*.

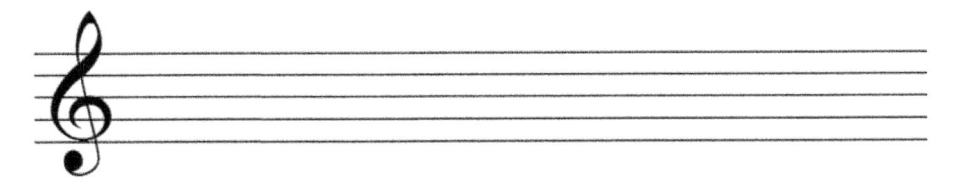

4. Write a one-octave D melodic minor scale with key signature in crotchets / *quarter notes* ascending.
   Mark the semitones / *half steps*.

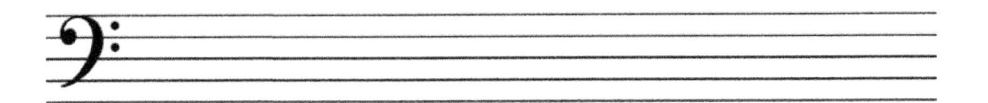

Book 2 page 54

Test 4

1. Here are four pieces of music. Add a time signature to each of them.

   (a)
   (b)
   (c)
   (d)

2. Write a higher note above each given note to make the named harmonic interval.

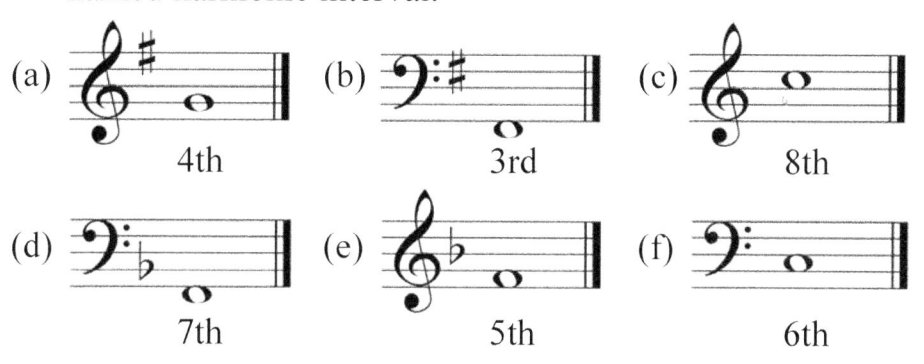

   (a) 4th (b) 3rd (c) 8th
   (d) 7th (e) 5th (f) 6th

3. Add the clef and any sharps or flats for this E♭ major scale.

Book 2 page 55

Test 5

1. Write the letter names for each of the notes marked *.
   Include the sharp or flat.

2. Write the notes in the correct order of the time values beginning with the longest and ending with the shortest.

3. Name the keys of these tonic triads.

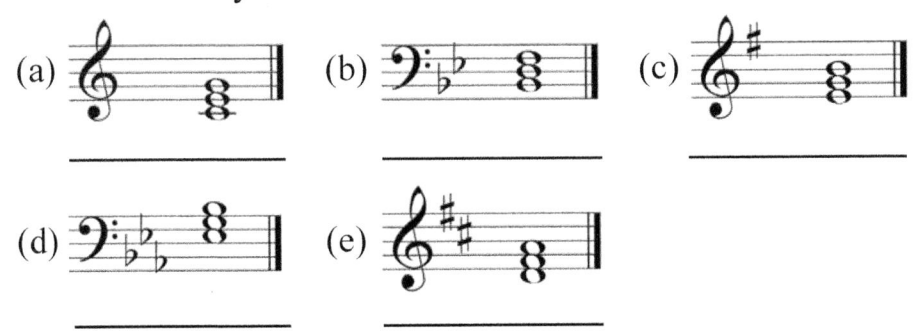

   (a)   (b)   (c)

   (d)   (e)

4. Write this passage of music in notes and rests of twice the value.

Book 2 page 56

Test 6

Look at this passage of music then answer the questions.

1. Name the key of this piece.

   _____

2. What type of beat is shown in the time signature?

   _____

3. How many beats are there in each bar / *measure*? _____

4. What is the meaning of Presto? _____

5. How should you play the two notes in bar 2?

       slowly ☐   smoothly ☐   quickly ☐

6. How many bars have staccato notes?

       6 ☐   5 ☐   4 ☐

7. How many accented notes are there in this piece?

       6 ☐   4 ☐   3 ☐

8. What does *ff* mean? _____

Book 2 page 57

Test 7

Look at this melody then answer the questions below.

1. Copy the music from bar 5 to the end just as it is written.

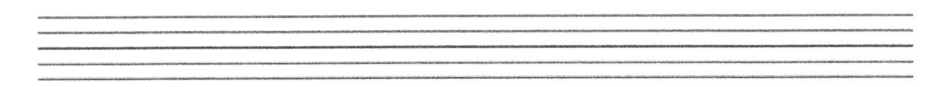

2. Name the first four notes in bar 6.

   (a) _____ (b) _____ (c) _____ (d) _____

3. Which two bars have the same rhythms? _____

4. What is the meaning of Allegro? _____

5. Write the letter name of the highest note. _____

6. How should the first two notes be played? _____

7. What does ⌒ mean over the note in bar 4?
   _____

8. Which bar has the note with the strongest accent? _____

9. Name the degree of the scale (e.g. 1st, 2nd) of the first note in bar 3. _____

Book 2 page 58

Test 8

1. This passage of music has no time signature. Work out what it should be and write it in the correct place.

2. Copy out bars 1-4 in the treble clef without a key signature. Remember to write an accidental if needed and to put in the time signature. Write neatly and accurately.

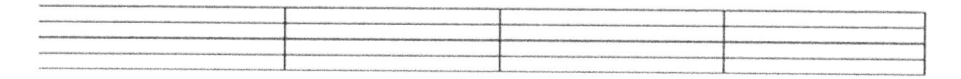

3. Name the major key of the melody. _____

4. Name the minor key with the same key signature. _____

5. Name the notes in bar 7. _____

6. Name the interval (number only) between notes 2 and 3 of bar 2. _____

7. Which bar has the same rhythm as bar 3? _____

8. Circle the note worth 3 crotchets / 3 *quarter notes* in the passage.

9. Circle two notes next to each other which make an octave interval.

Book 2 page 59

Test 9

Look at this melody and answer the questions below.

1. Find a triplet in the passage and copy it here.

2. Find in the passage two notes next to each other and a semitone / a *half step* apart. Copy them here.

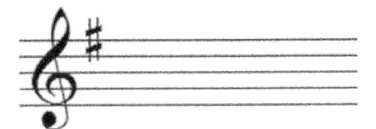

3. Raise each note in bar 1 a semitone / *a half step* and write them here.

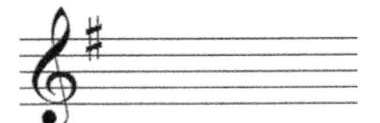

4. Lower each note in bar 5 a semitone / *a half step* and write them here.

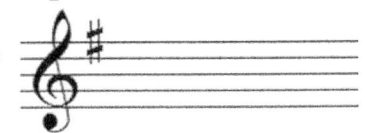

5. Copy out bar 4 in the bass clef and put in the key signature.

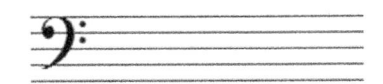

6. Give the meaning of the following:

mf _____

Lento _____ _____

Book 2 page 60

Test 10

1. This passage of music has no time signature. Work out what it should be and write it in the correct place.

2. Write the notes in bar 4 one octave lower in the bass clef. Put in the key signature.

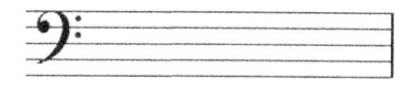

3. How many staccato notes are there? _____

4. Name the intervals in bar 11 between

    (a) notes 1 and 2 _____

    (b) notes 2 and 3 _____

5. Give the meaning of

    sfz _____

    mp _____

    $<$ _____

    Andante _____

    $>$ _____

    f _____

Book 2 page 61

MIM

Book 2 page 62

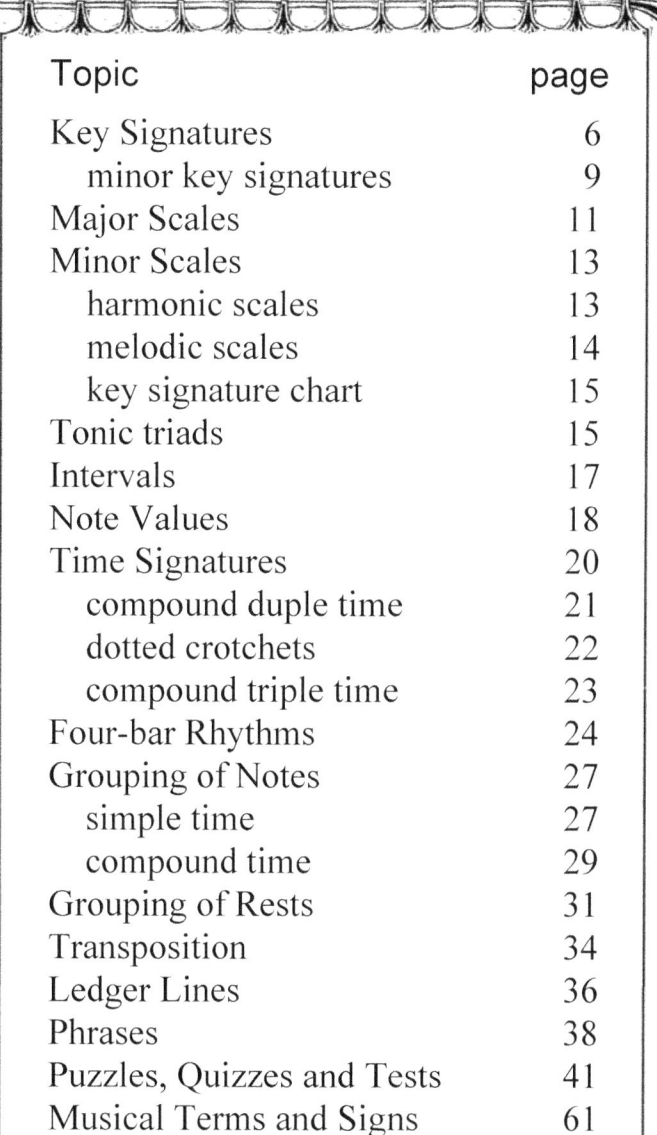

CONTENTS
Book 3

Topic	page
Key Signatures	6
minor key signatures	9
Major Scales	11
Minor Scales	13
harmonic scales	13
melodic scales	14
key signature chart	15
Tonic triads	15
Intervals	17
Note Values	18
Time Signatures	20
compound duple time	21
dotted crotchets	22
compound triple time	23
Four-bar Rhythms	24
Grouping of Notes	27
simple time	27
compound time	29
Grouping of Rests	31
Transposition	34
Ledger Lines	36
Phrases	38
Puzzles, Quizzes and Tests	41
Musical Terms and Signs	61

KEY SIGNATURES

Which key signatures do you need now? You will need major and minor key signatures. You already know some of the key signatures because you met them in my Music Theory is Fun Books 1 and 2.

Major Key Signatures

At this level you will need to know all major key signatures up to and including four sharps and four flats.

major	key signature
C	no sharps or flats
G	F♯
D	F♯ C♯
A	F♯ C♯ G♯
E	F♯ C♯ G♯ D♯
F	B♭
B♭	B♭ E♭
E♭	B♭ E♭ A♭
A♭	B♭ E♭ A♭ D♭

That's a lot to learn!

Important

The sharps and flats in the key signatures are always placed on the lines and in the spaces as shown below.

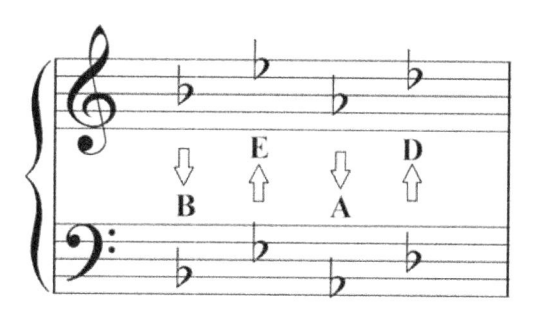

Important

Do not write the sharps and flats an octave higher or lower - this is a common mistake.

Book 3 page 7

Test yourself

Complete the following:-

1. D major has ____ sharps.
2. B♭ major has ____ flats.
3. E major has ____ sharps.
4. A♭ major has ____ flats.
5. A major has 3 _____
6. E♭ major has ____ flats.
7. ___ major has 1 flat.
8. ___ major has 1 sharp.

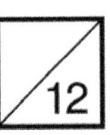

Fill in the key signatures:-

9. E major

10. E♭ major

11. A♭ major

12. A major

How many did you get right? /12

Book 3 page 8

Minor Key Signatures

Minor key signatures need to be known up to and including four sharps and four flats.

minor	key signature
A	no sharps or flats
E	F♯
B	F♯ C♯
F♯	F♯ C♯ G♯
C♯	F♯ C♯ G♯ D♯
D	B♭
G	B♭ E♭
C	B♭ E♭ A♭
F	B♭ E♭ A♭ D♭

Important

Remember to place the sharps and flats in their correct positions on the stave.

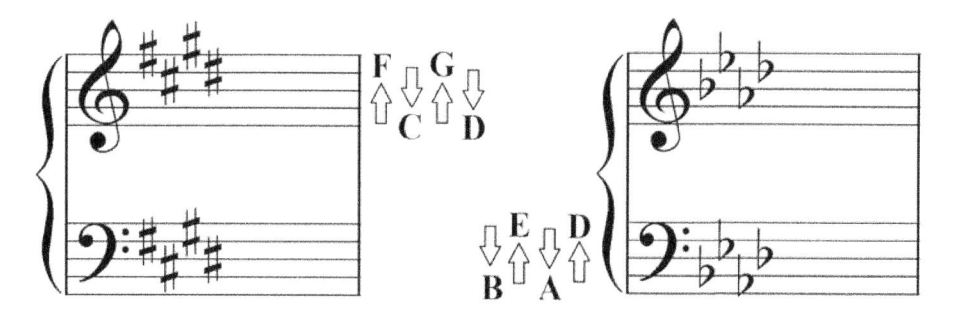

Book 3 page 9

Test yourself

Complete the following:-

1. B minor has ____ sharps.
2. C minor has ____ flats.
3. F♯ minor has ____ sharps.
4. F minor has ____ flats.
5. C♯ minor has 4 _____
6. G minor has ____ flats.
7. ___ minor has 1 flat.
8. ___ minor has 1 sharp.

Fill in the key signatures:-

9. C♯ minor

10. C minor

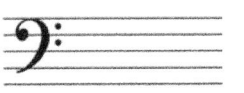

11. F minor

12. F♯ minor

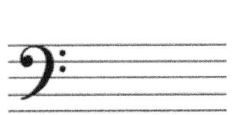

How many did you get right? ▢/12

Book 3 page 10

MAJOR SCALES

Which major scales do you need to know now? You will need all the major scales up to and including 4 sharps and 4 flats. You have already met all the key signatures, so the rest is easy.

All major scales have the same pattern of tones / *whole steps* and semitones / *half steps*:-

tone	tone	semitone	tone	tone	tone	semitone
whole step	*whole step*	*half step*	*whole step*	*whole step*	*whole step*	*half step*

You can remember it as:- **T T S   T T T S**
W W H   W W W H

Here is the scale of E major showing the order of tones and semitones.

Important
The first note of a scale is called the keynote or tonic.

Book 3 page 11

Test yourself

1. Write with key signature in the treble clef the scale of E major ascending in semibreves / *whole notes*.

2. Write without key signature in the bass clef the scale of A♭ major descending in crotchets / *quarter notes*.

3. Write with key signature in the bass clef the scale of A major ascending and descending in semibreves / *whole notes*. Mark the semitones / *half steps* with ⌐¬.

4. Write without key signature in the treble clef the scale of F major ascending and descending in semibreves / *whole notes*.

Book 3 page 12

MINOR SCALES

At this level you must know the minor scales in the harmonic and melodic forms up to and including 4 sharps and 4 flats.

Harmonic Minor Scales

Semitones / *half steps* occur between notes [2&3], [5&6] and [7&8]. Raise the 7th note one semitone / *one half step* ascending and descending.

1. Write with key signature in the treble clef the scale of F minor descending in semibreves / *whole notes*.

2. Write without key signature in the bass clef the scale of F♯ minor ascending in minims / *half notes*.

3. Write with key signature in the bass clef the scale of C minor descending and ascending in semibreves / *whole notes*. Mark the semitones / *half steps* with ⌐⌐.

Melodic Minor Scales

Semitones / *half steps* occur between notes [2&3] and [7&8] ascending and between notes [2&3] and [5&6] descending. Raise the 6th and 7th notes one semitone / *one half step* ascending. Lower them again when descending.

A minor

1. Write with key signature in the treble clef the scale of G minor ascending in crotchets / *quarter notes*.

2. Write without key signature in the bass clef the scale of C♯ minor descending in minims / *half notes*.

3. Write with key signature in the bass clef the scale of D minor descending and ascending in semibreves / *whole notes*.

Check your answers.

Key signature chart

major	key signature	minor
C	no sharps or flats	A
G	F♯	E
D	F♯ C♯	B
A	F♯ C♯ G♯	F♯
E	F♯ C♯ G♯ D♯	C♯
F	B♭	D
B♭	B♭ E♭	G
E♭	B♭ E♭ A♭	C
A♭	B♭ E♭ A♭ D♭	F

We should learn these key signatures.

Book 3 page 15

TONIC TRIADS

In my previous Music Theory is Fun books you learned that a tonic triad consists of notes 1, 3 and 5 of any scale.

Two examples without key signature:

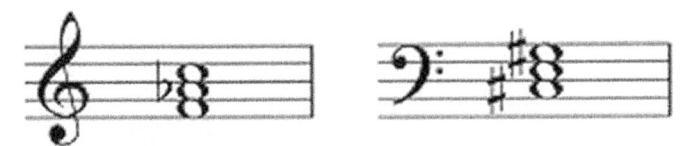

Write the tonic triads with key signature in the treble clef for:

A♭ major

D minor

G minor

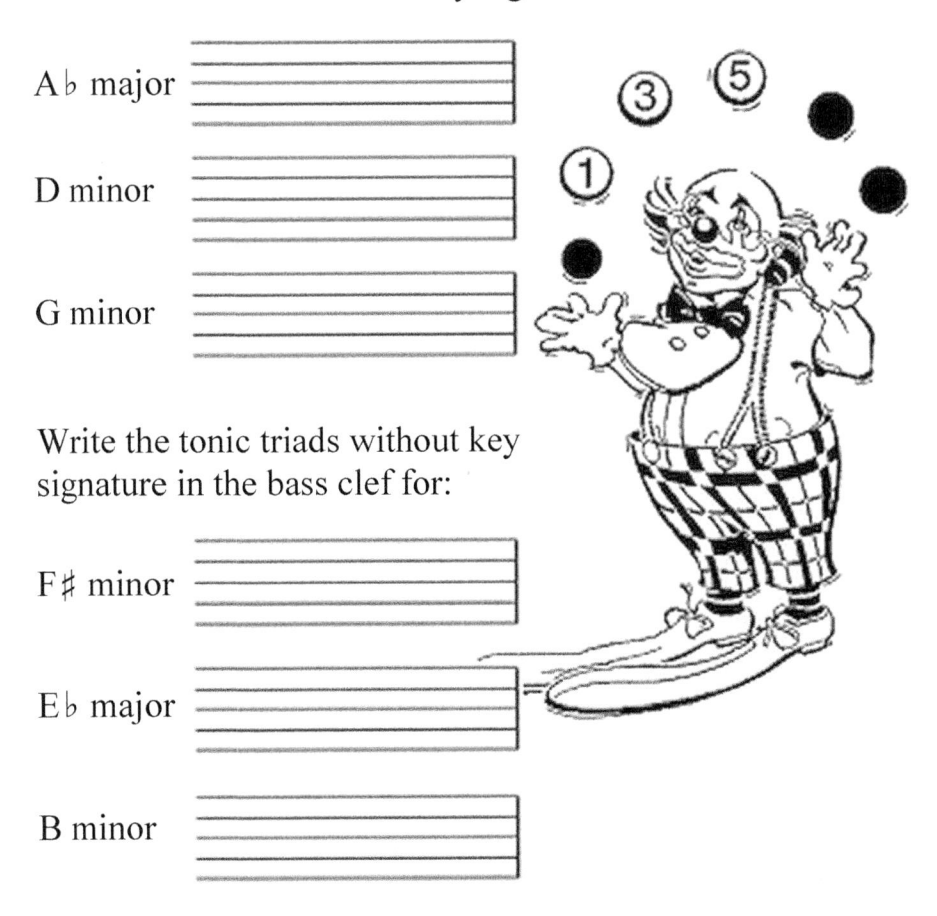

Write the tonic triads without key signature in the bass clef for:

F♯ minor

E♭ major

B minor

Book 3 page 16

INTERVALS

When you are working out an interval, always count both notes.

At this level you need to know these intervals:

major scales	minor scales
perfect 8th [or octave]	perfect 8th [or octave]
major 7th	major 7th
major 6th	minor 6th
perfect 5th	perfect 5th
perfect 4th	perfect 4th
major 3rd	minor 3rd
major 2nd	major 2nd

Write the following intervals, beginning on the tonic with key signature in the treble clef:

minor 3rd G minor   perfect 4th E major

without key signature in the bass clef:

minor 6th C minor   major 7th F♯ minor

NOTE VALUES

There is one more note to add to the note pyramid - the demisemiquaver / *thirty-second* (*32nd*) *note*.

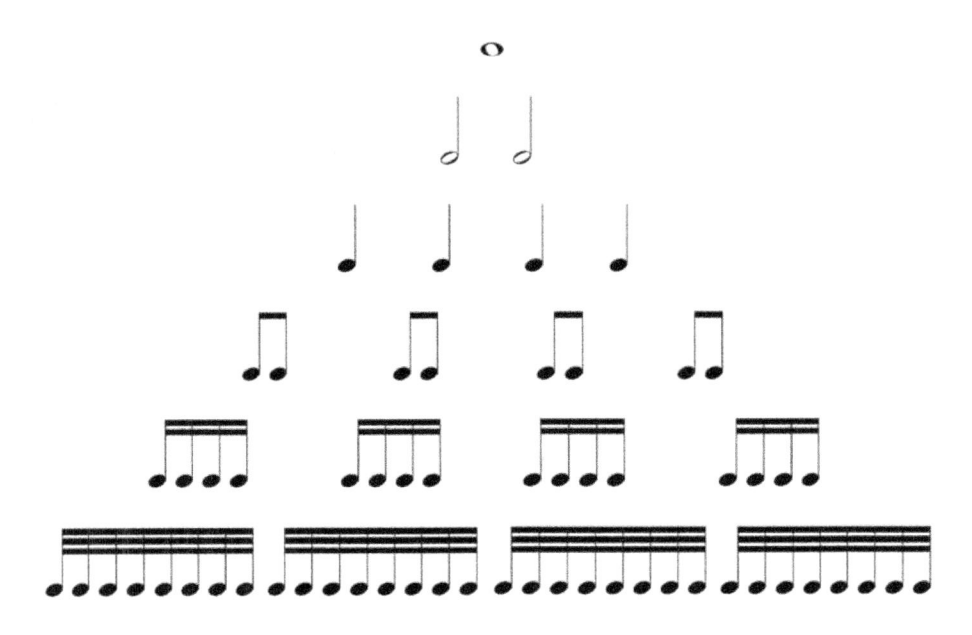

The demisemiquaver / *32nd* note looks like this

The demisemiquaver / *32nd* rest, like the note, also has three 'branches' on its stem.

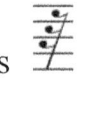

Demisemiquavers / *32nd notes* are often joined in groups, like this

Book 3 page 18

Test yourself

1. Two demisemiquavers / *32nd notes* are equal to one _____.

2. There are ___ demisemiquavers / *32nd notes* in a dotted quaver / *dotted 8th note*.

3. One crotchet is equal to ___ demisemiquavers / *32nd notes*.

4. A semibreve / *whole note* = ___ quavers / *8th notes* or ___ minims / *half notes*.

5. 𝅗𝅥 = ___ quavers / *8th notes*.

6. 𝅝 = ___ semiquavers / *16th notes*.

7. ♩. = ___ demisemiquavers / *32nd notes*.

8. ♬♬ = one _____

9. 𝅗𝅥. = ___ crotchets / *quarter notes*.

10. ♬♬♬ = one _____ _____

11. 𝅝. = ___ minims / *half notes*.

12. ♫♩ = one _____ _____

Use the note pyramid on page 18 to check your answers.

Book 3 page 19

TIME SIGNATURES

There are no new simple time signatures in this book.

Here is a reminder of the simple time signatures you have already met in Book 1 and Book 2.

Simple Time

duple	$\frac{2}{4}$		$\frac{2}{2}$ or ¢
triple	$\frac{3}{8}$	$\frac{3}{4}$	$\frac{3}{2}$
quadruple		$\frac{4}{4}$ or C	$\frac{4}{2}$

The top number of the time signature tells you how many beats there are in a bar. The bottom number tells you whether the beats are quavers / *eighth notes* (8), crotchets / *quarter notes* (4) or minims / *half notes* (2).

Compound time

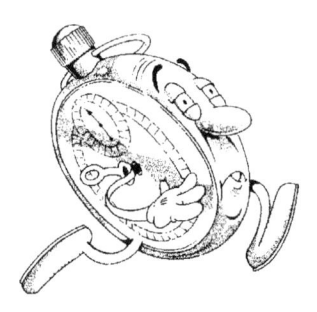

Oh no! This sounds too difficult for me. I'm off!

Wait! Compound time is easy. I'll show you!

Compound duple time

$^6_8$ is the only compound duple time in this book.

There are 6 quavers / 6 *8th notes* in each bar. Since there are 2 beats, you divide the quavers / *8th notes* into two groups.

3 quavers / 3 *8th notes* equal one dotted crotchet / *one dotted quarter note*.

There are 2 dotted crotchet beats / 2 *dotted quarter note beats* in a bar.

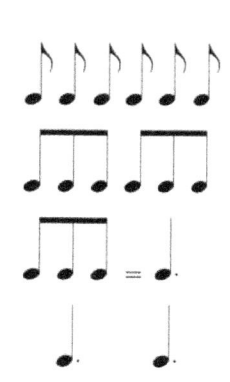

$^3_4$ or $^6_8$ - Which is it?

These two time signatures are very often confused because 6 quavers / *6 eighth notes* = 3 crotchets / *3 quarter notes*. You can tell the difference and choose the correct time signature if you remember these two rules:-

1. Group notes into beats:
   crotchets / *quarter notes* for simple time
   dotted crotchets / *dotted quarter notes* for compound time

2. Never join quavers / *8th notes* 3 and 4 in $^6_8$ time.

These examples show the difference between the grouping of notes in $^3_4$ and $^6_8$:-

Dotted crotchets / dotted quarter notes

You have seen that a dotted crotchet / *dotted quarter note* beat can be formed by grouping together three quavers / *three 8th notes*. There are other notes you can use.

Can you decide which of the groups below are worth a crotchet / *a quarter note* and which ones are worth a dotted crotchet / *a dotted quarter note*?

Book 3 page 22

Compound Triple Time

$\frac{9}{8}$ is the only compound triple time in this book.

It means that you can now divide each bar into 3 dotted crotchet / *dotted quarter note* beats:-

Write two bars of notes in $\frac{9}{8}$ time.
Use the bass clef and the note A.

Compound Quadruple Time

$\frac{12}{8}$ is the only compound quadruple time in this book.

This time signature gives us 4 dotted crotchet / *dotted quarter note* beats in a bar. If you remember to work out the groupings for dotted crotchets / *dotted quarter notes*, you will not find this time difficult.

As with simple quadruple time, you can beam together beats 1&2 and beats 3&4.

Book 3 page 23

FOUR-BAR RHYTHMS

When you wrote four-bar rhythms in Music Theory is Fun Book 2, you always began on the first beat of the first bar. Bars are always numbered from the first complete bar.

Now you need to be able to write rhythms that begin before the first beat of bar 1. When this happens it is called an anacrusis.

In the above example, bar 4 plus the anacrusis (the extra quaver / *eighth note* at the beginning) make a complete bar. Remember to subtract the anacrusis when you write bar 4.

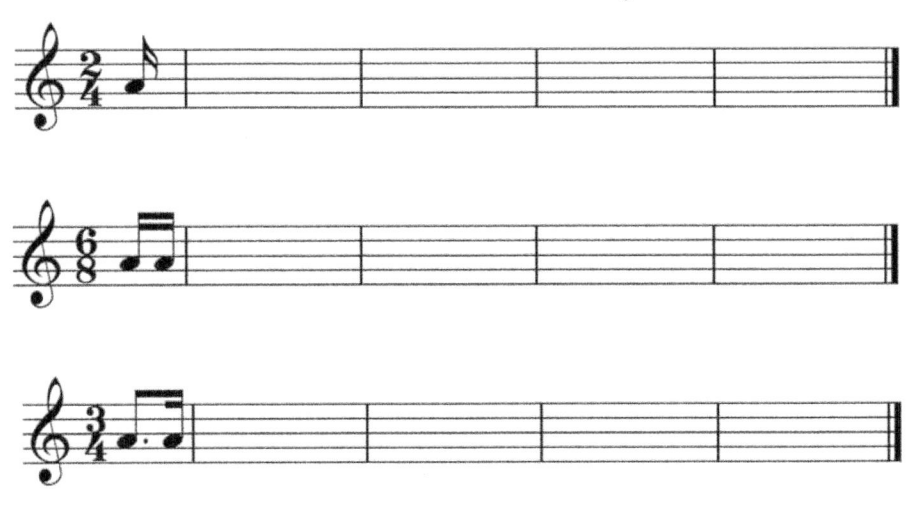

Test yourself

Write the time signature in each of the following passages. Choose from these time signatures:

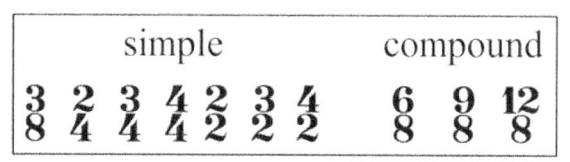

	simple		compound
$\frac{3}{8}$ $\frac{2}{4}$ $\frac{3}{4}$ $\frac{4}{4}$ $\frac{2}{2}$ $\frac{3}{2}$ $\frac{4}{2}$		$\frac{6}{8}$ $\frac{9}{8}$ $\frac{12}{8}$	

The first three will be $\frac{6}{8}$, $\frac{9}{8}$ or $\frac{12}{8}$.

Write three bars of notes in $\frac{6}{8}$ time. Use the treble clef and the note G on a line. Remember that each bar can be divided into 2 dotted crotchet / *dotted quarter note* beats.

Write two bars of notes in $\frac{9}{8}$ time. Use the bass clef and the note C in a space.

Write one bar of music in $\frac{12}{8}$ time. Use the treble clef and note F in a space. End with a dotted minim / *a dotted half note*.

Write three bars of notes in $\frac{4}{4}$ time. Use the bass clef and the note A on a line. Start with an anacrusis of a quaver / *8th note*.

Write four bars of notes in $\frac{3}{4}$ time. Use the bass clef and the note A on a line. Start with an anacrusis of a crotchet / *a quarter note*.

GROUPING OF NOTES

Simple time

I dealt with grouping notes in simple time in Music Theory is Fun Books 1 and 2. However, to help you avoid some common mistakes, here is a reminder of some important rules.

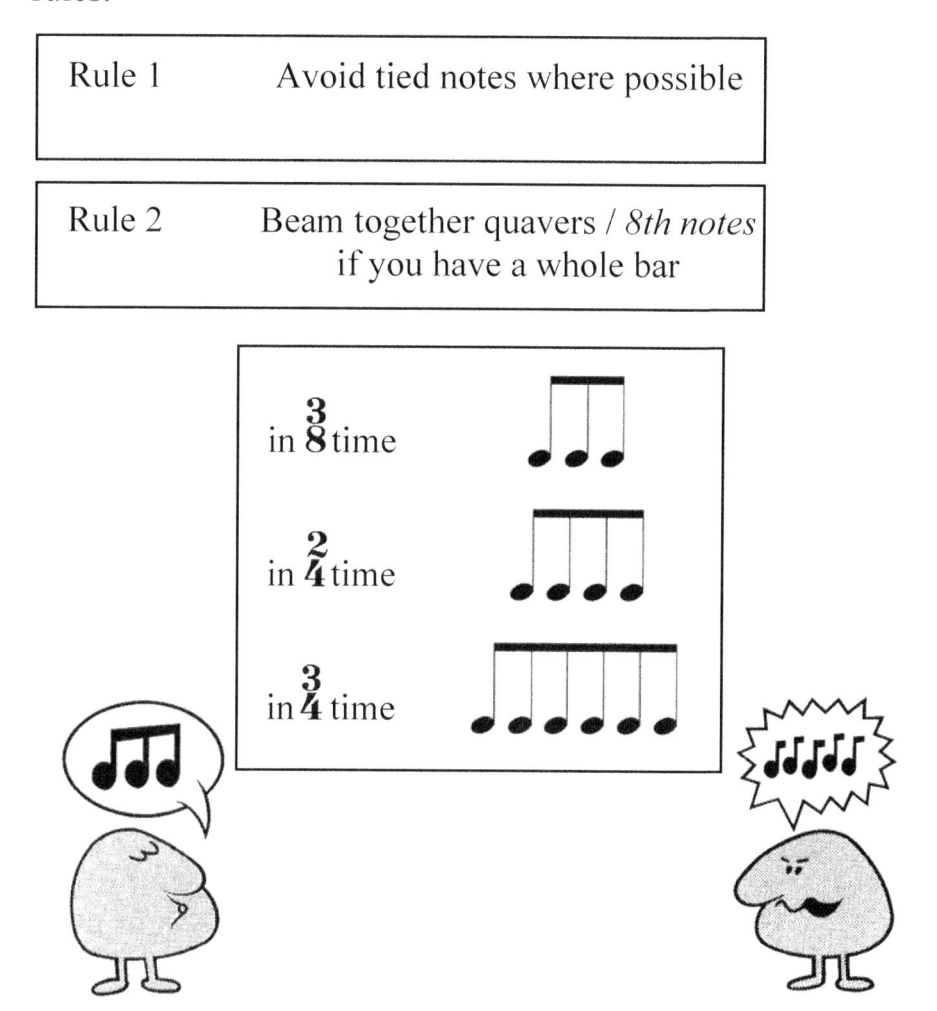

Rule 1	Avoid tied notes where possible

Rule 2	Beam together quavers / *8th notes* if you have a whole bar

in $\frac{3}{8}$ time

in $\frac{2}{4}$ time

in $\frac{3}{4}$ time

Book 3 page 27

| Rule 3 | Beam together half a bar of quavers / *8th notes* for beats 1 & 2 or 3 & 4 |

in 4/4 time

or

but **NOT**

| Rule 4 | Beam together in beats notes less than a quaver / *8th note* |

in 2/4 time

Demisemiquavers / *32nd notes*, however, may be beamed as whole beats or as half beats.

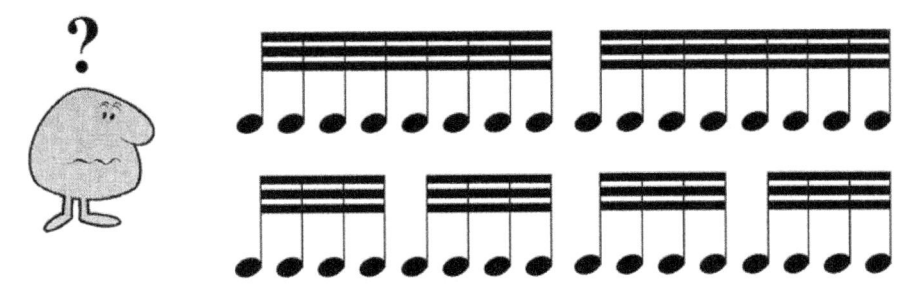

Book 3 page 28

Compound time

Compound rhythms are written so that you can usually see the groupings very easily.

Rule 1	Group notes into dotted beats

Rule 2	Write notes lasting 2 beats as a dotted minim / *dotted half note* instead of a tie

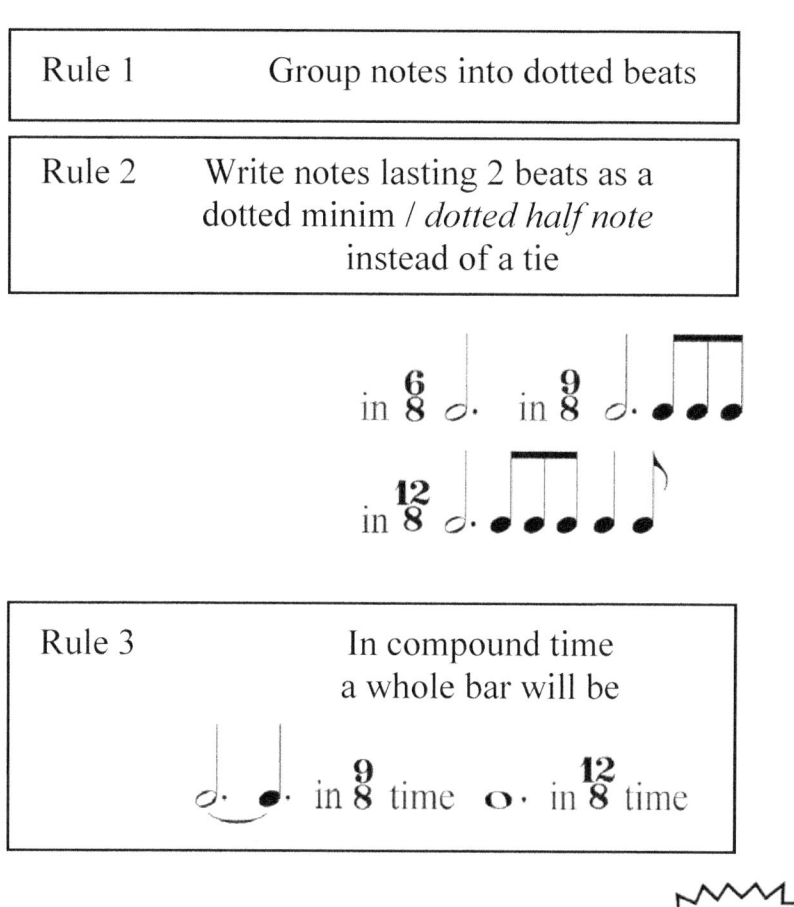

in 6/8 𝅗𝅥·   in 9/8 𝅗𝅥· ♩♩♩

in 12/8 𝅗𝅥· ♩♩♩♩♩

Rule 3	In compound time a whole bar will be 𝅗𝅥· ♩· in 9/8 time 𝅝· in 12/8 time

Book 3 page 29

Test yourself

Write a whole bar of quavers / *8th notes*

in $\frac{3}{4}$ time

in $\frac{4}{4}$ time

in $\frac{9}{8}$ time

Write a whole bar of semiquavers / *16th notes*

in $\frac{3}{4}$ time

in $\frac{6}{8}$ time

Write a whole bar of demisemiquavers / *32nd notes*

in $\frac{2}{4}$ time

Did you check your answers?

I forgot. I'll do that now.

GROUPING OF RESTS

Simple time

I dealt with the grouping of rests in simple time in my previous books. However, to avoid mistakes it is well worth reminding ourselves of some important points.

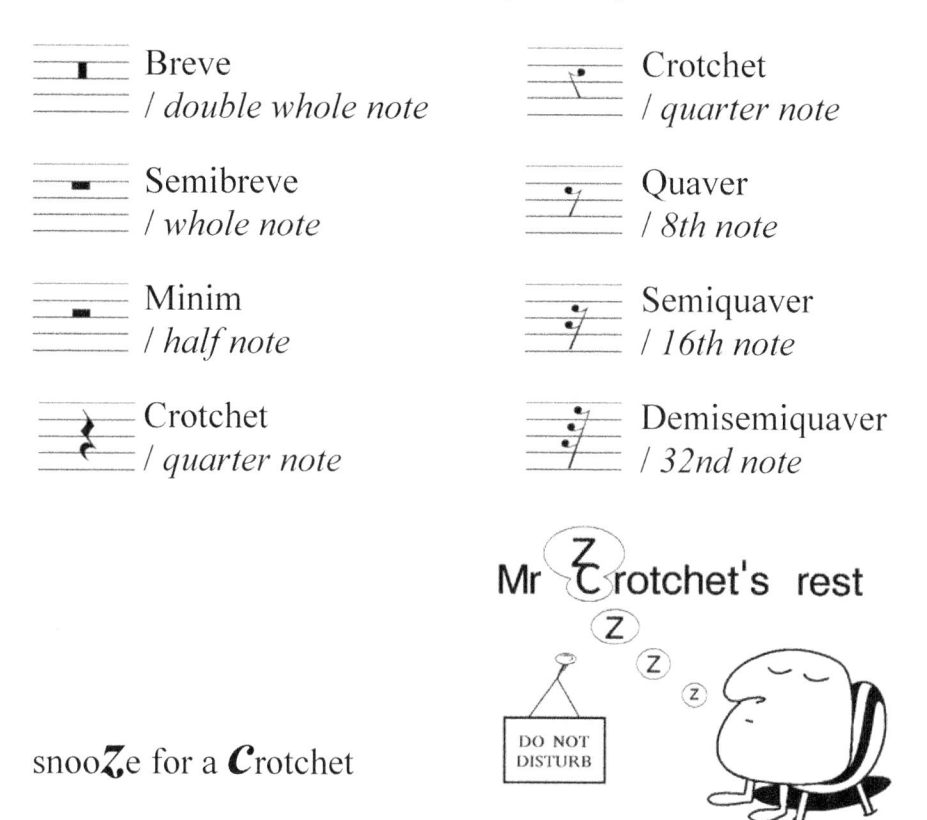

- Breve / *double whole note*
- Semibreve / *whole note*
- Minim / *half note*
- Crotchet / *quarter note*
- Crotchet / *quarter note*
- Quaver / *8th note*
- Semiquaver / *16th note*
- Demisemiquaver / *32nd note*

Mr Crotchet's rest

snoo**Z**e for a **C**rotchet

Important
For a **whole bar's rest** use a **breve rest** / *double whole note rest* in $\frac{4}{2}$ time. In **every other time** use a **semibreve rest** / *whole note rest* for a whole bar's rest.

In simple time, each beat should have its own rest.

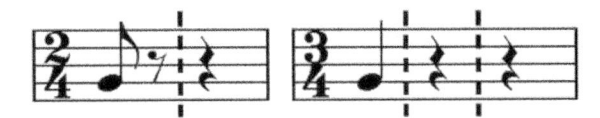

Exceptions
In triple time and quadruple time you can join beats 1&2. In quadruple time you can also join beats 3&4 with a single rest.

Do NOT join beats 2 & 3!

Compound time

You apply the same rules in compound time as in simple time but do remember - a whole beat is a dotted note!

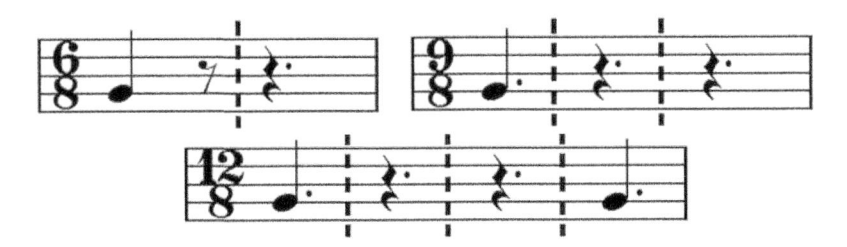

When using rests in compound time you may join quavers / *8th notes* 1&2 of a dotted crotchet / *dotted quarter note*.

You may NOT join quavers / *8th notes* 2&3 or 5&6!

Book 3 page 32

Test yourself

Fill in the missing words:
A whole bar's rest is shown by a
_____ in $\frac{3}{4}$ time,
_____ in $\frac{6}{8}$ time and
_____ in $\frac{4}{2}$ time,

Write a rest or rests under each * to complete a bar in the times given.

Book 3 page 33

TRANSPOSITION

At this level you might be given a simple melody in the treble clef and asked to write it an octave lower in the bass clef. For example: the given passage

transposed an octave lower

If the melody is in the bass clef, you might have to write it an octave higher in the treble clef. For example:-

Handy Hints

1. Make sure you put sharps and flats in the correct places when writing in a different clef.

2. Line up the key signature, the time signature and the bar lines under the original version you are transposing.

3. Write each note, each group of notes and each rest carefully, checking always that each transposed note has the same letter name as the original.

Book 3 page 34

Test yourself

Transpose this passage down an octave from the treble to the bass clef.

Transpose this passage up an octave from the bass to the treble clef.

Transpose this passage down an octave from the treble to the bass clef **without** key signature. Use accidentals.

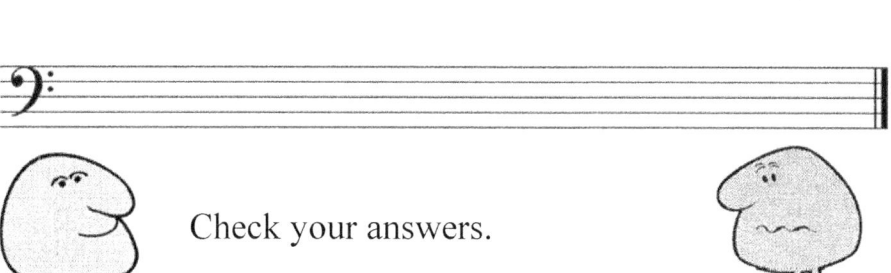

Check your answers.

Book 3 page 35

LEDGER LINES

At this level you have to be able to read notes that are more than two ledger lines above or below the stave. Practise ledger lines by filling in the names of the missing notes in CAPITALS to complete the poem.

TRIO CON BRIO

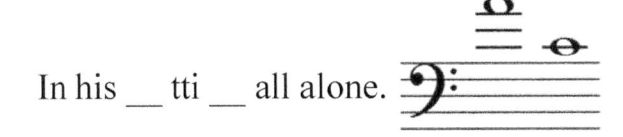

__ __ ward had a happy __ a __ e.

Liked to play the double __ __ ss.

__ er __ ld played the saxophone,

In his __ tti __ all alone.

Book 3 page 36

Then one day they
both met __re__

Who played piano and they s__i__,

"Join with us, let's __ __ a trio."

So now they play all thr__ __ con brio.

Book 3 page 37

PHRASES

A melody can be divided up into phrases.

If you have played a recorder, you will have noticed that there were sometimes marks to show where you should take a breath. These places were at the ends of phrases.

When you write a sentence, you put a comma if you need to take a breath. When you play a piece of music, you need to be able to 'shape' it. You have to know where to 'take a breath' in order to 'shape' a piece musically.

You may be asked to indicate where phrases should be in a piece of music. To do this you can use square brackets above the stave. Here are some bars of music with phrases marked.

When a poem is set to music the phrases usually occur at the beginning and end of each line of poetry.

Book 3 page 38

There once was a Martian from Mars,
Who dreamt all his life of fast cars.
When he came down to Earth,
He chuckled with mirth,
And drove one back up through the stars.

If this limerick were set to music, there would be a phrase mark between each comma or full stop.   For example,

⌐──────────────────┐
He chuckled with mirth,

Handy Hints

1. Phrases can begin anywhere in a bar.
2. Phrases often start with the same rhythm, or rhythms which are almost the same.
3. The most common examples you will be given will be four 2-bar phrases or four 4-bar phrases.

A slur shows that a group of notes is to be grouped together and played legato (smoothly) without a break. Do not call slurs 'phrase marks' unless they stretch from the beginning to the end of a phrase. Instead, call them articulation marks - this means 'joining' marks.

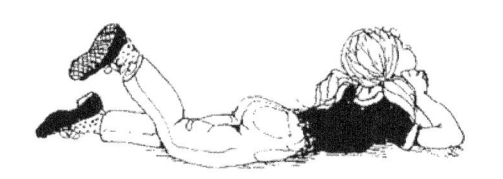

Mark the phrases with square brackets.

Book 3 page 40

PUZZLES

QUIZZES

TESTS

Book 3 page 41

Crossword

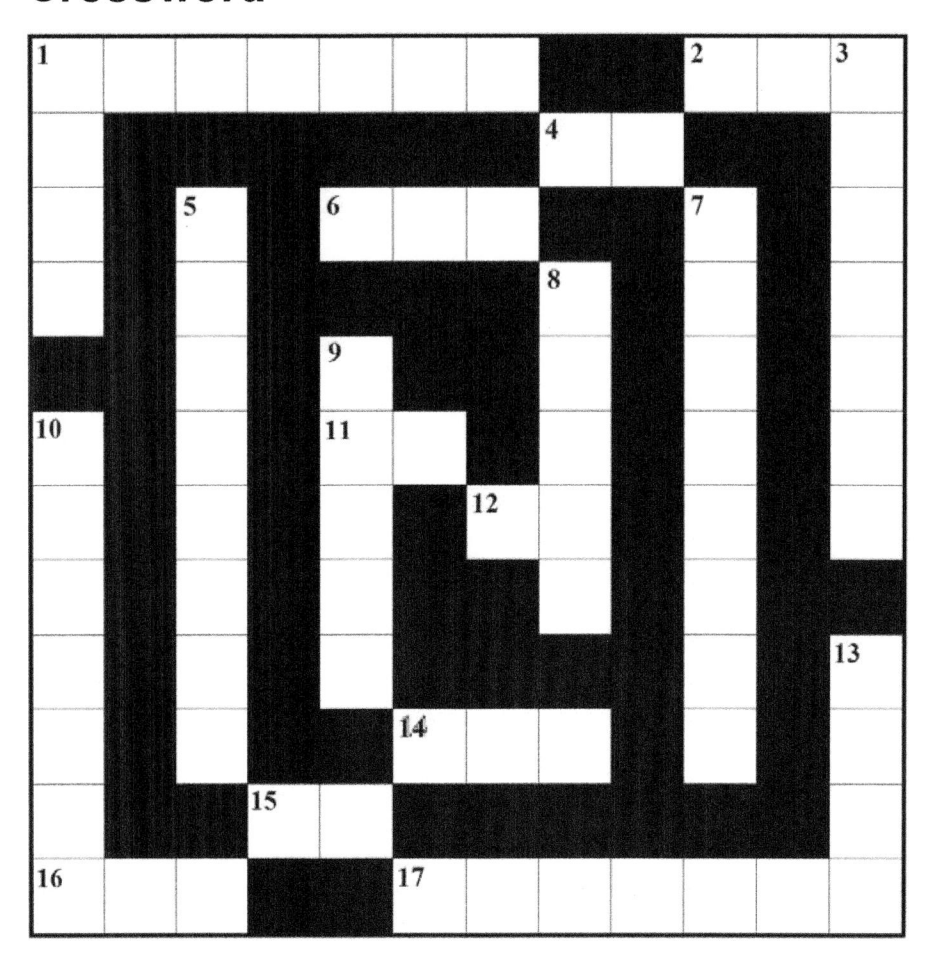

Clues

Across

1 dying away
2 1st, 2nd and 3rd degrees of G major
4 interval of a perfect 8th (an octave) in C Major, beginning on the tonic
6 from

Book 3 page 42

11 interval of a 4th in E major, starting on the keynote
12 interval of a 4th in G minor, starting on the keynote
14 with
15 interval of a 6th in D major, starting on the keynote
16 tonic triad of A minor
17 sadly

Down

1 movement
3 with boldness and spirit
5 in a singing style
8 fire
9 sign
10 go on immediately
13 the end

Answers?

Yes. Ready to check?

Book 3 page 43

Musical Matchword

Can you join the boxes to make ten musical words? I have joined the first one for you.

MEL	TONE	_____
COM	AVE	_____
INTER	ODIC	_____
TRI	NATURE	_____
HAR	POUND	_____
OCT	STEP	_____
SEMI	MONIC	_____
SIG	VAL	_____
QUAD	AD	_____
HALF	RUPLE	_____

Book 3 page 44

Musical Anagrams

noisetem / *lafh pest*

Clue: The interval between notes 2&3 in a minor scale.

charmion

Clue: You raise the 7th note one semitone / *half step* ascending and descending in this minor scale.

domicel

Clue: The interval between notes 5&6 is one semitone / *half step* when descending this minor scale.

citon driat

Clue: The 1st, 3rd and 5th notes of a scale.

trivalen

Clue: Always count both notes when working out one of these.

calendatics

Clue: Sharps, flats and naturals.

Book 3 page 45

Musical Boxes

Use these letters to complete the words in the musical boxes.

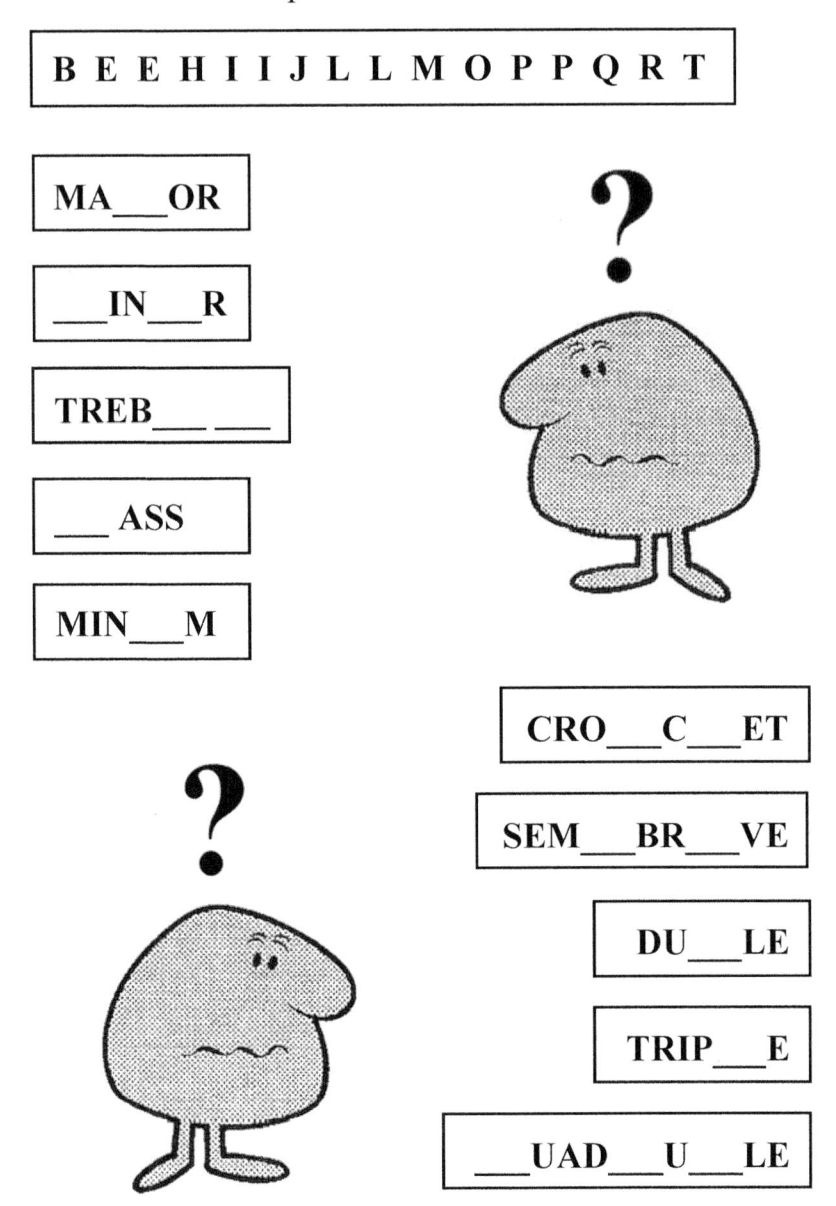

B E E H I I J L L M O P P Q R T

MA___OR

___IN___R

TREB___ ___

___ASS

MIN___M

CRO___C___ET

SEM___BR___VE

DU___LE

TRIP___E

___UAD___U___LE

Book 3 page 46

Musical terms word search

C	A	M	Y	L	O	A	F	S	E
O	L	A	G	M	X	U	Y	T	N
S	E	J	I	G	R	A	V	E	E
T	G	S	Q	I	Z	N	G	M	R
N	A	L	O	R	Z	T	O	P	G
I	T	S	O	R	E	A	I	O	I
A	O	F	S	C	R	N	G	P	C
S	L	O	I	C	G	T	A	H	O
S	M	E	N	O	R	O	D	G	T
A	N	A	D	N	T	P	A	I	U

Meaning	Musical term
less	meno
force, power	
with energy	
furiously	
smoothly	
slow, leisurely	
with	
very slow	
speed, time	
so much	
very	

Book 3 page 47

Quiz 1

1. How many sharps are in the E major key signature?

   1 ☐ 2 ☐ 3 ☐ 4 ☐ 5 ☐

2. How many flats are in the E♭ major key signature?

   1 ☐ 2 ☐ 3 ☐ 4 ☐ 5 ☐

3. How many sharps are in the C♯ minor key signature?

   1 ☐ 2 ☐ 3 ☐ 4 ☐ 5 ☐

4. How many demisemiquavers / *32nd notes* are in a crotchet / *quarter note*?

   8 ☐ 2 ☐ 4 ☐ 6 ☐ 7 ☐

5. Which notes in a melodic minor scale are raised one semitone when ascending and lowered when descending?

   3 and 4 ☐   5 and 6 ☐   6 and 7 ☐

6. Which beats can you not beam together in 4/4 time?

   1 and 2 ☐   2 and 3 ☐   3 and 4 ☐

7. Which time signature is a simple triple time?

   $\frac{3}{8}$ ☐ $\frac{6}{8}$ ☐ $\frac{9}{8}$ ☐

8. Which time signature is a compound quadruple time?

   $\frac{4}{2}$ ☐ $\frac{4}{4}$ ☐ $\frac{12}{8}$ ☐

9. Which rest is used for a whole bar in $\frac{4}{2}$ time?

   ☐   ☐   ☐

10. Which rest is used for a whole bar in $\frac{3}{4}$ time?

    ☐   ☐   ☐

Book 3 page 48

Quiz 2

Put a tick / *check mark* (✓) in the correct box.

1. adagietto
☐ at a walking pace
☐ rather slow
☐ slightly slower than allegro
☐ slow, leisurely

2. largamente
☐ in a broad style
☐ slow and stately
☐ very slow
☐ sad, sorrowful

3. gradually faster
☐ slentando
☐ sostenuto
☐ stringendo
☐ subito

4. grief, sorrow
☐ dolce
☐ dolente
☐ dolore
☐ lacrimoso

5. mesto
☐ less
☐ more
☐ much
☐ sadly

6. quaver / *8th note* rest
☐ 𝄽
☐ 𝄽
☐ ▬
☐ 𝄾

Book 3 page 49

Quiz 3

1. **morendo** means
   - dying away ☐
   - sad, sorrowful ☐
   - simple ☐
   - too much ☐

2. **scherzando** means
   - majestically ☐
   - gracefully ☐
   - playfully ☐
   - with feeling ☐

3. **sospirando** means
   - softly ☐
   - sad, sorrowful ☐
   - sustained ☐
   - sighing ☐

4. **vivace** means
   - lively, quick ☐
   - with feeling ☐
   - vibrating ☐
   - boldly ☐

5. **tempo rubato** means
   - with some freedom of time ☐
   - at a comfortable speed ☐
   - resume the original speed ☐
   - gradually faster ☐

6. *fp* means
   - loud then gradually softer ☐
   - with a strong accent ☐
   - loud then immediately soft ☐
   - furiously ☐

Book 3 page 50

Handy hints for tests

This section is for you to practise the different types of questions you could have in a test or an exam.

The questions could be on any topic covered in this book and in Music Theory is Fun Books 1 and 2.

Revise each topic in this book thoroughly.

Don't forget to study musical terms and signs – they are **always** included.

Practice makes perfect!

Practice makes perfect!

If you have worked through this book carefully and understood each topic, this will be an easy task for you.

> Before you begin any test, write out your key signature chart (see page 15). Always refer to the chart when tackling questions that require you to know a key signature.

Book 3 page 51

Test 1

Put a tick / *check mark* (✓) in the box next to the correct answer.

1. Name this note:

   C ☐   B♭ ☐   F ☐

2. How many beats of silence are in these bars?

   3 ☐   4 ☐   5 ☐

3. Which is the correct time signature?

   3/4 ☐   6/8 ☐   3/2 ☐

4. Which time signature is in simple time?

   C ☐   9/8 ☐   6/8 ☐

5. The relative major of C minor is:

   B♭ major ☐   A♭ major ☐   E♭ major ☐

6. The major scale with a key signature of three sharps is:

   D major ☐   A major ☐   E major ☐

7. Which degrees of the scale do you change to form melodic minor scales when ascending?

   5th & 6th ☐   5th & 7th ☐   6th & 7th ☐

8. Name this interval.

   perfect 5th ☐   major 6th ☐   major 7th ☐

Book 3 page 52

Test 2

1. ♪♪♪ = one _____

2. ♪♪♪♪ = one _____

3. ____ demisemiquavers / *32nd notes* = one semibreve / *whole note*

4. 𝅗𝅥. = ____ minims / *half notes*

5. A semibreve / *whole note* = ____ quavers / *8th notes*

6. Choose from the words simple, compound, duple, triple and quadruple to describe the following time signatures.

   $\frac{4}{4}$ _____

   $\frac{9}{8}$ _____

7. When a rhythm begins before the first beat of a bar 1, this is called an _____.

8. When you write the final bar, you must subtract the value of the _____.

9. Write a 2 bar rhythm to follow each anacrusis.

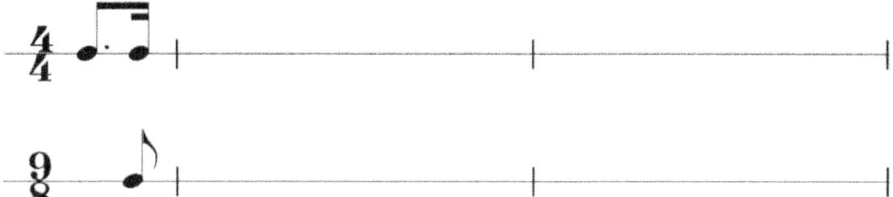

Book 3 page 53

Test 3

1. Name this triad.

   F♯ minor ☐   F minor ☐   A major ☐

2. Name this minor key signature.

   D minor ☐   C♯ minor ☐   E minor ☐

3. Write a one-octave G harmonic minor scale in minims / *half notes*, ascending in the treble clef, without key signature. Remember the accidentals.

4. Write a one-octave C melodic minor scale in crotchets / *quarter notes*, descending in the bass clef, with key signature.

5. There are mistakes in this piece of music. Rewrite it correcting them.

   Adanteo

   mf

Book 3 page 54

Test 4

1. Write a whole bar of quavers / *eighth notes* in the bottom space in each of these times shown.

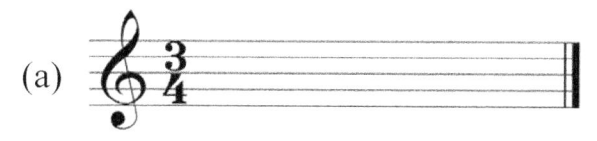

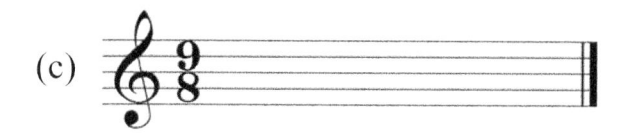

   (a) $\treble\;^3_4$

   (b) $\treble\;^4_4$

   (c) $\treble\;^9_8$

2. Write a whole bar of semiquavers / *sixteenth notes* in the top space in each of these times shown.

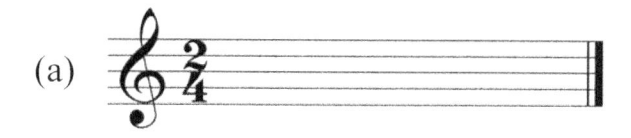

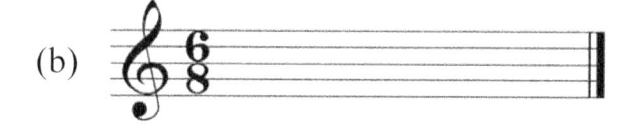

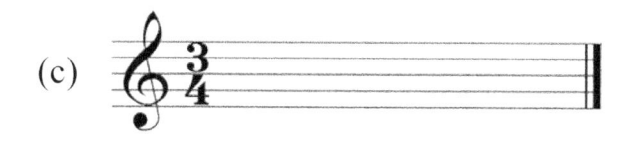

   (a) $\treble\;^2_4$

   (b) $\treble\;^6_8$

   (c) $\treble\;^3_4$

Book 3 page 55

Test 5

1. Add the missing bar lines to each of these melodies, all of which begin on the first beat.

2. Add the correct clef and any necessary sharp or flat signs to complete each of these scales. Do not use key signatures.

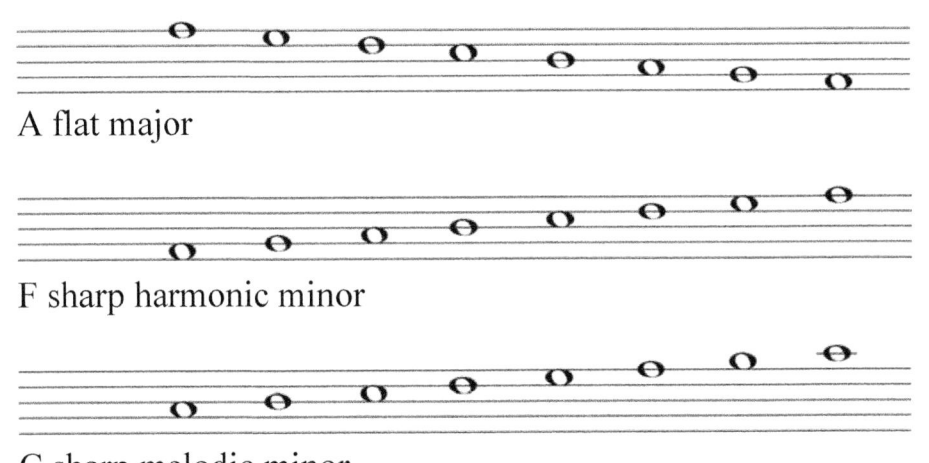

A flat major

F sharp harmonic minor

C sharp melodic minor

3. Write the letter name of each note on the lines below.

Book 3 page 56

Test 6

1. Name each of these intervals as shown in the first answer.

   major 6th   _____   _____

   _____   _____   _____

2. Add the correct rest(s) where you see * to make each bar complete.

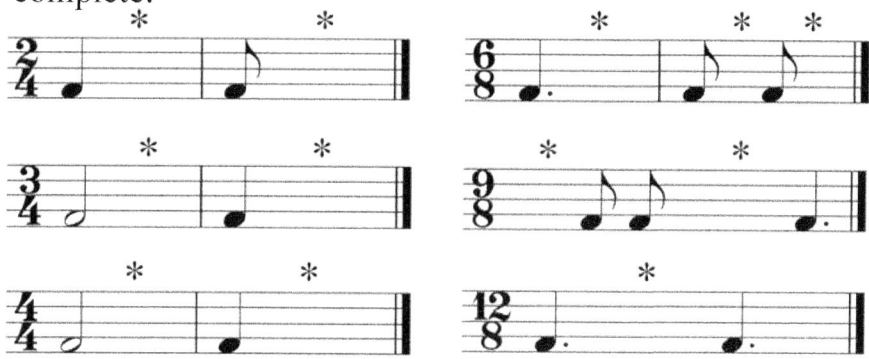

3. Rewrite this music with the notes correctly beamed.

4. Write the key signature and tonic triad in semibreves / *whole notes* for each of the following keys.

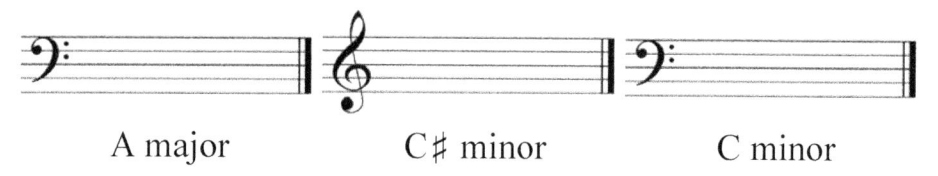

   A major   C♯ minor   C minor

Book 3 page 57

Test 7

1. Write these notes an octave higher in the treble clef.

2. Write the key signature and tonic triad in semibreves / *whole notes* for each of the following keys.

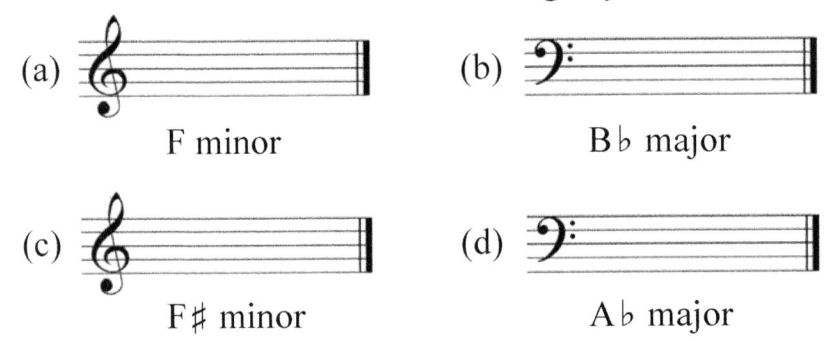

   (a) F minor

   (b) B♭ major

   (c) F♯ minor

   (d) A♭ major

3. Write in semibreves / *whole notes* the scale of B melodic minor ascending and descending without key signature.

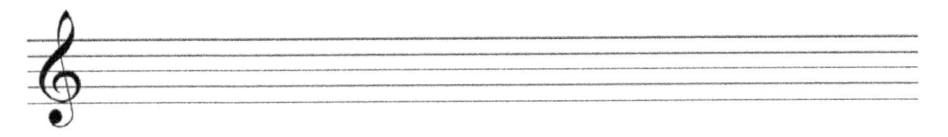

4. Write one bar of rhythm in each of the following compound times. Use the note G.

Book 3 page 58

Test 8

Look at these four bars then answer the questions below,

1. Using the blank stave above, write out bars 3 and 4 an octave lower and in the bass clef.
2. Name the key of this piece. _____
3. The time signature tells you that
   (a) there should be ___ beats in a bar and
   (b) that they are _____ beats.
4. Name the semiquaver / *16th notes* in bar 3.
   _____
5. Give the number of the bar that contains all the notes of the tonic triad. _____
6. Give the meaning of Presto: _____
7. How should you play the last note?
   _____
8. How should the first four notes in bar 1 be played?
   _____
9. How should the first four notes in bar 3 be played?
   _____

Book 3 page 59

Test 9

Look at the following piece then answer the questions below.

1. Using the blank stave below, write out bars 5 and 6 an octave lower and in the bass clef.

2. What does ⦂| mean at the end of bar 8?

3. In bar 3 how should you play notes 4 and 5 joined by ⌣ ?

4. What does **C** mean?

5. What is the loudest note in the piece? Name the note and bar number.

6. Name the lowest note in the piece.

Book 3 page 60

Test 10

Look at the following piece then answer the questions below.

1. What does > mean under the notes in bar 7?

2. Give the Italian words and the English meaning of *mp*.

3. How many staccato notes are there in the piece?

4. Name in order the rests at the beginning of the piece.

6. What does ∧ mean over the note in bar 8?

7. What does ⟍⟋ mean?

8. What is the meaning of Con brio?

Book 3 page 61

MIM

Book 3 page 62

CONTENTS
Book 4

Topic	page
Key Signatures	6
major and minor keys	7
Alto Clef	9
Scales	11
Technical Names	13
Chromatic Scales	15
Time Signatures	17
Primary Triads and Chords	22
Intervals	24
Ornaments	28
acciaccatura	28
appoggiatura	29
arpeggio	31
upper and lower mordent	32
upper turn	33
trill or shake	35
Words and Rhythm	38
Instruments of the Orchestra	40
Puzzles, Quizzes and Tests	47
Musical Terms and Signs	65

KEY SIGNATURES

In Music Theory is Fun Book 3 you learned the major and minor key signatures up to and including 4 sharps and 4 flats. You should know the minor scales in their harmonic and melodic forms.

In this book we meet the key signatures with 5 sharps and 5 flats.

Important

The A♯ is placed in the bottom space in the bass, not on the top line. If it were placed an octave higher, then in the treble clef the A♯ would be on a ledger line!

Book 4 page 6

Major and minor key signatures

major	key signature	minor
C	no sharps or flats	A
G	F♯	E
D	F♯ C♯	B
A	F♯ C♯ G♯	F♯
E	F♯ C♯ G♯ D♯	C♯
B	F♯ C♯ G♯ D♯ A♯	G♯
F	B♭	D
B♭	B♭ E♭	G
E♭	B♭ E♭ A♭	C
A♭	B♭ E♭ A♭ D♭	F
D♭	B♭ E♭ A♭ D♭ G♭	B♭

When you are ready to test yourself on these key signatures, turn over to page 8.

Test yourself

Name these ten keys.

___ major

___ major

___ minor

___ minor

___ major

___ major

___ minor

___ minor

Check your answers

___ minor

___ minor

Book 4 page 8

THE ALTO CLEF

The alto clef is also known as the C clef. This is because middle C is found on the middle line of the stave.

It is printed like this.

If you wish, you may write it in other ways.

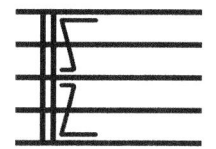

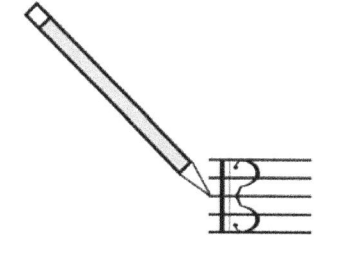

The important thing is that the two curved halves of the clef should be drawn either side of the middle line of the stave.

In former times the alto clef was found a great deal in vocal music. Nowadays the alto clef is used mainly for the viola.

Test yourself

Name these notes.

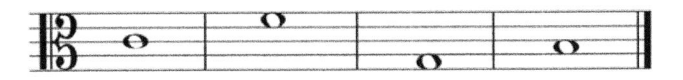

Write these key signatures in the alto clef.

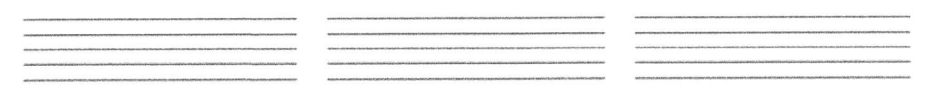

E major   F minor   B major

Rewrite the following treble clef passages in the alto clef, keeping the same pitch.

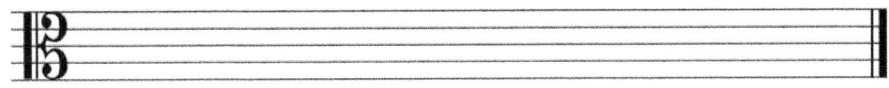

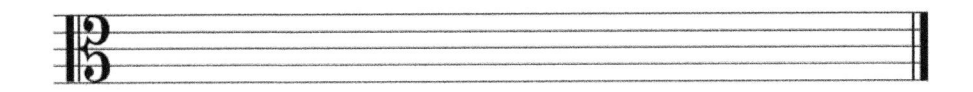

Book 4 page 10

SCALES

Now you are using my Music Theory is Fun Book 4, I shall assume that you understand the differences between the harmonic and melodic minor scales.

The major key with five sharps is _____

G♯ minor, the new scale in this book, also has five sharps. Its seventh note has a sharp. To raise the seventh note in minor scales you have to use a 'double sharp.'

The double sharp 𝄪

A double sharp raises a note one tone or whole step.

Here are the scales of G♯ minor to remind you of the differences between the harmonic and melodic minors.

Harmonic ascending

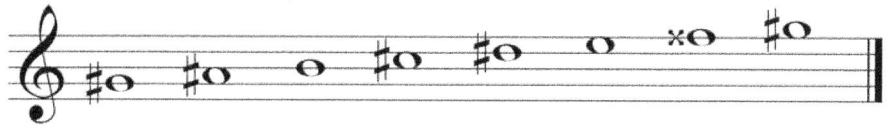

Melodic ascending

Melodic descending

Turn to the next page when you are ready for a test.

Book 4 page 11

Test yourself

Write with key signature in the treble clef the scale of D♭ major ascending and descending in minims / *half notes*. Mark the semitones / *half steps* with ⌐⌐.

Write with key signature in the bass clef the scale of G♯ harmonic minor ascending and descending in semibreves / *whole notes*. Mark the semitones / *half steps* with ⌐⌐.

Write without key signature in the treble clef the scale of G♯ melodic minor ascending and descending in semibreves / *whole notes*. Mark the semitones / *half steps* with ⌐⌐.

Check your scales test. You might have made a small mistake which you have not noticed.

The Double Flat ♭♭

Now that you have mastered the double sharp, I shall introduce you to the double flat. When placed in front of a note, it simply lowers that note one tone / *a whole step*.

TECHNICAL NAMES

Each note of the scale has a different **technical** name. You have already met the **tonic** - the first note. Each note is also given a **Roman numeral**.

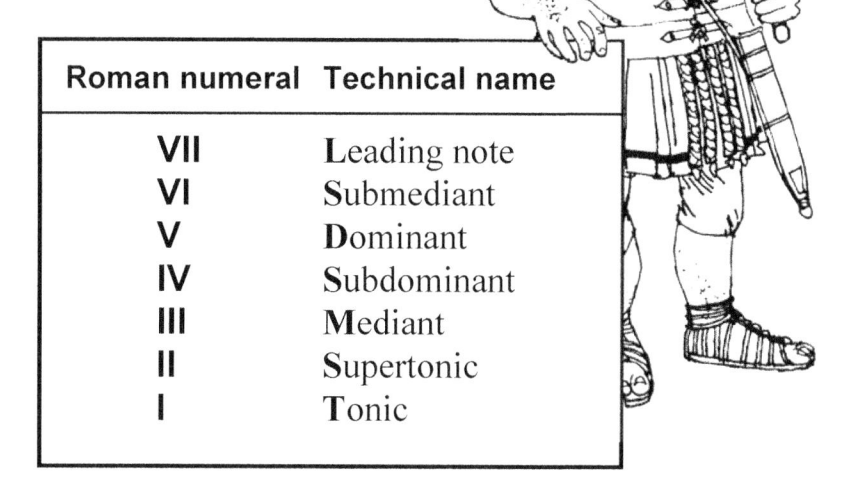

Roman numeral	Technical name
VII	**L**eading note
VI	**S**ubmediant
V	**D**ominant
IV	**S**ubdominant
III	**M**ediant
II	**S**upertonic
I	**T**onic

How can you remember these? One way is to make up a sentence. For example:

Two **S**peedy **M**otorists **S**low **D**own **S**eeing **L**ights

Now you make up a sentence.

L _____
S _____
D _____
S _____
M _____
S _____
T _____

Book 4 page 13

In exams you are often asked to give the technical names of notes in a short passage. Decide on the key and write out the scale. Let's say that the passage is in F harmonic minor.

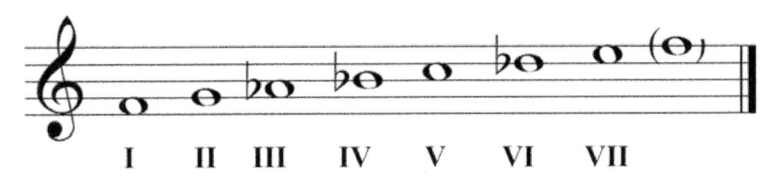

I   II   III   IV   V   VI   VII

Test yourself

Give the technical names of the notes (a) to (f) in the following passage. The key is D♭ major.

(a) _____ (b) _____ (c) _____
(d) _____ (e) _____ (f) _____

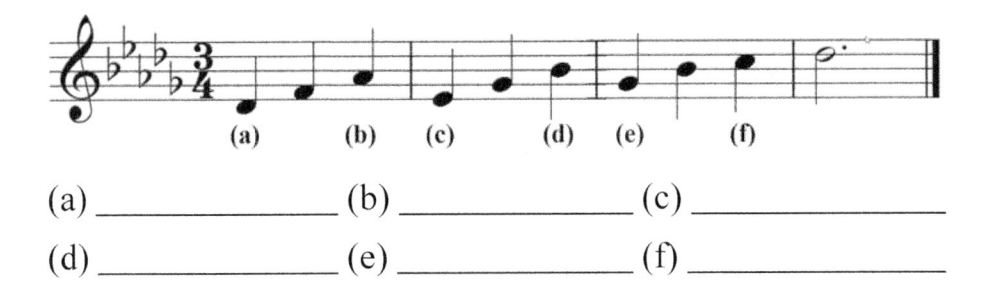

Name the key of this passage and write the technical names of the notes (a) to (f).

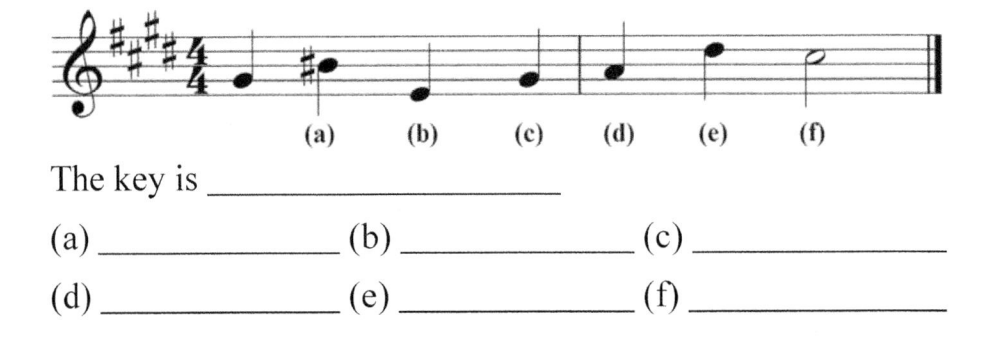

The key is _____
(a) _____ (b) _____ (c) _____
(d) _____ (e) _____ (f) _____

Book 4 page 14

CHROMATIC SCALES

A chromatic scale is composed entirely of semitones / *half steps* in which a note may appear twice but never three times.

You could be asked to write a chromatic scale with or without key signature, in the treble, bass or alto clef, ascending, descending or both.

Without key signature

1. Put at least one note but not more than two notes on each line and in each space.
2. Usually use sharps ascending and flats descending.

With key signature

There is more than one way to write the scale **with** a key signature. Here is an example.

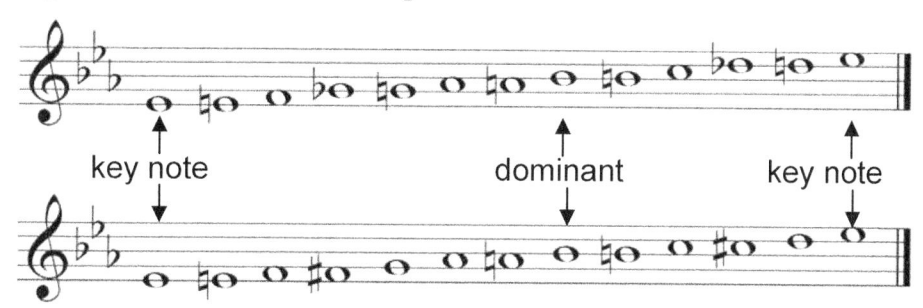

key note   dominant   key note

1. Put the key note at both ends of the scale.
2. Write the dominant **once only**.
3. Do **not** change the key note or the dominant note.
4. Do **not** put more than **two** notes on all the other lines and in all the other spaces.

Test yourself

Write one octave of a chromatic scale, in semibreves / *whole notes*, beginning on the key note or tonic

without a key signature, ascending

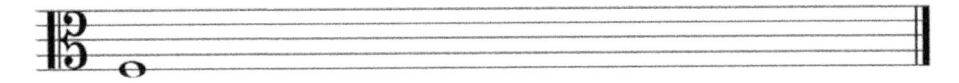

without a key signature, descending

with a key signature for C minor, ascending

with a key signature for G♯ minor, descending

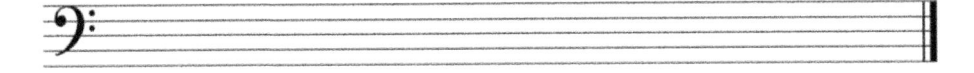

Checking your answers?

Yes. I always do.

Book 4 page 16

TIME SIGNATURES

$\frac{4}{8}$ is the only new simple time signature in this book. Students are sometimes confused between $\frac{2}{4}$ and $\frac{4}{8}$ time. There is no difference in notation between pieces written in $\frac{2}{4}$ and $\frac{4}{8}$. The difference is in how they are played. In $\frac{2}{4}$ time the composer wants two beats in the bar. In $\frac{4}{8}$ time the piece should have four beats in the bar.

Here is a quick reminder of simple time signatures.

duple $\frac{2}{4}$ $\frac{2}{2}$ or ¢   triple $\frac{3}{8}$ $\frac{3}{4}$ $\frac{3}{2}$ quadruple $\frac{4}{8}$ $\frac{4}{4}$ or C $\frac{4}{2}$

Duplets

In simple time you met the triplet which divided a simple beat into 3 equal parts. Now you will meet the duplet. It is found in compound time when a dotted beat is divided into 2 equal parts.

There are two ways of writing the duplet.

using dotted notes	using a ² above the pair of notes
𝅝. = 𝅗𝅥. 𝅗𝅥.	𝅝. = 𝅗𝅥 𝅗𝅥 (2)
𝅗𝅥. = ♩. ♩.	𝅗𝅥. = ♩ ♩ (2)
♩. = ♫. ♫.	♩. = ♫ (2)
♪. = ♬. ♬.	♪. = ♬ (2)

Double dots

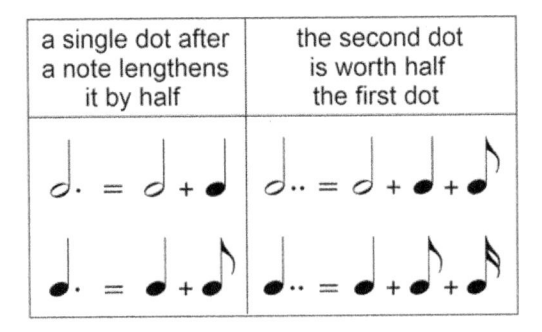

a single dot after a note lengthens it by half	the second dot is worth half the first dot
$\unicode{x1D15E}. = \unicode{x1D15E} + \unicode{x1D15F}$	$\unicode{x1D15E}.. = \unicode{x1D15E} + \unicode{x1D15F} + \unicode{x1D160}$
$\unicode{x1D15F}. = \unicode{x1D15F} + \unicode{x1D160}$	$\unicode{x1D15F}.. = \unicode{x1D15F} + \unicode{x1D160} + \unicode{x1D161}$

Try these:

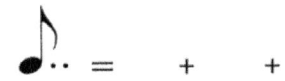

𝅝 ·· =   +   +   ♩·· =   +   +

Add the missing bar lines to the following:

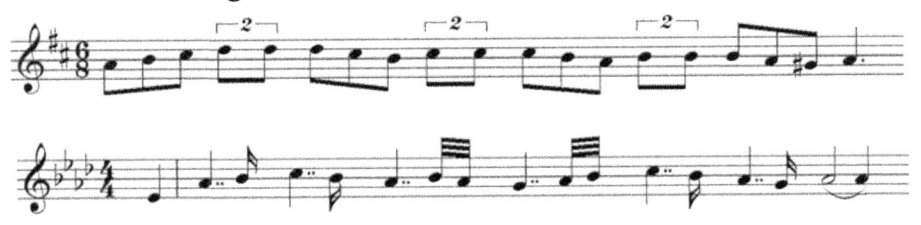

Here are some new compound time signatures. You will not find them difficult because you mastered the principles of compound time in Music Theory is Fun Book 3.

You will remember $\frac{6}{8}$ time. 6 quavers / *6 eighth notes* in a bar gave 2 dotted crotchet / *2 dotted quarter note* beats. This is compound duple time. Now we meet compound triple time with 3 dotted crotchet / *3 dotted quarter note* beats in a bar and compound quadruple time with 4 dotted crotchet / *4 dotted quarter note* beats in a bar.

Book 4 page 18

Compound duple time

Compound triple time

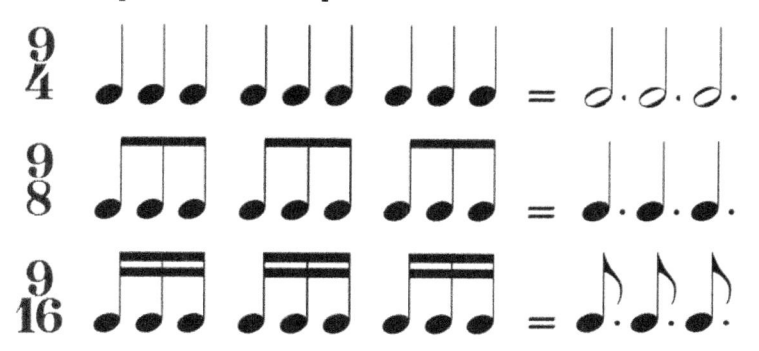

Compound quadruple time

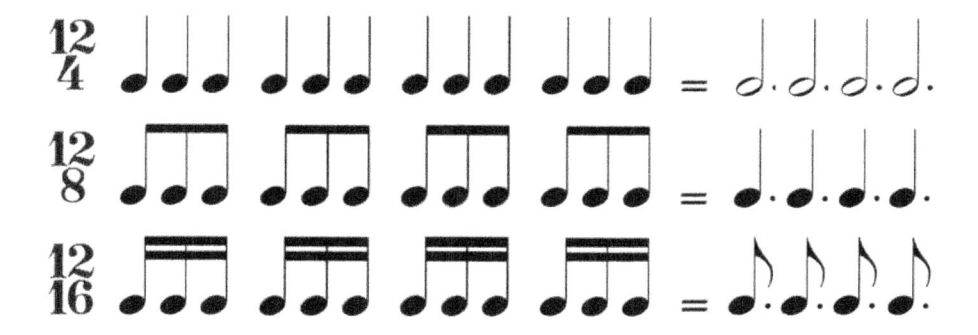

Grouping notes and rests

Study again pages 27 to 32 in my Music Theory is Fun Book 3 to revise the rules for the grouping of notes and rests.

The only difference with the compound times in this book is that the note values are doubled for $\frac{6}{4}$, $\frac{9}{4}$ and $\frac{12}{4}$ (crotchets / *quarter notes* instead of quavers / *8th notes*) and halved for $\frac{6}{16}$, $\frac{9}{16}$ and $\frac{12}{16}$ (semiquavers / *16th notes* instead of quavers / *8th notes*).

The breve / *double whole note*

We have already met the breve / *double whole note* rest in Book 3. This is what it looks like.

It is used to show a whole bar's rest in $\frac{4}{2}$ time. Written as a note it looks like this ‖o‖. It is worth two semibreves / *two whole notes*.

‖o‖ = o + o

Rewrite this passage doubling the time values.

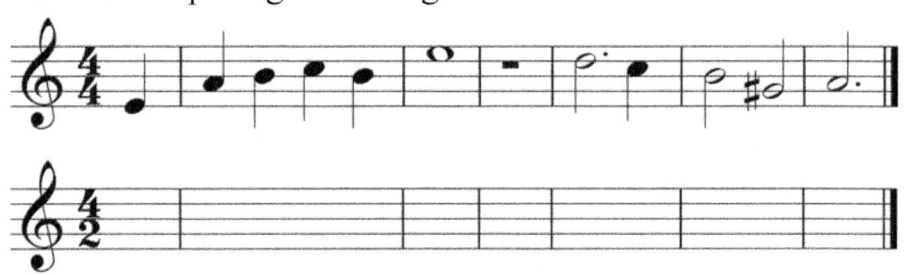

Test yourself

Add time signatures and bar lines where necessary.
The first one has been done for you as an example.

Time to check the answers.

Book 4 page 21

PRIMARY TRIADS AND CHORDS

Primary triads are formed on the **tonic – I**
subdominant – IV
dominant – V

D major
I   IV   V

D minor
I   IV   V

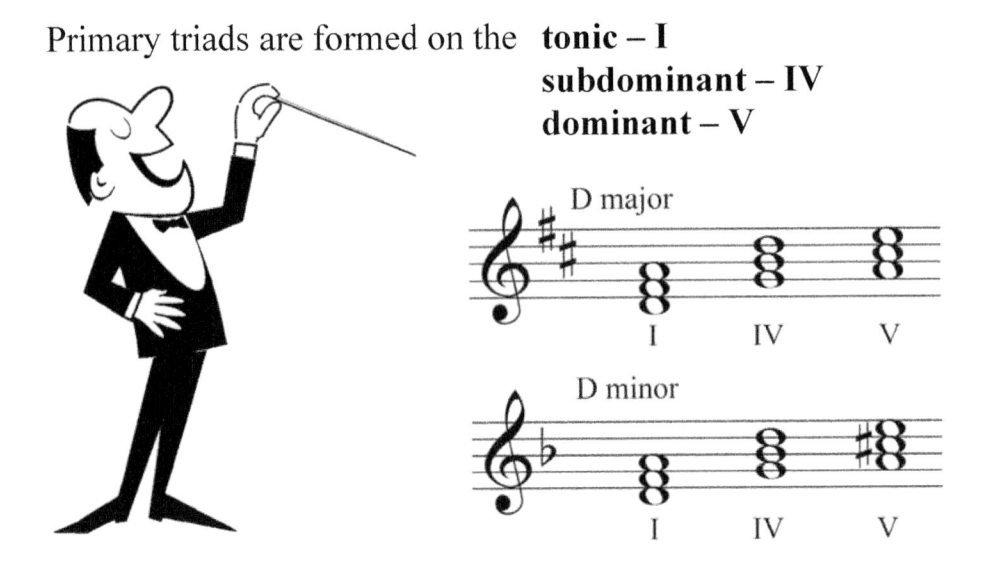

Important

The dominant triad in a minor scale contains the leading note which needs to be raised a semitone / *half step*.

Root, third (3rd) and fifth (5th) refer to the notes of a triad.

Tonic (I), supertonic (II), mediant (III), subdominant (IV), dominant (V), submediant (VI) and leading note (VII) refer to the notes of a scale.

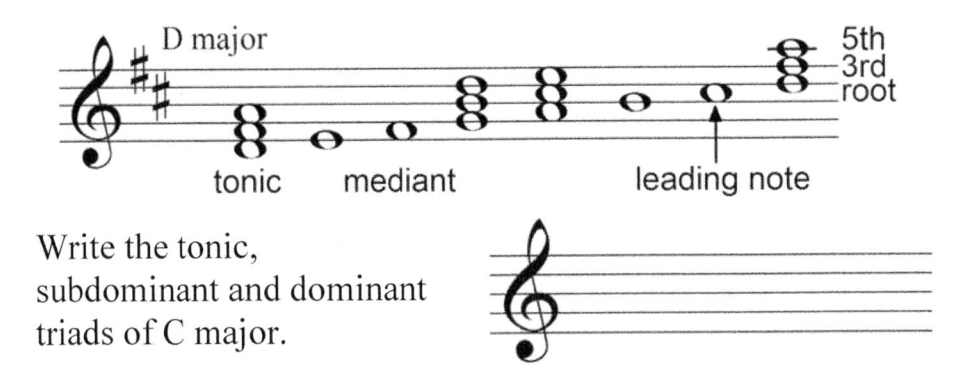

D major
tonic   mediant   leading note
5th
3rd
root

Write the tonic, subdominant and dominant triads of C major.

Book 4 page 22

Write the tonic, subdominant and dominant triads of C minor with key signature.

Primary chords

At the level reached in this book you could be asked to name chords that have been formed from the three primary triads. You would not have to write them. You would only have to recognise them. This is easy because the lowest note of the triad – the root – is always at the bottom of the chord in questions at this level.

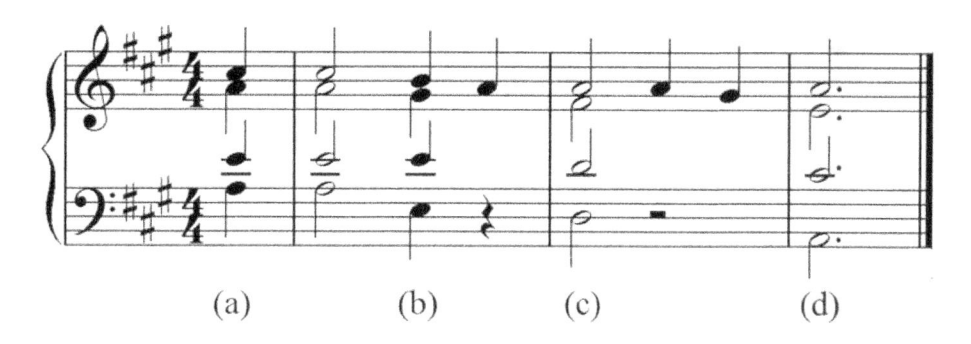

(a)   (b)   (c)   (d)

Name each of the chords (a) to (d) as tonic, subdominant or dominant.

(a) _____

(b) _____

(c) _____

(d) _____

Book 4 page 23

INTERVALS

In my previous books you met major, minor and perfect intervals. Name these. I have done the last one for you.

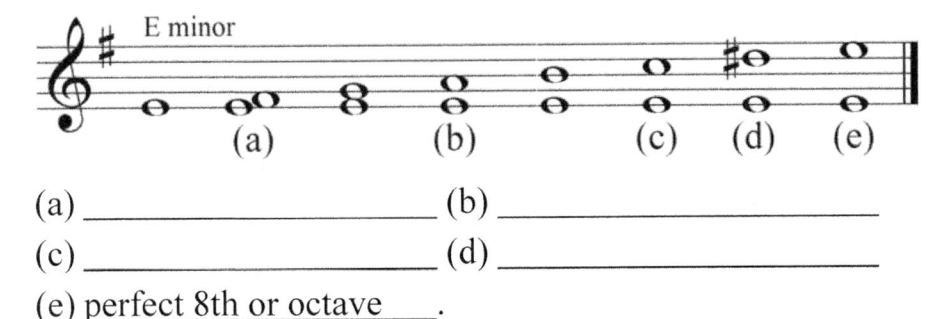

(a) _____ (b) _____
(c) _____ (d) _____
(e) <u>perfect 8th or octave</u>   .

You will now meet augmented and diminished intervals.

Augmented means BIGGER. An augmented interval is one semitone / *one half step* more than a major interval or a perfect interval.

A diminished interval is SMALLER. It is one semitone / *one half step* less than a minor interval or one semitone / *one half step* less than a perfect interval.

Handy hints

major + 1 semitone (½ step)	=	augmented
perfect + 1 semitone (½ step)	=	augmented
minor - 1 semitone (½ step)	=	diminished
perfect - 1 semitone (½ step)	=	diminished
major - 2 semitones (1 step)	=	diminished

Book 4 page 24

Here is a method to take the worry out of intervals so that you can always get the right answer! Follow these instructions to name this interval for example.

Step by Step

1. Decide whether the interval is a 2nd, 3rd, 4th, etc. by counting the letter names. In this example, GABCD = 5 so this is a 5th.

2. Draw a piano keyboard and name the keys.

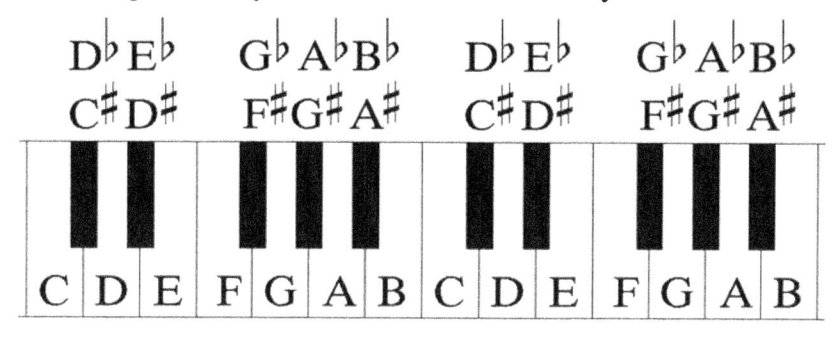

3. Find the lower note of the interval on the keyboard.

4. Count the semitones / *half steps* by walking your fingers (o) on the keys until you reach the upper note.

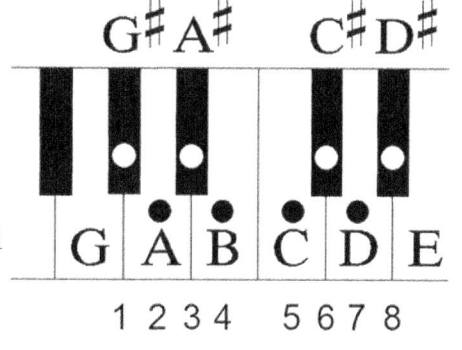

One Final Step

The chart on the next page shows you how many semitones there are in each interval. Look at the chart to name the interval. There are 8 semitones / *8 half steps* in this example so it is an augmented 5th. Remember – 7 semitones / *7 half steps* in a perfect 5th.

Interval Chart

Interval		Semitones / *Half steps*
8ve / Perfect	8th	12
Augmented	7th	12
Major	7th	11
Minor	7th	10
Diminished	7th	9
Augmented	6th	10
Major	6th	9
Minor	6th	8
Diminished	6th	7
Augmented	5th	8
Perfect	5th	7
Diminished	5th	6
Augmented	4th	6
Perfect	4th	5
Diminished	4th	4
Augmented	3rd	5
Major	3rd	4
Minor	3rd	3
Diminished	3rd	2
Augmented	2nd	3
Major	2nd	2
Minor	2nd	1
Diminished	2nd	-

Test yourself

Use the interval chart to find the following intervals.

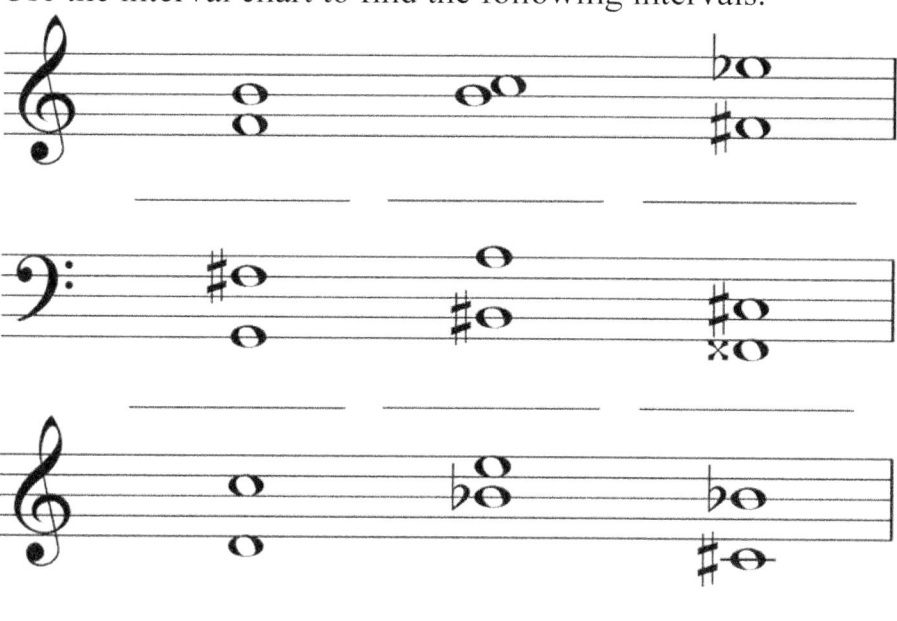

Describe the intervals (a) to (e) in this passage

(a) _____

(b) _____

(c) _____

(d) _____

(e) _____

Check your answers

Book 4 page 27

ORNAMENTS

Many candidates 'run away' from facing ornaments. Don't be one of them. The correct playing of ornaments is so important to music that I'm sure you will want to make the effort to understand them. I shall take you through each one very carefully to give you confidence.

For each ornament in this book you will learn to

1. *Recognise* the *sign*.
2. *Write* its name.
3. *Know* how it is *played*.

You will **not** have to write out the notes.

The acciaccatura

It looks like this:- ♪
Acciaccatura is an Italian word meaning 'squeezed in'.

You play it as quickly as possible on the beat, just before you play the main note. We sometimes call the acciaccatura a 'short grace note'.

Note Values

Grace note: = a demisemiquaver / *a 32nd note*
Main note: minus a demisemiquaver / *a 32nd note*

If the main note is longer than a crotchet / *a quarter note*:-

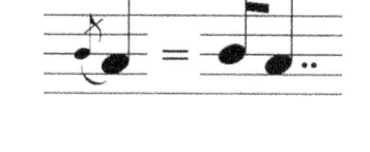

If the main note is dotted:-

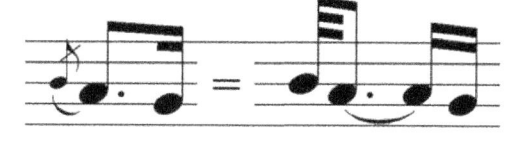

The appoggiatura

It looks like this ♪ and it has no line through it.

The appoggiatura takes different values, depending on the main note.

Note values

If the main note is not dotted, the grace note is half the value of the main note.

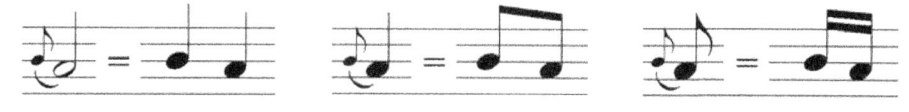

If the main note is dotted, the grace note is two thirds the value of the main note.

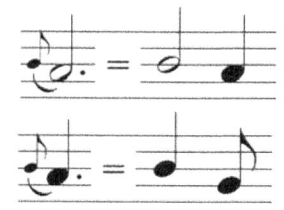

The double or triple appoggiatura

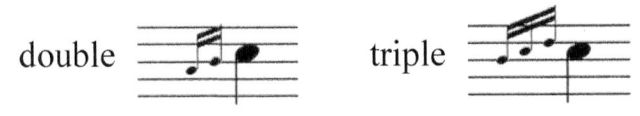

double   triple

note values

If the main note is not dotted, the grace note is half the value of the main note.

If the main note is dotted, the grace note is two thirds the value of the main note.

So far we have two ornaments:
the acciaccatura (4 letter c's) and
the appoggiatura (2 p's and 2 g's)

Book 4 page 30

Test yourself

Write an acciaccatura before the notes marked with *. Put them a note higher than the given note.

Write an appoggiatura before each note.

Which do you think is the best way to play the following? Put a tick in the box of your choice.

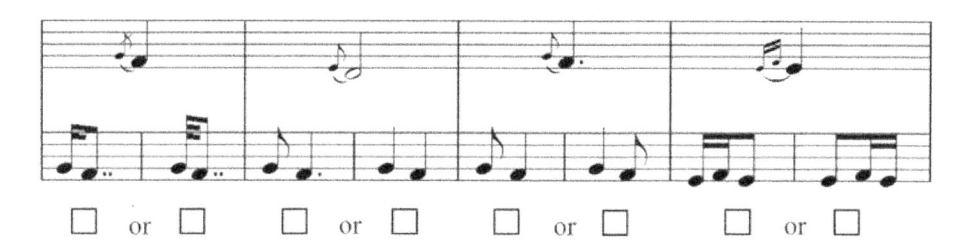

☐ or ☐   ☐ or ☐   ☐ or ☐   ☐ or ☐

The arpeggio

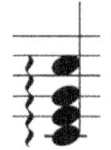

The wavy line tells you to ripple the chord in a harp-like manner from bottom to top. Arpeggio is Italian for harp-like.

When written, the notes take the smallest sensible value and are tied to the notes of the chord.

Each note of the chord is played in turn and held.

The upper mordent

It looks like this 〰

and it is played like this

The main note: a demisemiquaver / *a 32nd note*
The note above: a demisemiquaver / *a 32nd note*
The main note: minus two demisemiquavers / *two 32nd notes.*

When an upper mordent is above a minim / *half note*, add an extra tied crotchet / *quarter note*.

When an upper mordent is above a dotted crotchet / *dotted quarter note*, add an extra tied quaver / *8th note*.

The lower mordent

The main note: a demisemiquaver / *a 32nd note*
The note above: a demisemiquaver / *a 32nd note*
The main note: minus two demisemiquavers / *two 32nd notes.*

It looks like this 〰

and it is played like this

Accidentals and mordents

The accidental is written above the sign with an upper mordent and below the sign with a lower mordent. The middle note is given the accidental indicated.

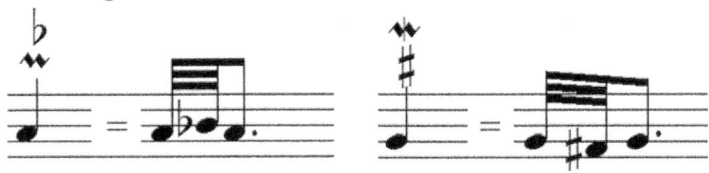

Book 4 page 32

The upper turn

It looks like this ∽

If **above** a note, it is played like this.

The note above
The main note
The note below
The main note

Divide the main note into 4 equal notes.

If **after** a note
    the main note = half its value
    the remainder = 4 equal notes

After a **dotted** note which is a **whole** beat, the turn = the value of the dot.
For example, in $\frac{6}{8}$ time

After a **dotted** note which is **part** of a beat, a triplet is needed in the turn. For example, in $\frac{3}{4}$ time

Book 4 page 33

Accidentals and turns

Accidentals obey the same rules for turns as for mordents.

If above a turn, accidentals apply to the note above.

If below, accidentals apply to the note below.

Test yourself

Tick the box showing the best way to play these ornaments.

□ or □   □ or □

□ or □   □ or □

□ or □

Book 4 page 34

The trill or shake

It looks like this **tr** or **tr**〰〰
It is played with the main note and the note above.
With early composers, start a trill on the note above.

Bach   value of a crotchet / *quarter note*

Use semiquavers / *16th notes* for fast pieces and demisemiquavers / *32nd notes* for slower pieces.

If a trill begins with an acciaccatura, start on the note above.

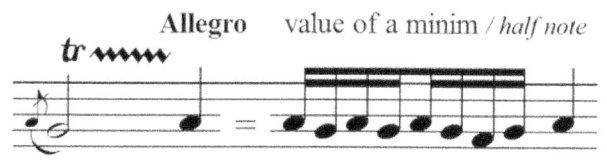

Allegro   value of a minim / *half note*

With modern composers, start a trill on the main note.

Dvorak

Avoid repeated notes at the beginning or the end of a trill. If this means adding an extra note, you will need a triplet before the last two notes of the trill (see above).

Grace notes are included in the trill.

Ready to test yourself? Turn over.

Book 4 page 35

Test yourself

Put a tick / *check mark* in the box showing the best way to play these trills or shakes.

Name these ornament signs.

Write the signs for the ornaments

	upper turn
	trill or shake
	lower mordent
	appoggiatura
	upper mordent
	acciaccatura.

Time to check your answers.

Book 4 page 37

WORDS AND RHYTHM

In my Music Theory is Fun Book 3 you met four-bar rhythms. A musical phrase is often four bars in length. In this book we shall look at writing a rhythm to words. Here is an example:-

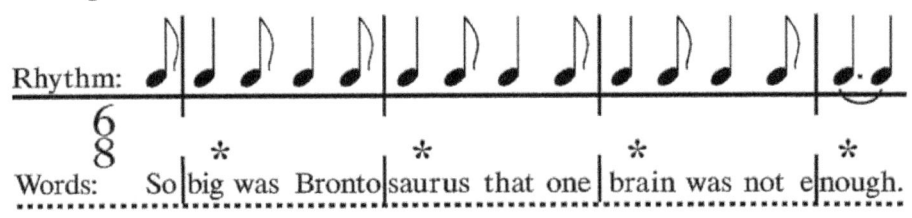

Rhythm: ♪ ♩ ♪ ♩ ♪ | ♩ ♪ ♩ ♪ | ♩ ♪ ♩ ♪ | ♩. ♩ ♪

$\frac{6}{8}$

Words: So |big was Bronto|saurus that one| brain was not e|nough.

- I put bar lines in front of important syllables (see *)
- I chose a time $\frac{6}{8}$ signature since it combines duple time and the possibility of dividing a beat into 3.
- I wrote separate notes for each syllable.

Test yourself

Compose rhythms for the following words.

>Give thought, now, to the dinosaurs,
>Whom no-one fears today.

rhythm _____

words ....

rhythm _____

words ....

Book 4 page 38

Whenever you look at moon and stars,
Whenever the wind is wild.

rhythm _____

words ....

rhythm _____

words ....

Write four-bar rhythms in the times given. Begin with an anacrusis before bar 1. You met the anacrusis in Book 3.

$\frac{4}{4}$ _____

_____

$\frac{6}{8}$ _____

_____

"Hurry! Take me to the next topic!"

INSTRUMENTS OF THE ORCHESTRA

Instrument	treble	alto	tenor	bass
violin	●			
viola		●		
cello	(●)		(●)	●
double bass				●
flute	●			
oboe	●			
bassoon			(●)	●
clarinet	●			
trumpet	●			
horn	●			●
trombone			(●)	●
tuba				●

(●) this clef is sometimes used. Knowledge of the tenor clef is not expected at this level.

A note about notes

String instruments can play more than one note at a time - sometimes two, three or even four notes. Wind instruments can play only one note at a time.

The string family

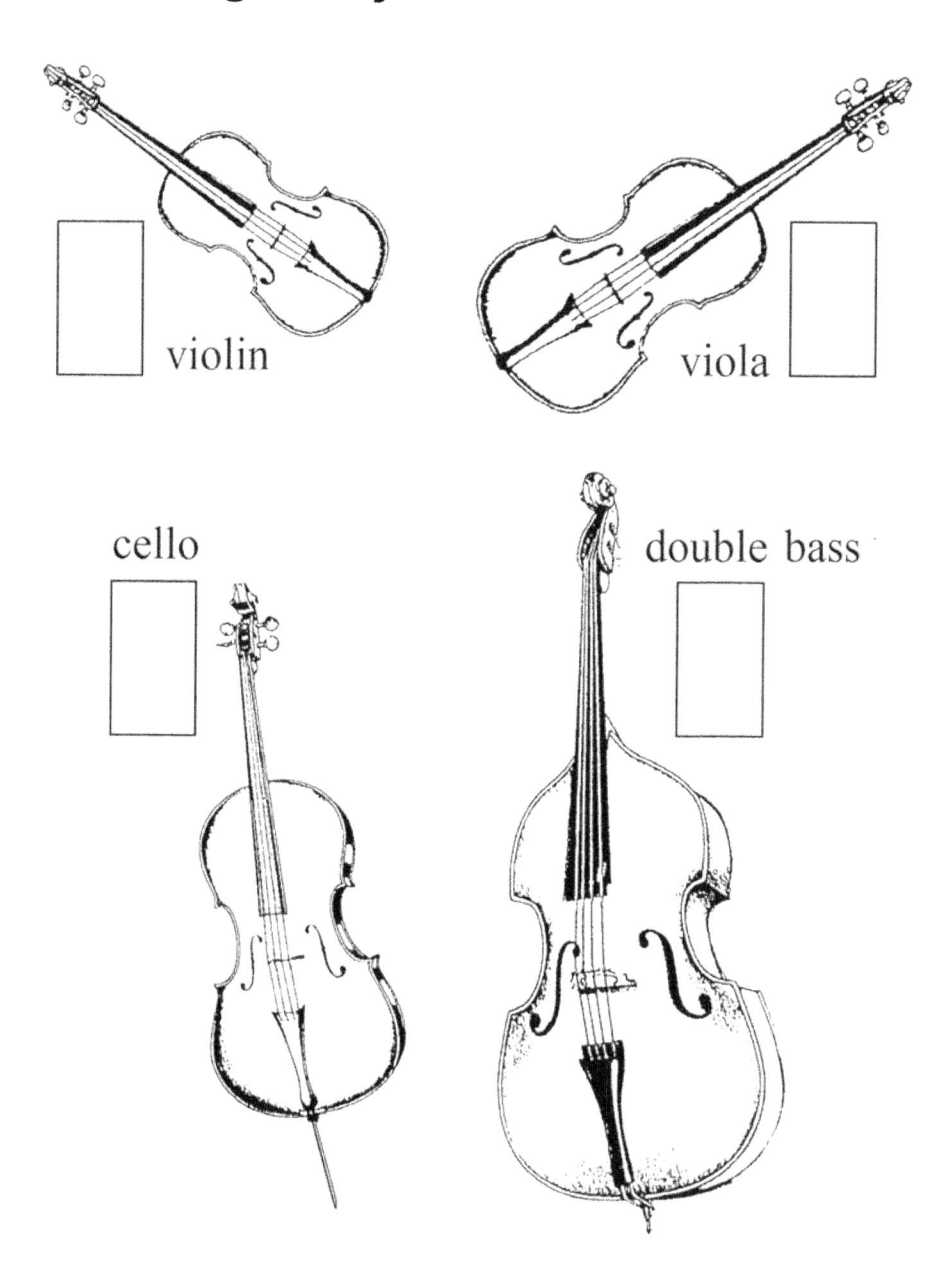

violin

viola

cello

double bass

In each box draw the main clef for the instrument.

The woodwind family

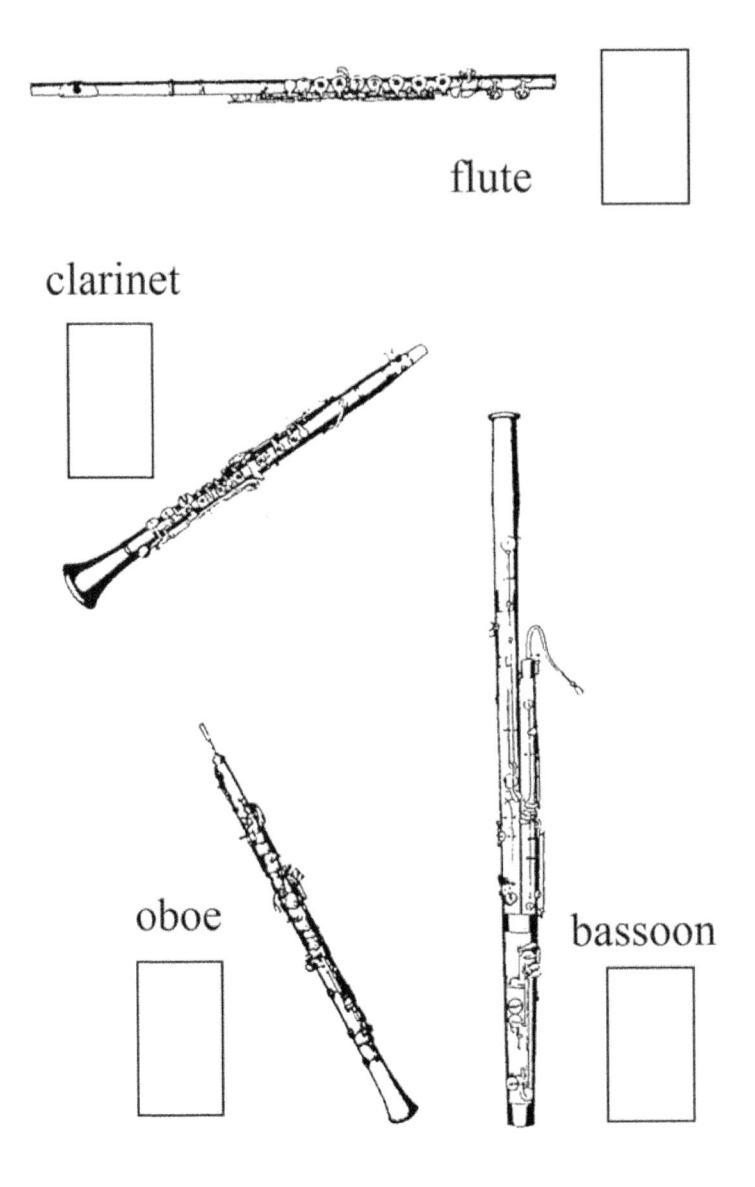

flute

clarinet

oboe

bassoon

In each box draw the main clef for the instrument.

Book 4 page 42

The brass family

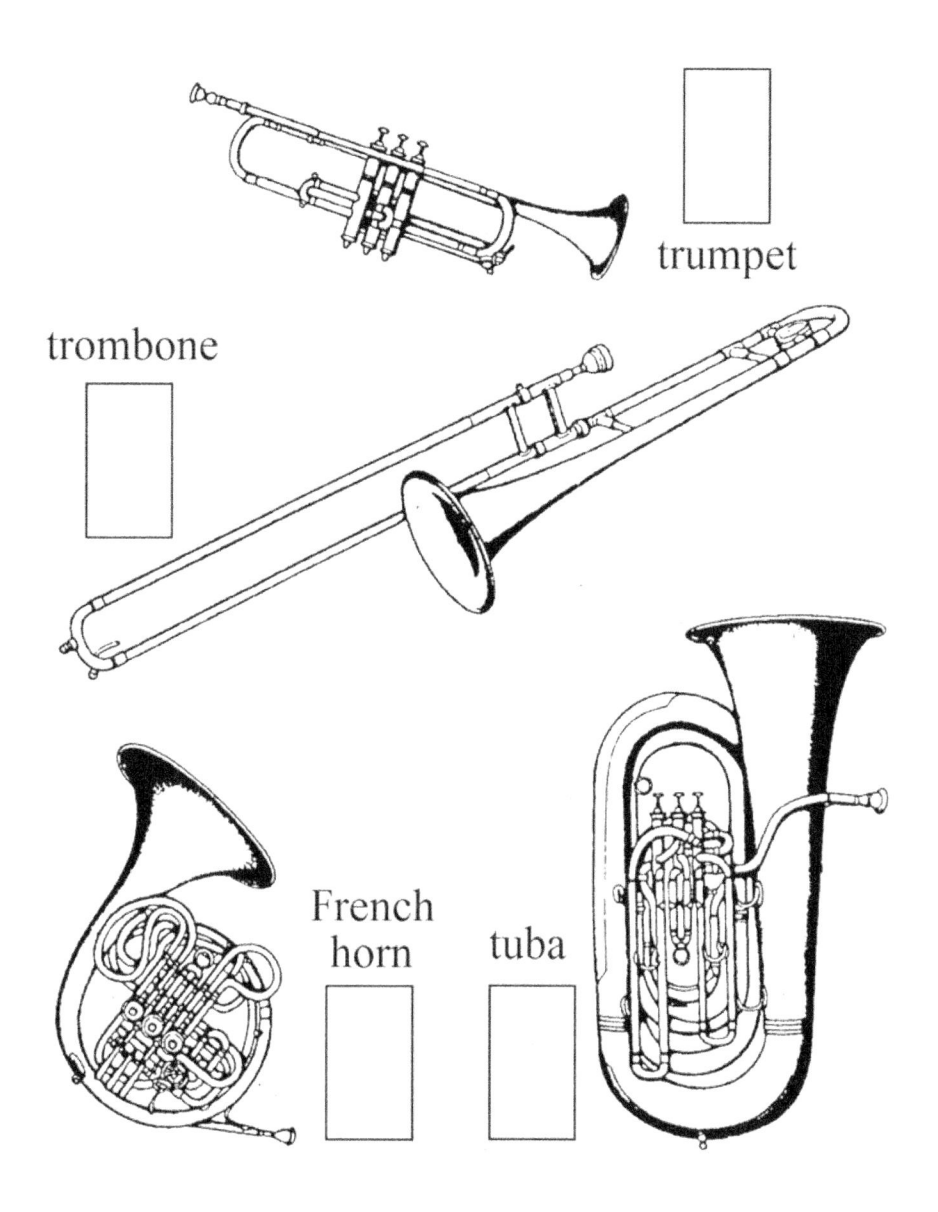

trumpet

trombone

French horn   tuba

In each box draw the main clef for the instrument.

Book 4 page 43

The percussion family

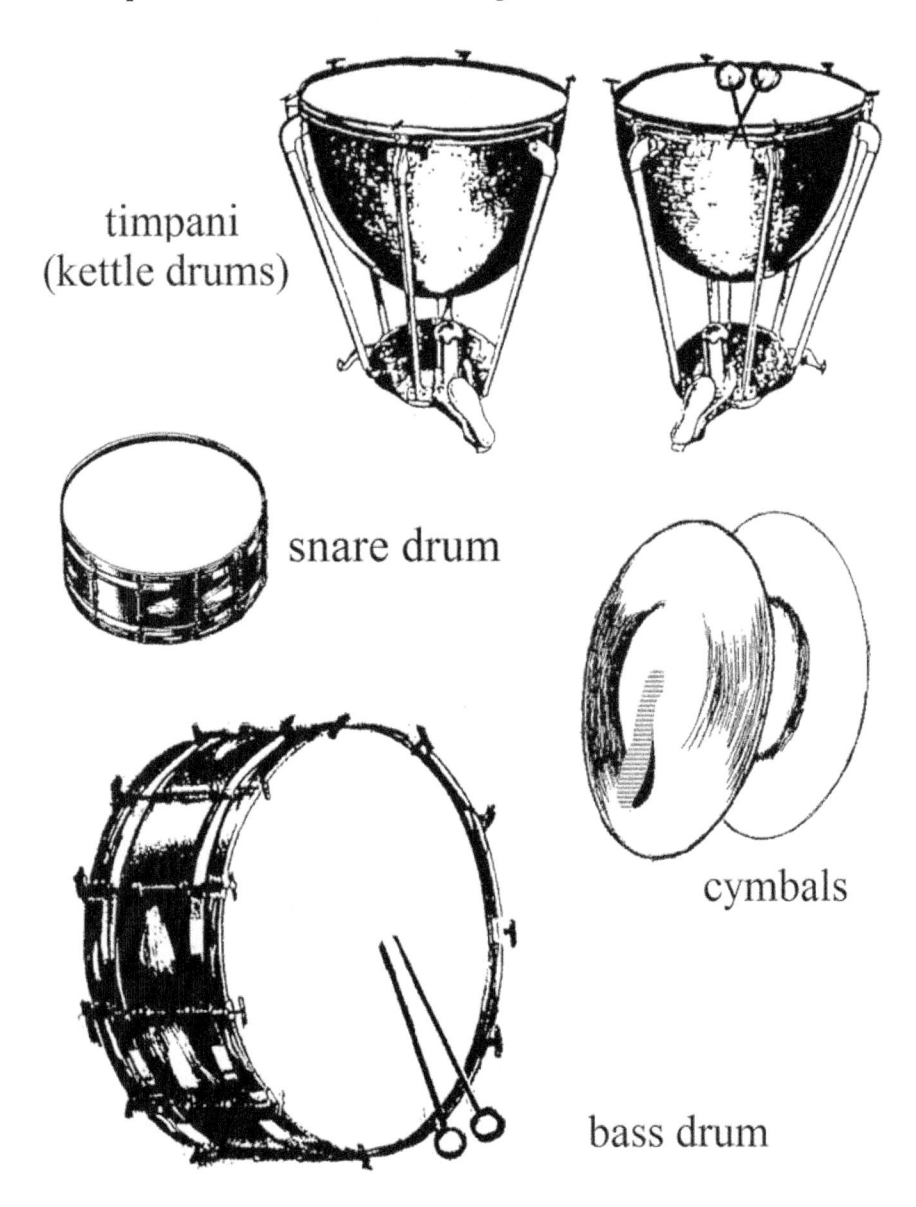

timpani
(kettle drums)

snare drum

cymbals

bass drum

Some members of the percussion family contribute to the rhythm and dynamics of a piece of music. Others can play notes of varying pitch. We shall look more closely at this family in Book 5.

Book 4 page 44

Performance Directions

Brass and string instruments can use a mute to play quietly.

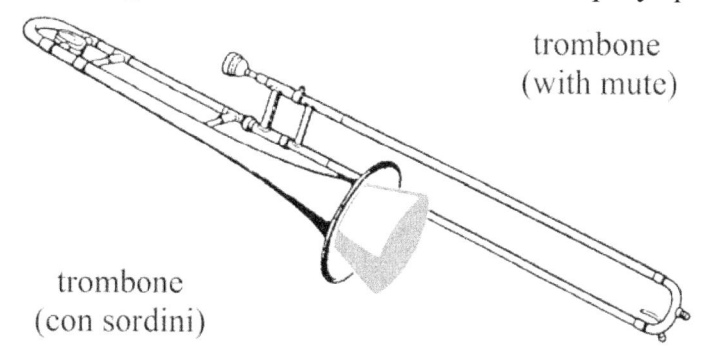

trombone
(with mute)

trombone
(con sordini)

The term **senza sordini** tells you to play without a mute.

To a violinist, ⊓ means 'down' bow and V means 'up' bow. Here are some other directions for string players:

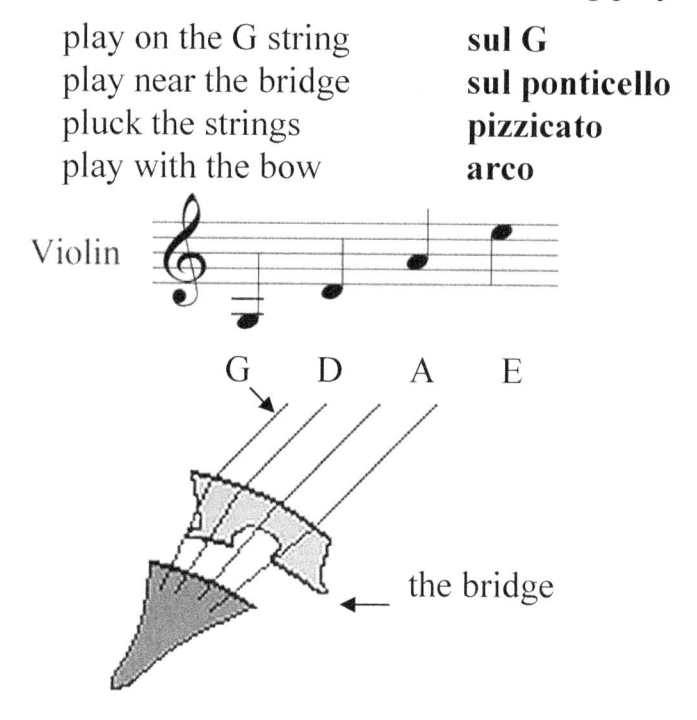

play on the G string	**sul G**
play near the bridge	**sul ponticello**
pluck the strings	**pizzicato**
play with the bow	**arco**

Violin

G D A E

← the bridge

Book 4 page 45

Test yourself

Name the family for each instrument.

1. violin   _____
2. oboe   _____
3. trombone   _____
4. bassoon   _____
5. clarinet   _____
6. tuba   _____
7. timpani   _____

Name the main clef for each instrument.

8. cello   _____
9. clarinet   _____
10. flute   _____
11. trumpet   _____
12. tuba   _____
13. viola   _____
14. French horn   _____

Check your answers.   /14

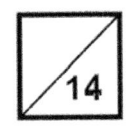

Book 4 page 46

PUZZLES

QUIZZES

TESTS

Book 4 page 47

Fun Page

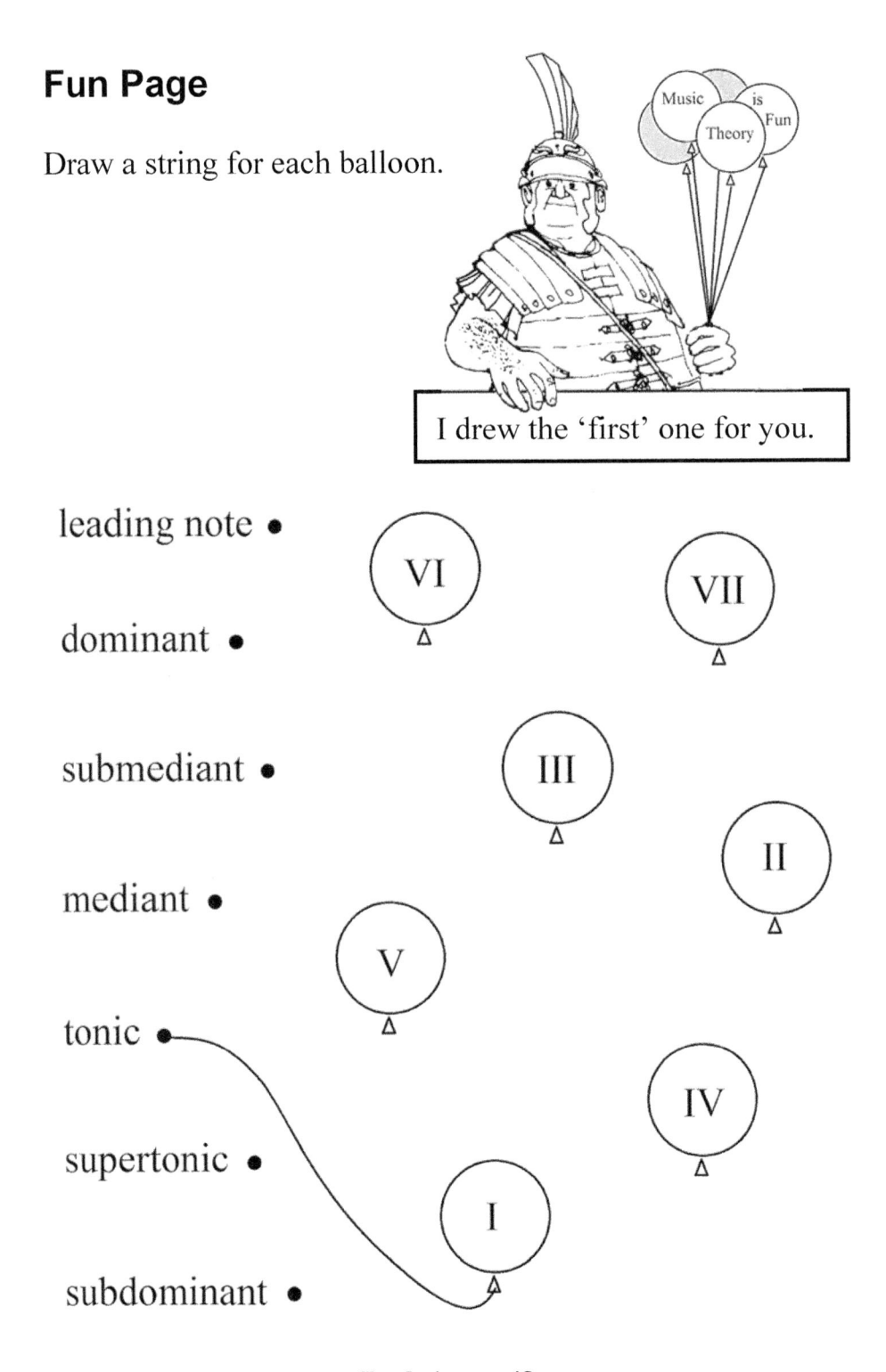

Draw a string for each balloon.

I drew the 'first' one for you.

leading note •

dominant •

submediant •

mediant •

tonic •

supertonic •

subdominant •

VI VII III II V IV I

Book 4 page 48

Anagrams

caratacacuci

Clue: This ornament is played as quickly as possible on the beat and just before the main note.

ograpige

Clue: This wavy line means ripple the chord like on a harp.

frecept hofurt

Clue: This is an interval of 5 semitones / *5 half steps*.

rajmo veenths

Clue: This is an interval of 11 semitones / *11 half steps*.

hiddinmeis

Clue: These intervals are 1 semitone / *1 half step* less than a minor interval.

tombudanins

Clue: This is also called chord IV.

Crossword

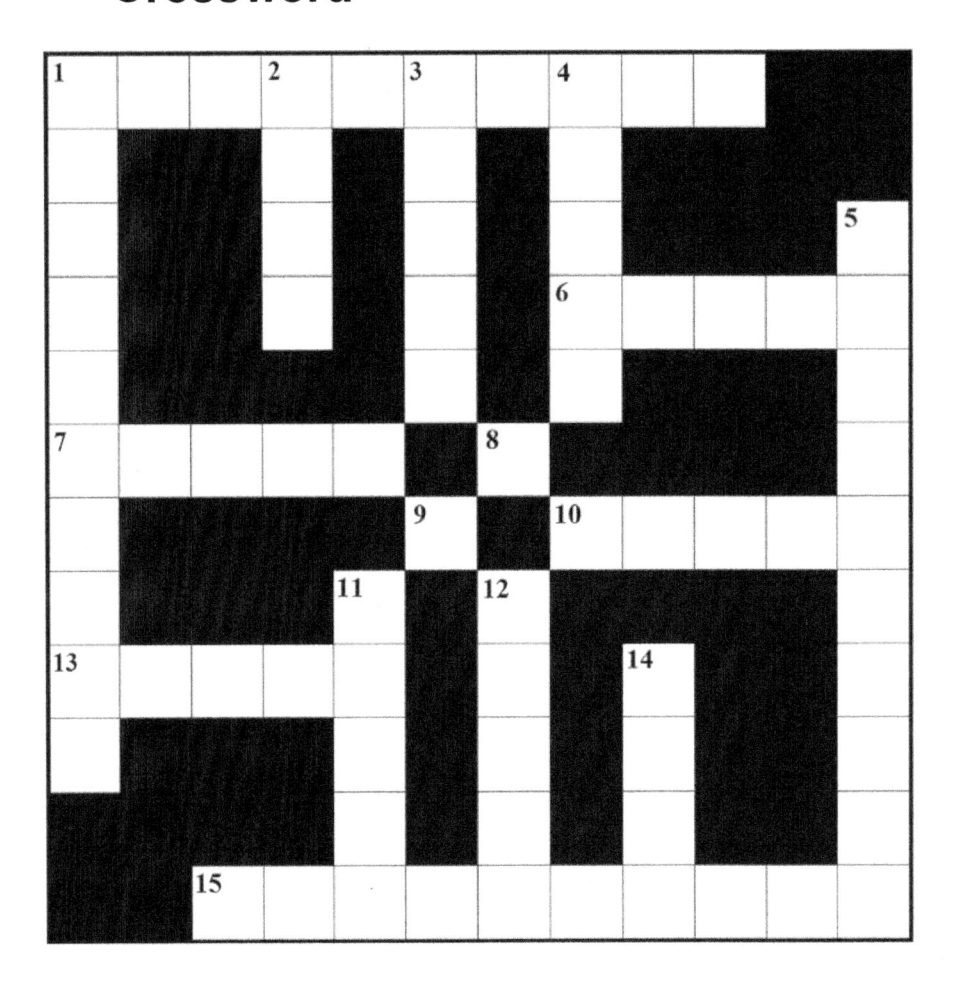

Across

1 hammered out

6 sadly

7 hold back [ritenuto]

8 minor key with 4 flats

9 major key with 5 sharps

Book 4 page 50

10 sweetly
13 below
15 sighing

Down
1 mysteriously
2 very
3 slowly
4 animated, lively
5 loud then immediately soft
11 less
12 as if, resembling
14 in the style of

Book 4 page 51

Musical terms word search

I	B	A	S	O	P	R	A	E	S
A	R	W	O	U	K	A	C	Y	A
X	A	E	T	X	I	O	R	B	N
Y	L	Q	T	G	L	Y	Q	V	S
M	E	N	O	E	L	U	I	S	N
E	N	C	V	G	N	P	Z	K	I
Q	T	K	B	G	I	U	S	T	O
Y	I	F	V	F	V	O	Q	X	M
O	R	O	N	O	S	B	G	I	G
H	B	X	B	V	I	F	P	E	U

Meaning	Musical term
lively	vif
slow down	_____
held back	_____
exact, proper	_____
with rich tone	_____
without	_____
above	_____
below	_____
swift	_____
less	_____
little	_____

Book 4 page 52

Quiz 1

Put a tick / *check mark* (✓) for the correct answer.

1. **marcato**
- ☐ majestically
- ☐ in a military style
- ☐ hammered out
- ☐ marked, accented

2. **sadly**
- ☐ dolente
- ☐ dolce
- ☐ dolore
- ☐ delicato

3. **with a strong accent**
- ☐ forte
- ☐ fortissimo
- ☐ forzando
- ☐ pesante

4. 𝄿
- ☐ upper turn
- ☐ upper mordent
- ☐ lower mordent
- ☐ shake

5. **with vigour**
- ☐ con anima
- ☐ con brio
- ☐ con moto
- ☐ con spirito

6. **meno**
- ☐ less
- ☐ more
- ☐ moderately
- ☐ much

7. **from the beginning**
- ☐ dal segno
- ☐ a tempo
- ☐ da capo
- ☐ prima volta

8. 𝄈
- ☐ short, detached
- ☐ accent the note
- ☐ staccatissimo
- ☐ staccato

Book 4 page 53

Quiz 2

Do you know these orchestral instruments? Write in the box the name of the instrument being played.

Book 4 page 54

Handy hints for tests

This section is for you to practise the different types of questions you could have in a test or an exam.

The questions could be on any topic covered in this book and in Music Theory is Fun Books 1, 2 and 3.

Revise each topic in this book thoroughly.

Don't forget to study musical terms and signs – they are **always** included.

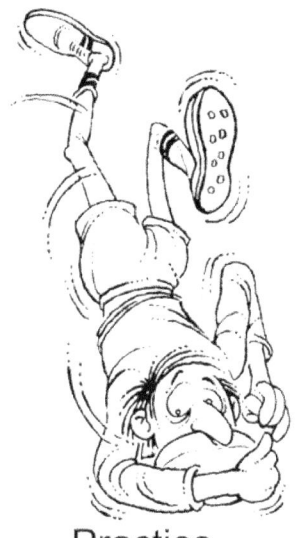

Practice makes perfect!

Practice makes perfect!

If you have worked through this book carefully and understood each topic, this will be an easy task for you.

Before you begin any test, write out your key signature chart (see page 7). Always refer to the chart when tackling questions that require you to know a key signature.

Test 1

1. Name this interval.

   major 7th ☐   augmented 6th ☐   diminished 7th ☐

2. Smorzando means

   gradually slower ☐   dying away ☐   tearfully ☐

3. Which minor key has 5 sharps in its key signature?

   F ☐   C ☐   G♯ ☐

4. Which minor key has 4 flats in its key signature?

   F ☐   C ☐   B ☐

5. Which note is the mediant in this minor key?

   G ☐   A ☐   D ☐

6. This note is

   lowered one semitone / *one half step* ☐
   lowered one tone / *one whole step* ☐
   raised one semitone / *one half step* ☐

7. Which is the correct time signature for this bar?

   3/8 ☐   5/8 ☐   5/4 ☐

8. How many semiquavers / *16th notes* are there in this note?

   5 ☐   6 ☐   7 ☐

Book 4 page 56

Test 2

1. Put a Roman numeral under each note in this D major scale.

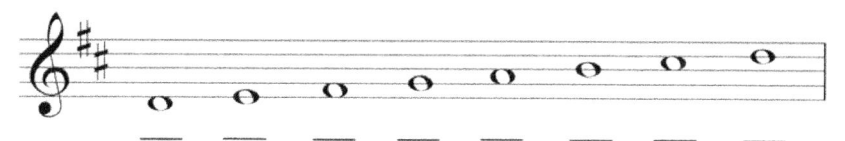

2. How many quavers / *8th notes* are there in these notes?

3. Name these ornament signs.

    (a) _____

    (b) _____

    (c) _____

    (d) *tr*____ _____

    (e) _____

4. What does this metronome setting mean? ♩ = 80

    _____

5. Write the chromatic scale of G major in the treble clef ascending in semibreves / *whole notes* with key signature.

Book 4 page 57

Test 3

1. Name the four main families of orchestral instruments.

   _____   _____

   _____   _____

2. What is the meaning of

   (a) sul ponticello _____

   (b) pizzicato _____

   (c) arco _____

3. (a) What is the meaning of senza sordini?

   _____

   (b) Name an instrument that might have this direction.

   _____

4. Write in semibreves / *whole notes* the scale of D♭ major ascending in the treble clef with key signature.

5. Write in semibreves / *whole notes* the scale of G♯ melodic minor descending in the bass clef without key signature.

Book 4 page 58

Test 4

1. Write a note above the given note to form the named melodic intervals.

   (a) augmented 4th (b) diminished 7th.

2. Put accidentals in front of the notes that need them to make the scale of C melodic minor. Do not use a key signature.

3. Write the scale of G♯ harmonic minor ascending in minims / *half notes* using the bass clef. Do not put a key signature. Add any necessary accidentals.

4. **patetico** means
   dying away ☐
   with feeling ☐
   tearfully ☐
   sadly ☐

5. ♪ is the sign for
   upper mordent ☐
   appoggiatura ☐
   acciaccatura ☐
   trill ☐

Book 4 page 59

Test 5

1. Name the family for each instrument.

   oboe   _____

   cello   _____

   trumpet _____

   timpani _____

2. Write the scale of F melodic minor in the bass clef ascending in minims / *half notes* with key signature.

3. Write the letter names of the notes on the white keys.

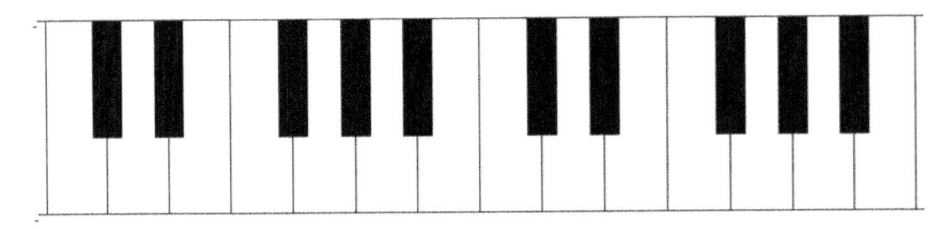

4. Write above the black keys the letter names of (a) the flats and (b) the sharps.

   (a) — —   — — — (b) — —   — — —

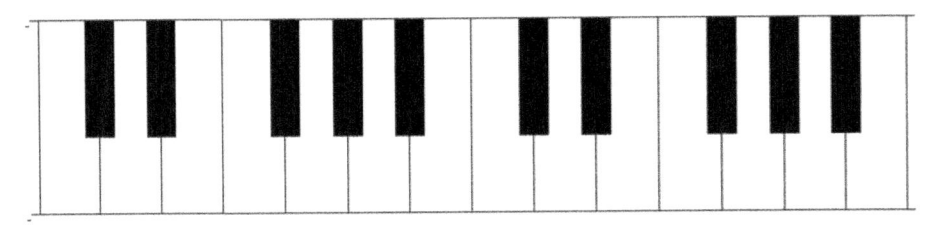

Test 6

1. Write these alto clef notes at the same pitch in the treble clef.

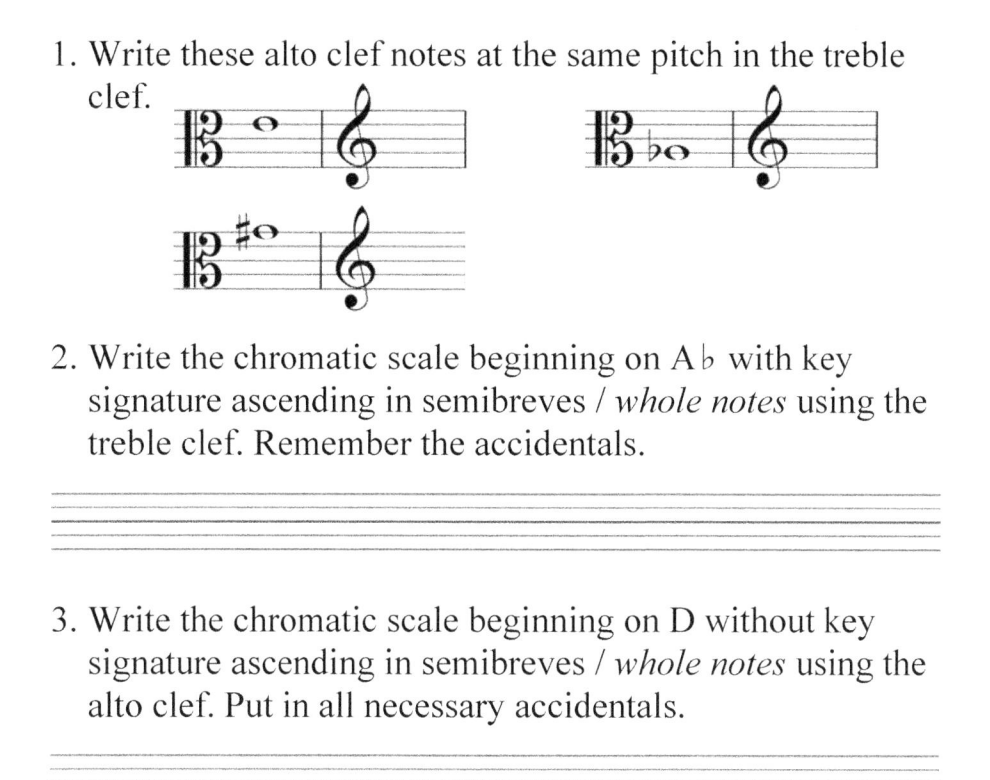

2. Write the chromatic scale beginning on A♭ with key signature ascending in semibreves / *whole notes* using the treble clef. Remember the accidentals.

3. Write the chromatic scale beginning on D without key signature ascending in semibreves / *whole notes* using the alto clef. Put in all necessary accidentals.

4. Describe each of these harmonic intervals fully e.g. major 3rd, perfect 4th.

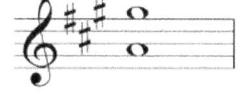

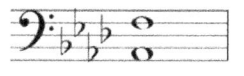

5. Name these notes.

Book 4 page 61

Test 7

1. Find the mistakes in this piece of music and then write it out correctly on the stave below.

2. Write the tonic, subdominant and dominant triads of F major in the treble clef with key signature.

4. Write the tonic, subdominant and dominant triads of F minor in the treble clef with key signature.

5. Compose rhythms to these words from a poem by Robert Frost.   The woods are lovely, dark and deep
But I have promises to keep

    Begin with an anacrusis. Add a time signature.

    rhythm   _____

    words   _____

    rhythm   _____

    words   _____

Test 8

1. Give the meaning of Patetico. _____

2. Transpose this melody up one octave using the treble clef.

3. Name the notes in bar 3 in order. ___ ___ ___ ___

4. How many demisemiquavers / *32nd notes* is the last note of bar 1 worth? _____

5. Name two orchestral instruments, one string and one woodwind, that could play this melody so that the pitch sounds the same.
   string _____ woodwind _____

6. Which member of the string family normally uses the alto clef? _____

7. Tick / *check* the boxes beside two instruments that are not members of the orchestral woodwind family.
   bassoon ☐   tuba ☐   oboe ☐   trombone ☐   flute ☐

Test 9

Look at the following piece of music and answer the questions that follow.

1. Add a key signature in the bass clef and add a time signature in the treble and bass clefs.

2. Copy the treble part in bar 1 and mark the beats with a stroke (|) between each beat.

3. What is the Italian word for the ornament ( ) at the beginning of bar 2 and what does it mean? Is it played quickly or slowly?

   _____

   _____

4. Give the meaning of ♩ = 120

   _____

5. Name the notes in the last chord in the treble clef in bar 2.

   _____   _____

6. Name the number and type of interval between the notes in the last chord in the treble clef in bar 2.

   number _____   type _____

Book 4 page 64

Test 10

Look at this melody and then answer the questions below.

1. Add the time signature of this melody in the correct place.

2. Describe the time signature as simple, compound duple, triple or quadruple. _____

3. What is the key of the piece? _____

4. Give the letter names of the first three notes in bar 1.

   ____   ____   ____

5. Give the letter name of the highest note in the melody.

   ____

6. Name the ornaments in bars 3 & 4. _____

7. Look at bar 5 then give the meaning of
   (a) ⌢ _____
   (b) ⌢̇ _____

8. How should the notes in bar 4 be played?
   _____

Book 4 page 65

Book 4 page 66

CONTENTS
Book 5

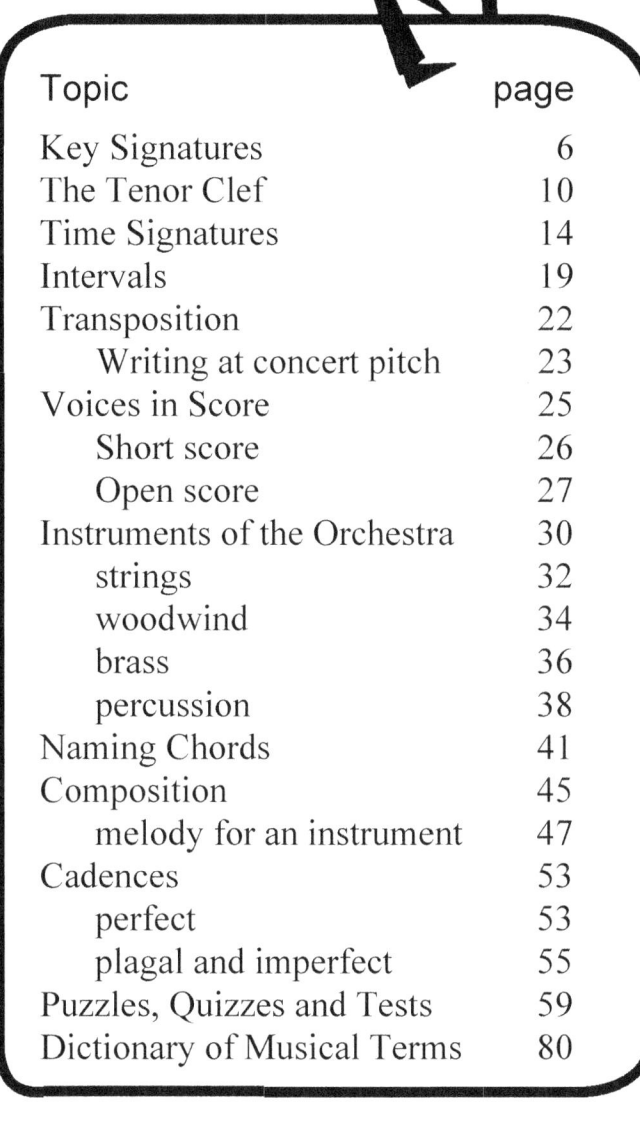

Topic	page
Key Signatures	6
The Tenor Clef	10
Time Signatures	14
Intervals	19
Transposition	22
Writing at concert pitch	23
Voices in Score	25
Short score	26
Open score	27
Instruments of the Orchestra	30
strings	32
woodwind	34
brass	36
percussion	38
Naming Chords	41
Composition	45
melody for an instrument	47
Cadences	53
perfect	53
plagal and imperfect	55
Puzzles, Quizzes and Tests	59
Dictionary of Musical Terms	80

KEY SIGNATURES

I expect you have met many methods for learning key signatures. My method is quite straightforward, so do try it - it works for me! Let it work for you too.

Follow this plan

1. Put a "1" under the key which has 1 sharp or 1 flat. Continue to number from left to right until you can go no further.
2. Go back to the beginning and carry on numbering.
3. Give a sharp or flat to each letter before the "1".

The patterns for the major key signatures with 7 sharps and 7 flats are easy to remember.

F C G D A E B   B E A D G C F

G major has 1 sharp and F major has 1 flat.

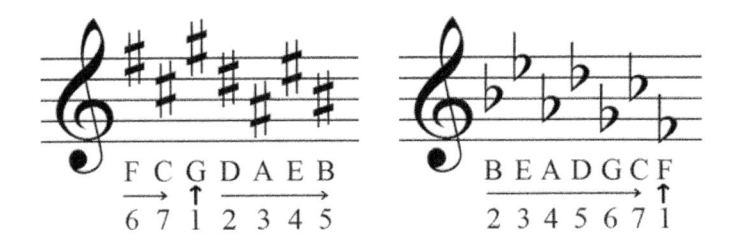

F C G D A E B   B E A D G C F
→ ↑ → →   → ↑
6 7 1 2 3 4 5   2 3 4 5 6 7 1

You can do the same for the minor keys. Just remember that E minor has 1 sharp and D minor has 1 flat.

Here are the charts following my rules. Remember them.

Major Sharps						
F♯	C♯	G	D	A	E	B
6	7	1	2	3	4	5

Minor Sharps						
F♯	C♯	G♯	D♯	A♯	E	B
3	4	5	6	7	1	2

Major Flats						
B♭	E♭	A♭	D♭	G♭	C♭	F
2	3	4	5	6	7	1

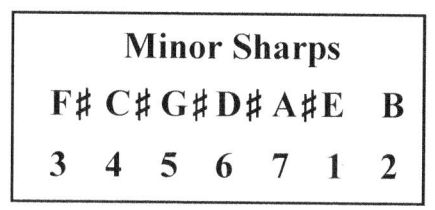

Minor Flats						
B♭	E♭	A♭	D	G	C	F
5	6	7	1	2	3	4

Important

You now know the order of sharps and the order of flats. Here is a reminder of where they come on the staves in the treble **and** bass clefs.

Test yourself

Complete the charts for all the key signatures in the spaces below, from memory!

major sharps

minor sharps

major flats

minor flats

Key signatures? They're a worry of the past.

Test yourself

Using your completed charts, name the keys shown below.

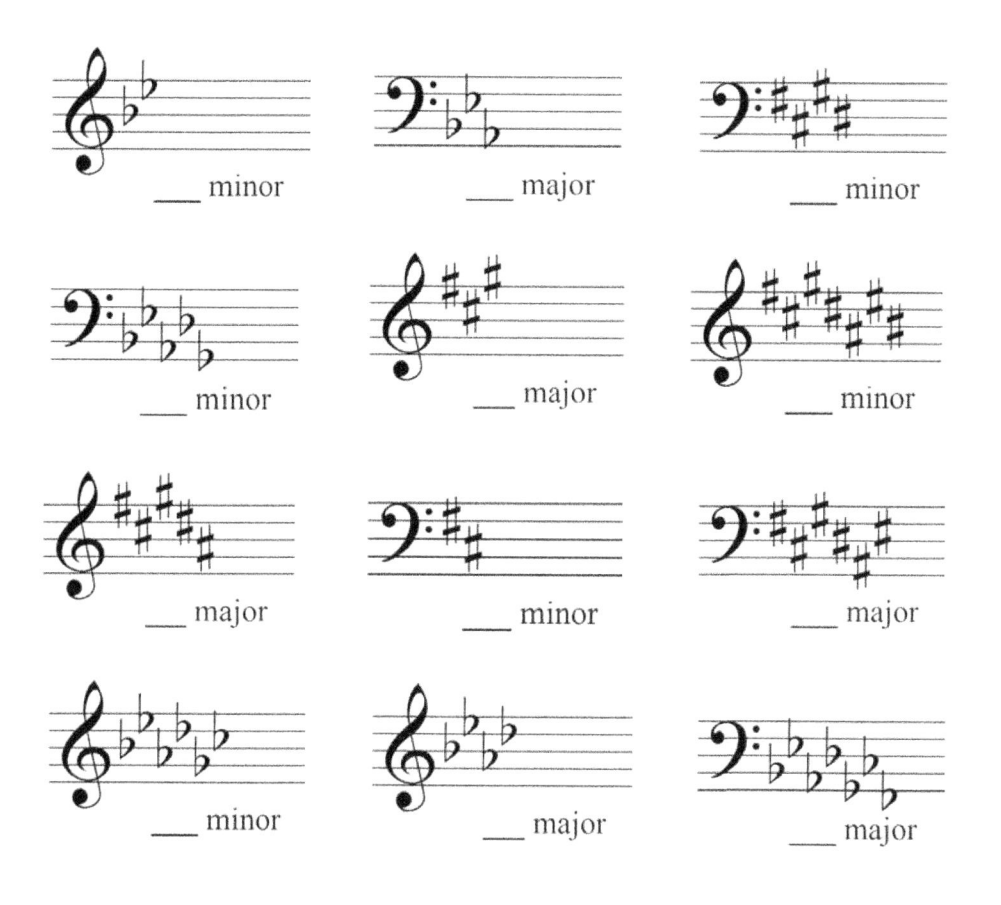

___ minor

___ major

___ minor

___ minor

___ major

___ minor

___ major

___ minor

___ major

___ minor

___ major

___ major

Now key signatures are a worry of the past for you too.

THE TENOR CLEF

The tenor clef can be used for these three instruments:-

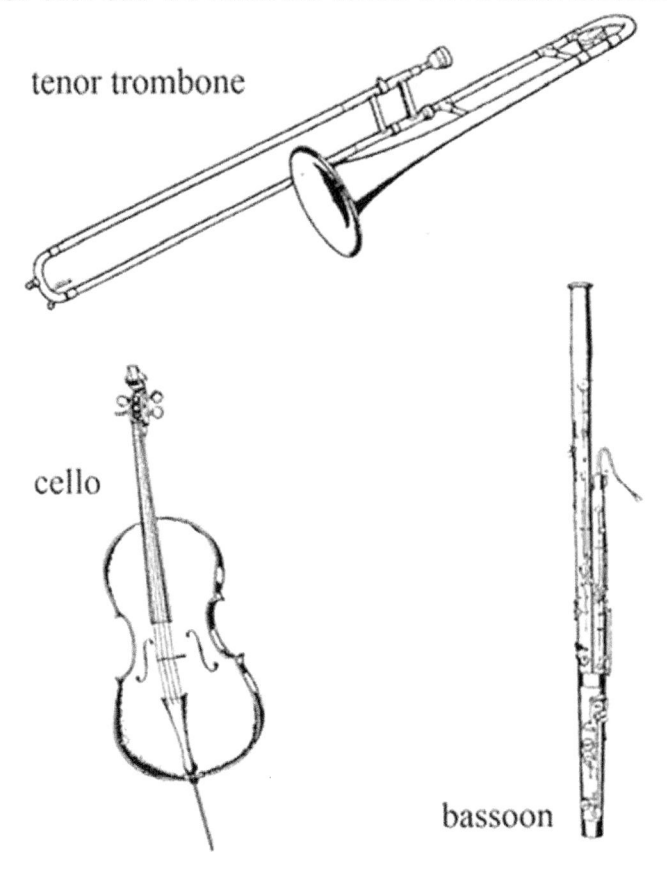

tenor trombone

cello

bassoon

Like the alto clef which you met in my Music Theory is Fun Book 4, the tenor clef is a **C clef**. The only difference is that middle C is on the 4th line.

Name these notes:

This is how the key signatures of seven sharps and seven flats are written in the tenor clef.

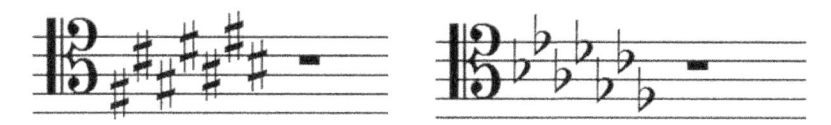

Test yourself

1. Write the required key signatures in the tenor clef:-

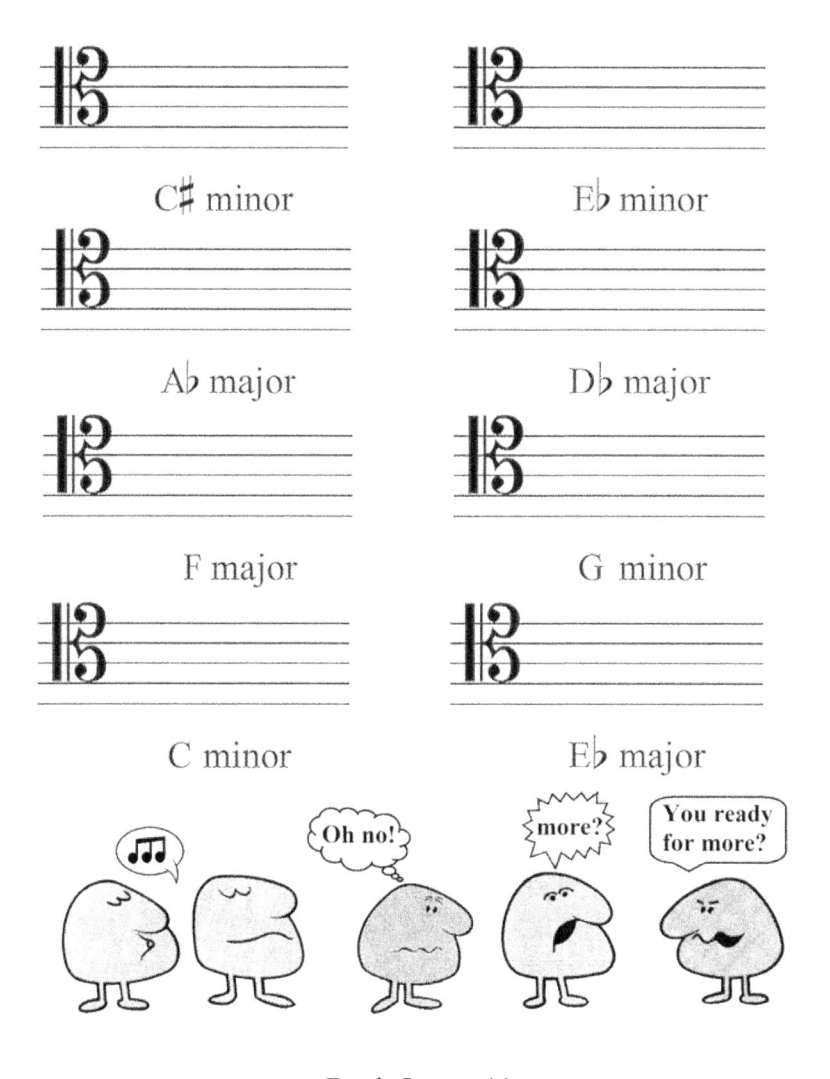

C# minor

E♭ minor

A♭ major

D♭ major

F major

G minor

C minor

E♭ major

Book 5 page 11

2. Write **with** key signature the tonic triads of:

   Db Major				C# Minor

3. Write **with** key signature the scales

   B major **ascending** in minims / *half notes*

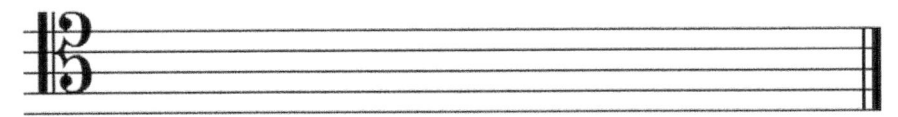

   F# Major **descending** in crotchets / *quarter notes*

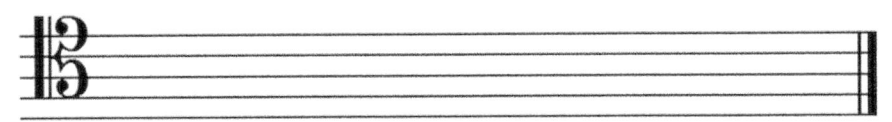

4. Write **without** key signature the scales

   G# melodic minor **ascending** in semibreves / *whole notes*

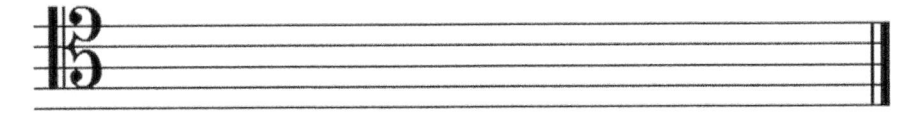

   Eb harmonic minor **descending** in semibreves / *whole notes*

Book 5 page 12

5. Rewrite each passage at the **same pitch** in the clef indicated – treble, bass or tenor.

TIME SIGNATURES

You should know all the simple and compound time signatures which you have met so far. Here is a reminder:

Simple Time

duple $\frac{2}{4}$ $\frac{2}{2}$ or ¢   triple $\frac{3}{8}$ $\frac{3}{4}$ $\frac{3}{2}$ quadruple $\frac{4}{8}$ $\frac{4}{4}$ or c $\frac{4}{2}$

Compound Time

duple $\frac{6}{16}$ $\frac{6}{8}$ $\frac{6}{4}$ triple $\frac{9}{16}$ $\frac{9}{8}$ $\frac{9}{4}$ quadruple $\frac{12}{16}$ $\frac{12}{8}$ $\frac{12}{4}$

If you are not too sure of compound time, read that section again in my Music Theory is Fun Book 4.

Irregular time signatures

In addition to the time signatures which you have met already, there are some new ones in this book. These are **irregular** time signatures.

Quintuple Time

$\frac{5}{8}$ [5 quaver / *eighth note* beats in a bar]

$\frac{5}{4}$ [5 crotchet / *quarter note* beats in a bar]

Septuple Time

$\frac{7}{8}$ [7 quaver / *eighth note* beats in a bar]

$\frac{7}{4}$ [7 crotchet / *quarter note* beats in a bar]

No other irregular time signatures will need to be known at this level.

Grouping of notes

In quintuple time notes are grouped in combinations of two or three beats: [2+3] or [3+2].

Here are examples in each of the quintuple times. Show how the notes have been grouped. The first bar has been done for you.

In septuple time, notes are grouped in combinations of three beats or two beats: [2+2+3], [2+3+2], [3+2+2], [4+3] or [3+4]. Notice that two groups of two beats can be joined to make a group of four.

Here are examples in each of the septuple times. Show how the notes have been grouped. The first bar has been done for you.

Book 5 page 15

Irregular time divisions

You met triplets in Book 2 and duplets in Book 4. In each of the further examples you are now going to meet, groups of 5, 6 or 7 notes use the same time values as a group of 4. A group of 9 uses the same time values as a group of 8.

Examples for you to study

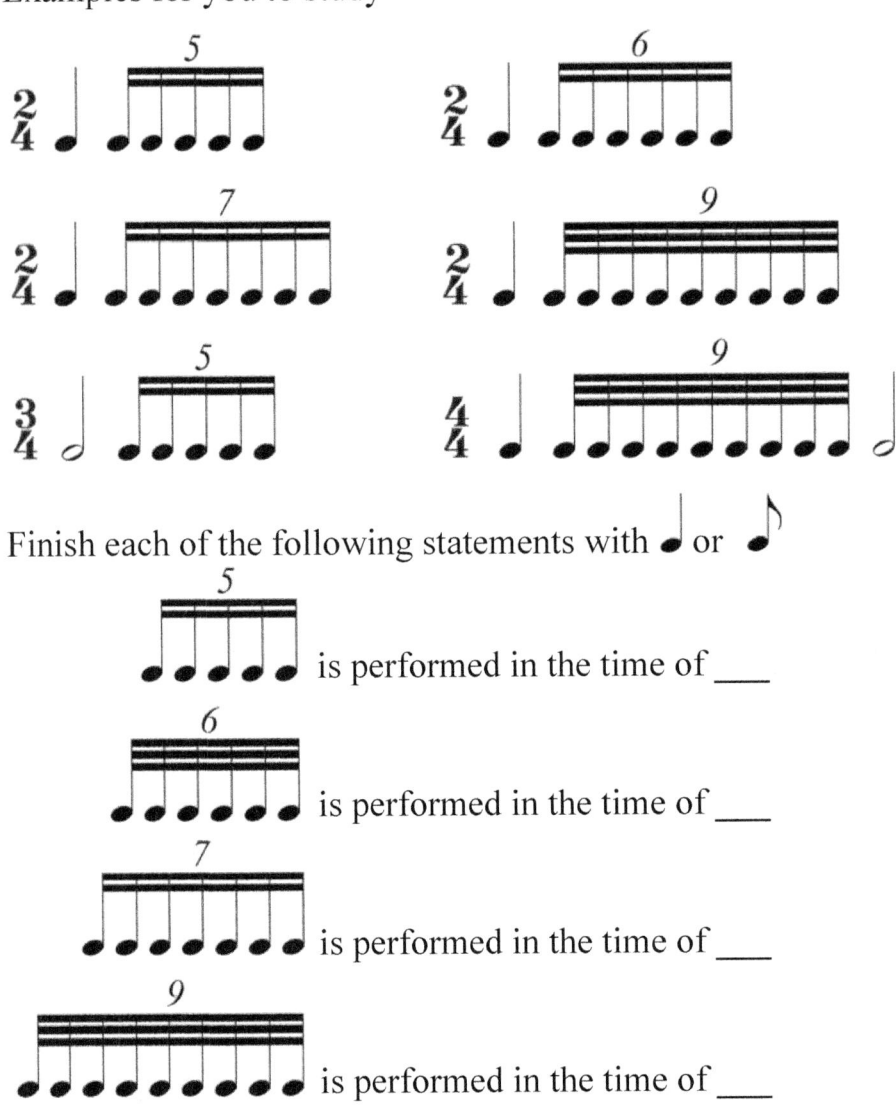

Finish each of the following statements with ♩ or ♪

 is performed in the time of ___

 is performed in the time of ___

 is performed in the time of ___

 is performed in the time of ___

Book 5 page 16

Test yourself

Add bar-lines and time signatures where needed. Each example begins on the first beat of the bar.
Take care - this is a 'mixed bag'!

Time signature changes

The following examples all contain changes of time. They all begin on the first beat of the bar. Put time signatures **where they are needed**. You may be asked to do this in an exam so **be prepared!**

Any of you not ready for a new topic?

Book 5 page 18

INTERVALS

In my Music Theory is Fun Book 4 you had to be able to describe intervals of less than an octave. There was a chart drawn for you. It has been drawn again for you here because it is so useful.

Step by Step
1. Draw a piano keyboard and name the keys
2. Find the lower note of the interval on the keyboard
3. Walk your fingers in semitones / *half steps* until you reach the upper note
4. Decide whether the interval is a 3rd, 4th, 5th, etc.

One Final Step
Look at the interval chart. Check in the semitone / *half step* column for the correct answer.

Interval		Semitones *half steps*
Perfect	8th	12
Augmented	7th	12
Major	7th	11
Minor	7th	10
Diminished	7th	9
Augmented	6th	10
Major	6th	9
Minor	6th	8
Diminished	6th	7
Augmented	5th	8
Perfect	5th	7
Diminished	5th	6

Interval		Semitones *half steps*
Augmented	4th	6
Perfect	4th	5
Diminished	4th	4
Augmented	3rd	5
Major	3rd	4
Minor	3rd	3
Diminished	3rd	2
Augmented	2nd	3
Major	2nd	2
Minor	2nd	1
Diminished	2nd	-

At this level you must be able to describe intervals of more than an octave. Using the 'chart' method this will not be a problem for you. Simply ignore the octave and begin your 'semitone count / *half step count*'.

An interval greater than an octave can be named in two ways:-

   1. a 9th, 10th, 11th, 12th, etc.
   2. a compound 2nd, 3rd, 4th, 5th, etc.

9, 10, 11, 12...

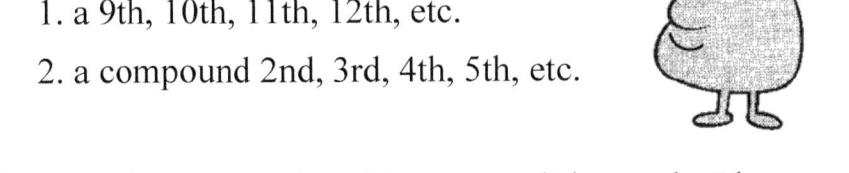

Here are three examples of 'compound' intervals. I have named them in the two ways just described.

major 9th
or
compound
major 2nd

perfect 12th
or
compound
perfect 5th

major 14th
or
compound
major 7th

Test yourself

Write a note above the given note to produce the required interval.

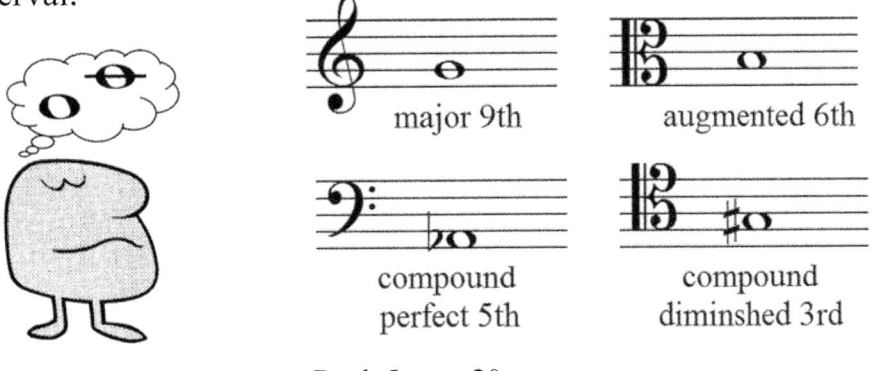

major 9th

augmented 6th

compound
perfect 5th

compound
diminished 3rd

Book 5 page 20

Describe the given intervals.

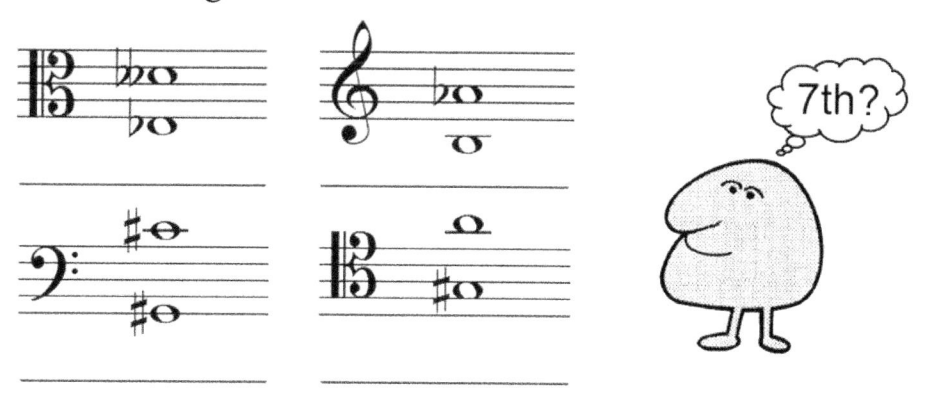

Describe each of the intervals.

Important
Look at the key signature and any accidentals in the bar.

a _____ b _____ c _____

d _____ e _____ f _____

A new topic?   Yes. Hurry up!

Book 5 page 21

TRANSPOSITION

You met transposition up or down an octave in my Music Theory is Fun Book 3. Now you will be asked to transpose a piece of music in one of the following ways:-

a) up or down an **octave** [12 semitones / *12 half steps*]
b) up or down a **major 2nd** [2 semitones / *2 half steps*]
c) up or down a **minor 3rd** [3 semitones / *3 half steps*]
d) up or down a **perfect 5th** [7 semitones / *7 half steps*]

These intervals are the ones most commonly used by transposing instruments in an orchestra.

Handy Hints

1. Decide on the new key signature.
   If the music to be transposed is in a major key, the new version will be in a major key. If the original is in a minor key, the new version will be in a minor key.

2. Take care with accidentals!
   If there is a key signature, any note with an accidental in the original version will need an accidental in the transposed version.

3. Odd-numbered intervals [3rds & 5ths]
   Notes on lines transpose to notes on lines.
   Notes in spaces transpose to spaces.

4. Even-numbered intervals [2nds]
   Notes on lines transpose to notes in spaces.
   Notes in spaces transpose to lines.

Test yourself

Write this melody an octave **higher** in each of the given clefs. Include the key signature and time signature.

Writing at concert pitch

Instruments in B♭, such as clarinets in B♭ or trumpets in B♭, produce sounds a major 2nd lower than the written notes. So, for example, if middle C is played on one of these instruments, then the B♭ below the C is heard.

> The pitch at which we hear an instrument is known as **'concert pitch'**.

This passage is for a clarinet in B♭. Write it below at concert pitch [major 2nd lower] with a new key signature.

The concert pitch of instruments 'in A' (clarinet in A, cornet in A, trumpet in A, etc.) is a minor 3rd lower than written. Transpose the following passage so that it will sound at concert pitch when played by instruments in A [down a minor 3rd].

The French horn and the cor anglais / *English horn* are two instruments which produce the note F when C is played.

Their notes sound a perfect 5th lower than the written notes.

Transpose the following up a perfect 5th so that the notes will sound at concert pitch when played by instruments in F.

Book 5 page 24

VOICES IN SCORE

Music for choirs is often written in **four** parts. Voices can be divided into four groups – **SATB**.

Soprano, Alto, Tenor and Bass

In an exam or test you might be asked for the approximate range of one of the voices. You will find this chart useful.

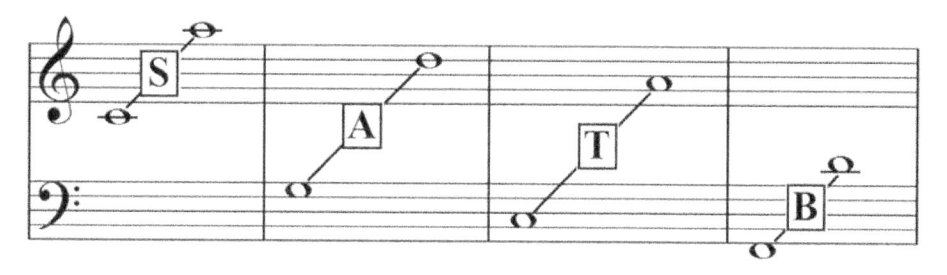

I say approximate range because individual voices often lie between ranges. The mezzo-soprano voice is between alto and soprano. The baritone voice lies between bass and tenor.

Short score

Music for SATB is written either on two staves or on four. If it is written on **two staves**, we say that it is written in **short score**. Here is an example in short score.

Checklist

1. The soprano and alto parts are on the upper stave.

2. The tenor and bass parts are on the lower stave.

3. The stems of the soprano and tenor notes go up.

4. The stems of the alto and bass notes go down.

Open score

When a passage is written on four staves and each part therefore has its own stave, we say it is written in '**open score**'. Here is an example of a passage in open score.

Notice that separate bar-lines are used in both short score and open score.

The tenor voice

In short score the **tenor** part is written in the bass clef at its true pitch. In open score it is written in the treble clef an **octave higher** than it sounds. This is the reason for the *small 8* written below the treble clef.

Book 5 page 27

Test yourself

Rewrite the following in open score.

Book 5 page 28

Transcribe the following into short score.

Book 5 page 29

INSTRUMENTS OF THE ORCHESTRA

strings

brass

percussion

woodwind

Clef chart

Instrument	treble	alto	tenor	bass
violin	●			
viola		●		
cello			●	●
double bass				●
harp	●			●
flute	●			
piccolo	●			
oboe	●			
cor anglais	●			
bassoon	[●]		●	●
double bassoon				●
clarinet	●			
saxophone	●			
trumpet	●			
French horn	●			●
trombone			●	●
tuba				●
timpani				●
tubular bells	●			
vibraphone	●			
xylophone	●			
glockenspiel	●			
piano	●			●

The string family

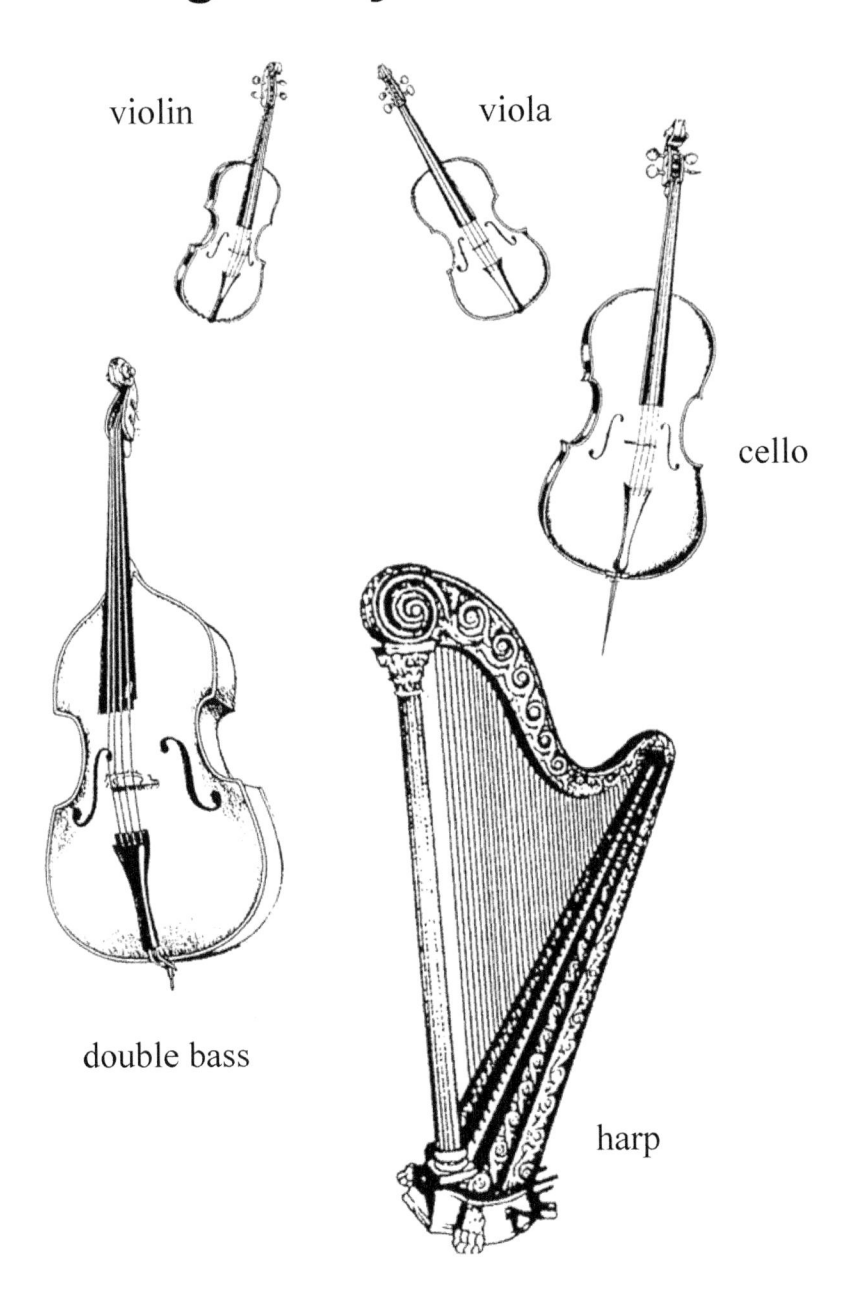

violin

viola

cello

double bass

harp

You could be asked to give the letter names for the strings of one of the four instruments played with a bow. Write the letter names for these 16 notes.

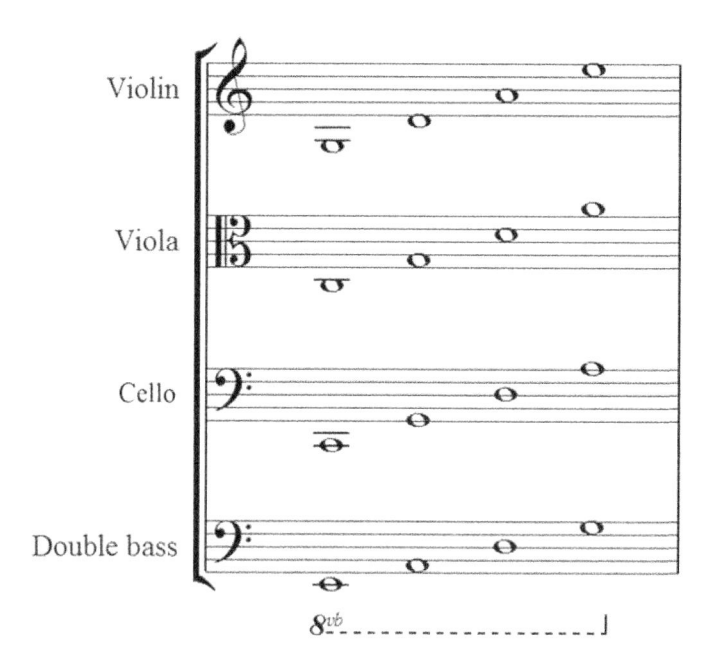

A stringed instrument can produce two notes at the same time because the bow may engage two notes simultaneously.

A string **trio** consists of a violin, viola and cello.

A string **quartet** is made up of 2 violins, a viola and cello.

A string **quintet** may add a second viola or another cello.

The harp has 47 strings and 7 pedals. Arpeggios take their name from the harp and are very well suited to the instrument.

The woodwind family

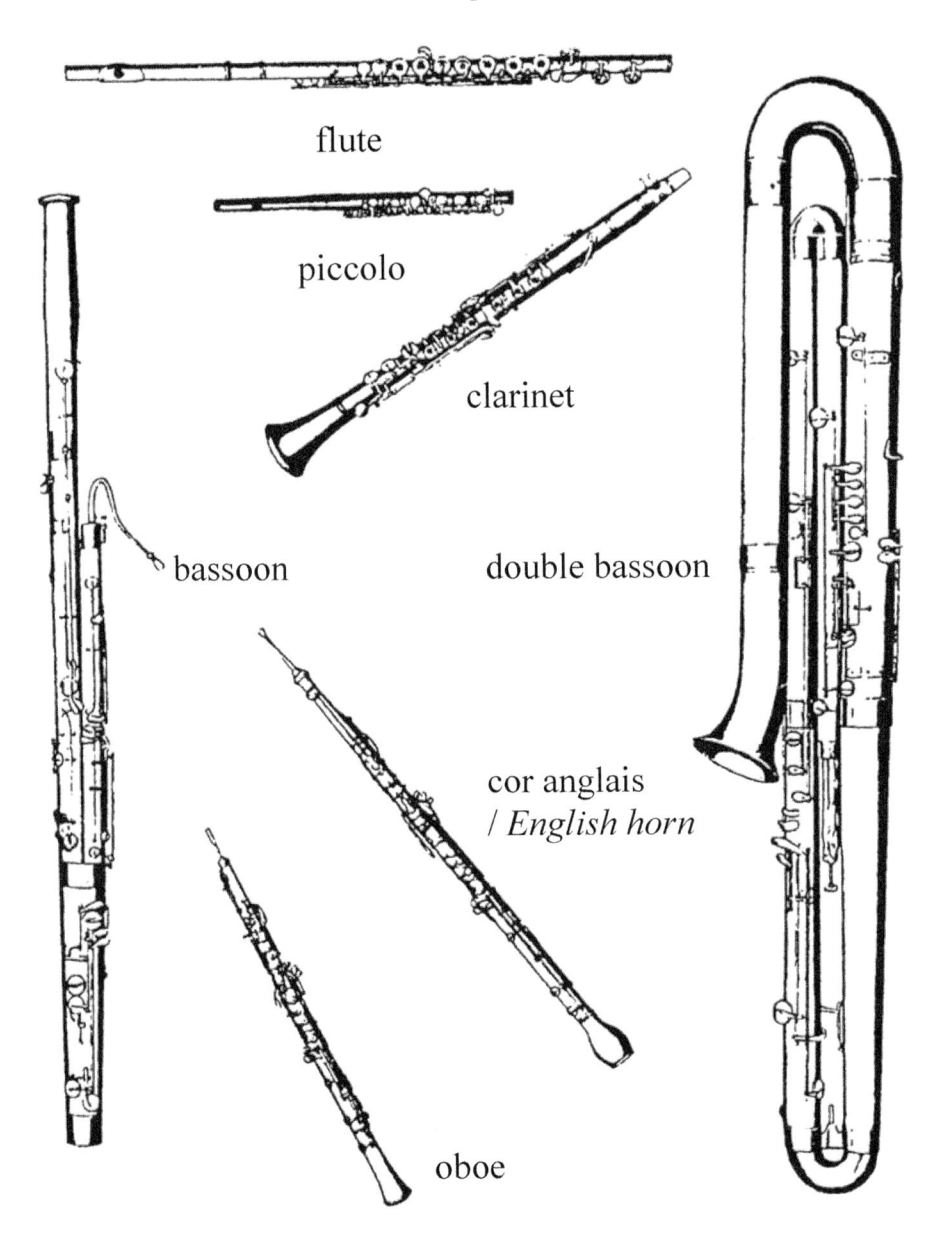

flute

piccolo

clarinet

bassoon

double bassoon

cor anglais
/ *English horn*

oboe

Players of wind instruments make the air in the tube vibrate by tonguing a piece of reed at the end of the instrument.

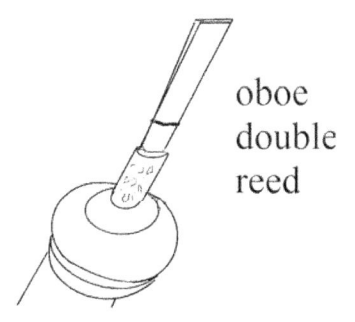

oboe double reed

Some members of the woodwind family are double-reed instruments. They are the oboe, cor anglais, bassoon and double bassoon. A double reed consists of two pieces of cane bound together.

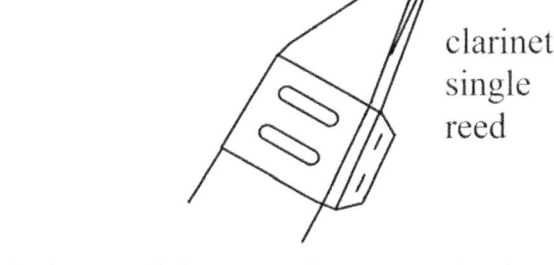

clarinet single reed

The clarinet and the saxophone are single-reed instruments. The saxophone is not a regular member of the orchestra and is found mainly in jazz, dance or military bands.

The flute player produces sound by blowing across the edge of a hole and doing so at the correct angle. The flute is held sideways, as is the smaller version, the piccolo, whose notes sound an octave higher.

flute tone hole and lip plate

The brass family

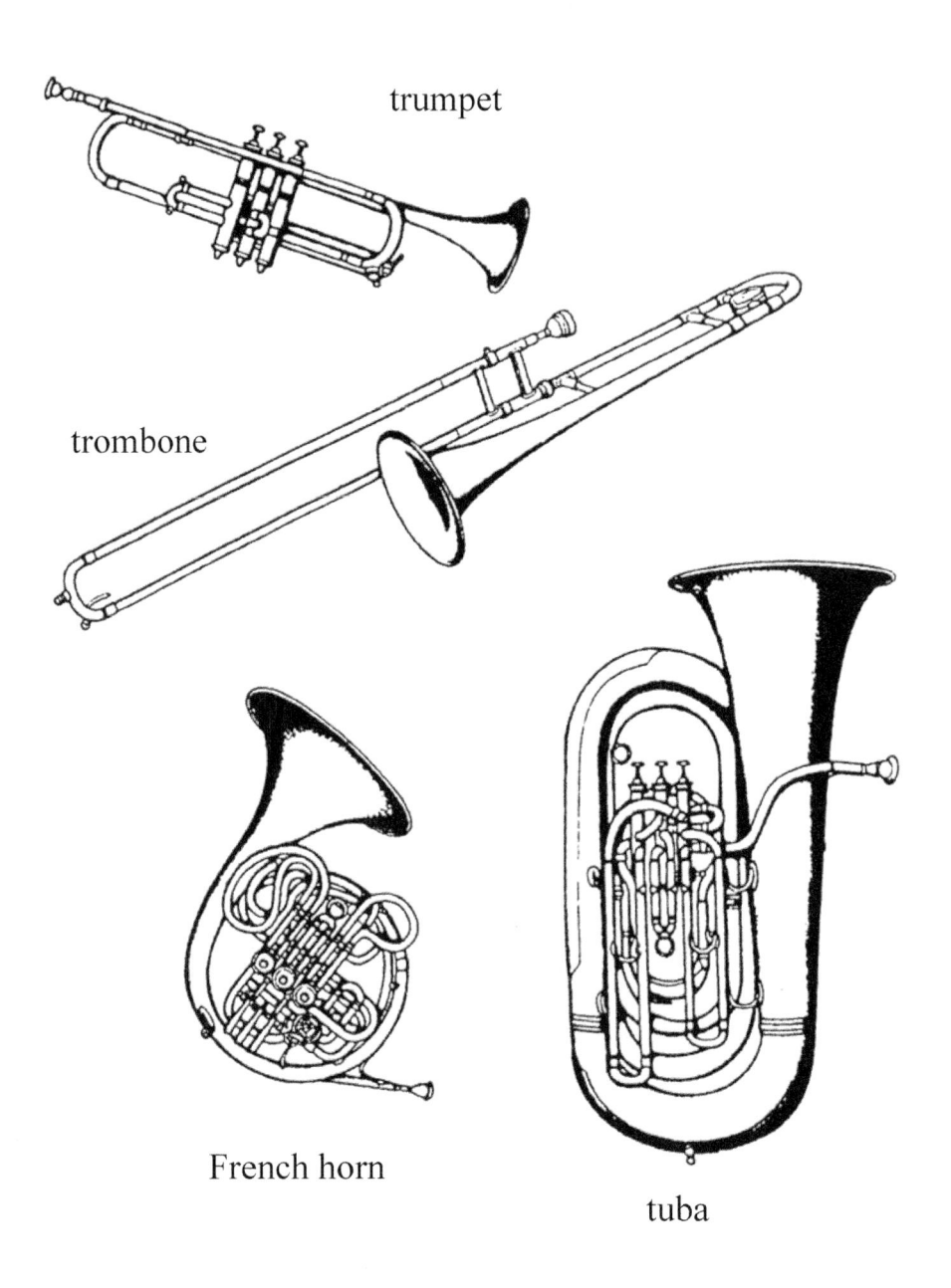

trumpet

trombone

French horn

tuba

The trombone is a slide instrument. The slide is pulled in or pushed out to alter the length of the tubing and therefore the pitch of the note. A player has to judge how far to extend the slide to move from one note to the next. There are various sizes of trombones, the most common being the B♭ trombone or B♭ tenor trombone.

The trumpet, French horn and tuba have valves which the player uses to open or close loops in the tubing and produce notes of differing pitch. In all brass instruments, the sound is produced by the vibration of the lips against the mouthpiece.

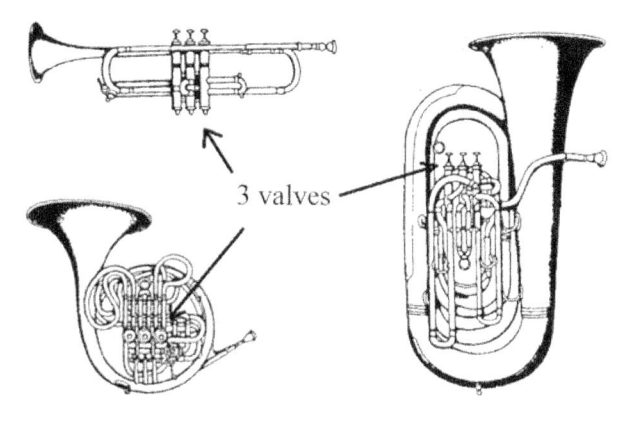

3 valves

Brass players are sometimes given the performance directions **con sord.** (with mute) or **senza sord.** (without mute). A mute is a cone-shaped object which the player inserts into the bell of the brass instrument to soften the sound of the notes it is producing.

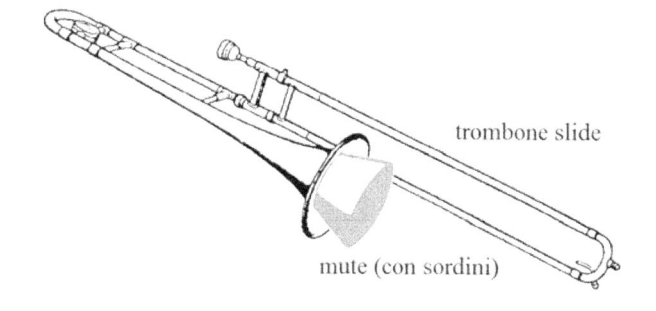

trombone slide

mute (con sordini)

Book 5 page 37

The percussion family

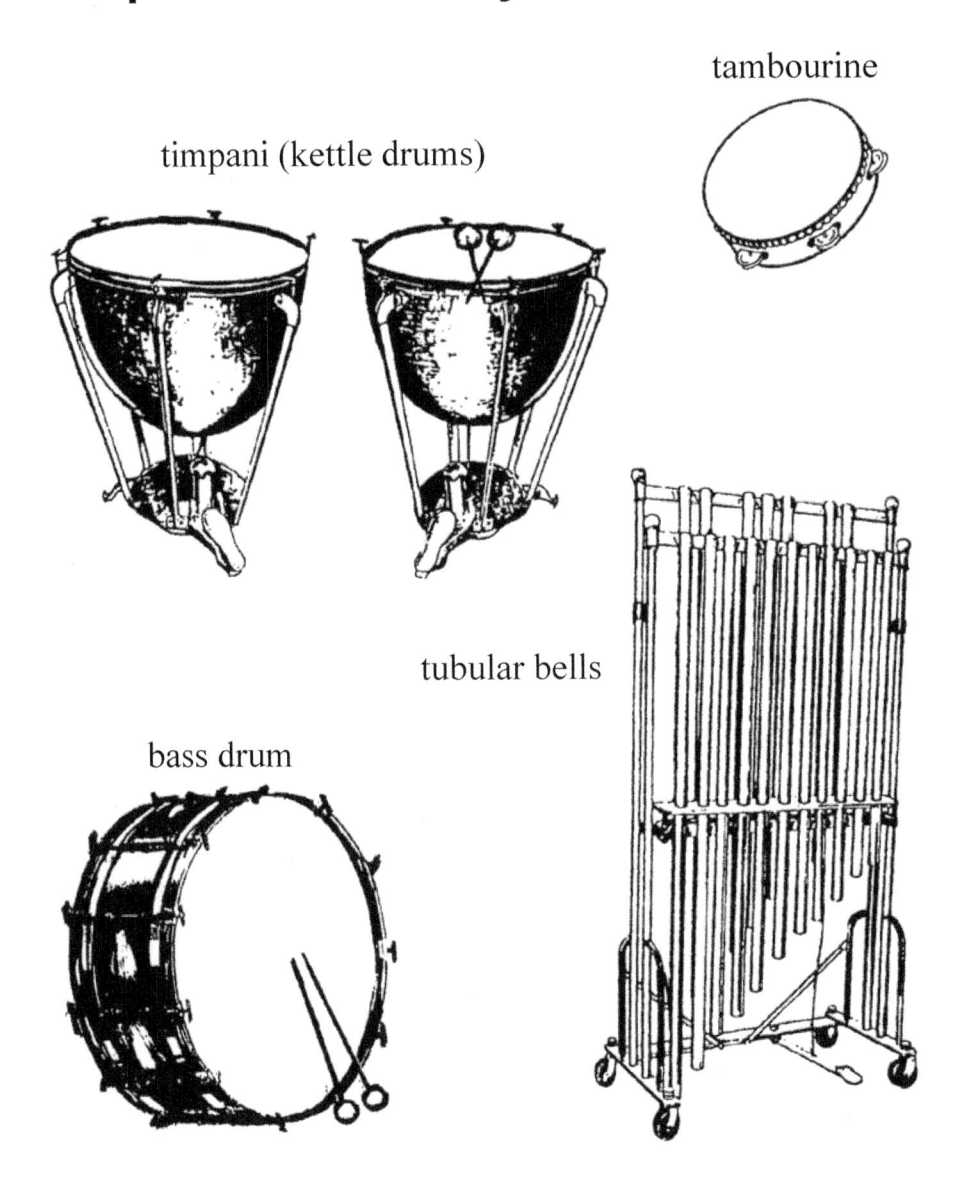

timpani (kettle drums)

tambourine

tubular bells

bass drum

The most important percussion instruments in the orchestra are the timpani. Each drum of these **pitched** percussion instruments has a range of a perfect 5th or slightly more.

The drums are made of copper and shaped as shown on page 38 opposite. They are scarcely ever used singly. Two, three or even four are used for some pieces of music.

The xylophone is also a **pitched** percussion instrument. It has two sets of wooden bars arranged like piano keys. The bars are struck with wooden sticks. The notes sound an octave higher than written. The xylophone has a range of up to 4 octaves. The marimba is similar to the xylophone but its range is an octave lower.

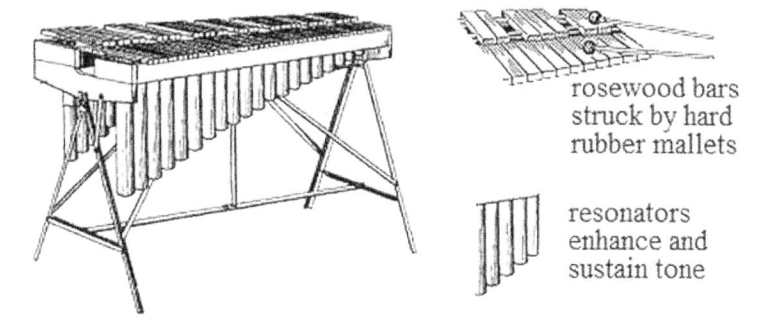

rosewood bars struck by hard rubber mallets

resonators enhance and sustain tone

The vibraphone sounds at the pitch written and the glockenspiel sounds two octaves higher. Both instruments have metal bars which may be struck by a variety of mallets.

Tubular bells are metal tubes which are struck with a mallet. **Unpitched** percussion includes bass drum, snare drum, tambourine, crash cymbals, suspended cymbal, gong and triangle.

Test yourself on the orchestra

1. Name the four main families of instruments.
   _____   _____
   _____   _____

2. Name one instrument, apart from the piano, which can produce two notes at the same time.
   _____

3. Name the three instruments which make up a string trio.
   _____   _____   _____

4. How many pedals does a harp have? _____

5. Give the letter names of the strings of a cello.
   _____   _____   _____   _____

6. Name two double-reed instruments.
   _____   _____

7. Name a single-reed instrument. _____

8. Name two instruments which have valves.
   _____   _____

   To which family do they belong? _____

9. Give the meaning of 'senza sord.' _____

10. Name three pitched percussion instruments.
    _____   _____   _____

NAMING CHORDS

In my Music Theory is Fun Book 4 you had to name chords formed from the three primary triads: the tonic [I], the subdominant [IV] and the dominant [V].

Now you have to add one more chord, the supertonic [II], formed on the second note of the scale. Here are these four chords for F Major.

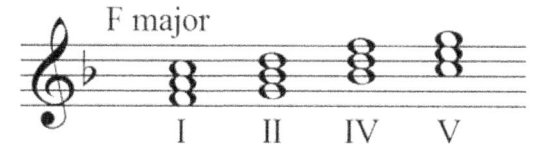

So far you have only met chords in **root** position [1 3 5]. Chords can also be written as **first** or **second inversions**.

Inversions

A **first** inversion is when the bottom note of the chord [the root] is an octave higher.

For the **second** inversion you write the bottom note of the first inversion [3] an octave higher.

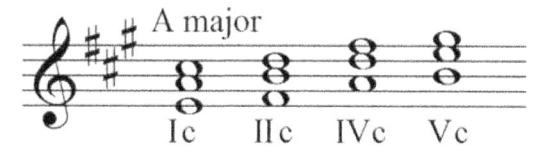

Each chord can be written in
(a) **root position**   [1 3 5]
(b) **first inversion**   [3 5 1]
(c) **second inversion** [5 1 3]

Tackling exam questions

As well as deciding if a chord is I, II, IV or V, you may be asked to say whether the root, 3rd or 5th of the chord is in the bass. I shall describe two ways of writing the answer.

First method

    a). If the chord is in root position, put a small letter 'a' after it: Ia, IIa, IVa or Va

    b). Put 'b' if the 3rd is in the bass (1st inversion): Ib, IIb, IVb or Vb

    c). If the 5th is in the bass (2nd inversion) put a 'c': Ic, IIc, IVc or Vc

Practice

Describe each of the following chords as I, II, IV or V. Indicate by means of Ia, IIb, IVc, etc., whether the root, the 3rd or the 5th of the chord is in the bass. The first four chords in G major are in root position.

Book 5 page 42

Second method

$\frac{5}{3}$ instead of 'a' $\frac{6}{3}$ instead of 'b' $\frac{6}{4}$ instead of 'c'

The figures tell you the *intervals* from the bass note to the notes above. In a 2nd inversion the two other notes which are used in the chord are the **4**th and the **6**th notes above the bass note.

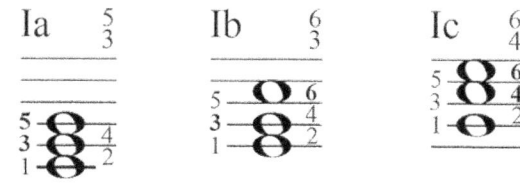

Practice

In the first passage of three chords, indicate by means of Ia, IIb, IVc, etc., whether the root, the 3rd or the 5th of the chord is in the bass. In the second passage of five chords, write underneath each chord $\frac{5}{3}$, $\frac{6}{3}$ or $\frac{6}{4}$ as appropriate.

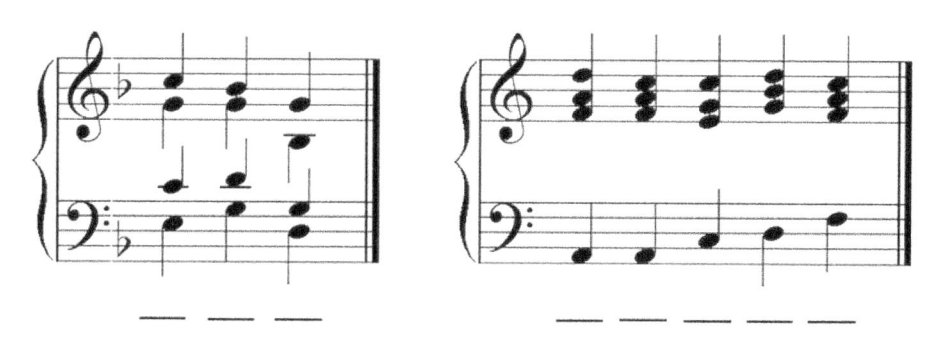

Important

If you put I, II, IV or V without 'a', 'b', 'c' or , $\frac{5}{3}$, $\frac{6}{3}$, $\frac{6}{4}$ it will be assumed that you mean root position.

Test yourself

Describe each chord as I, II, IV or V. Indicate whether the root, third or fifth of the chord is in the bass. In the third example you may choose to use letters or figures.

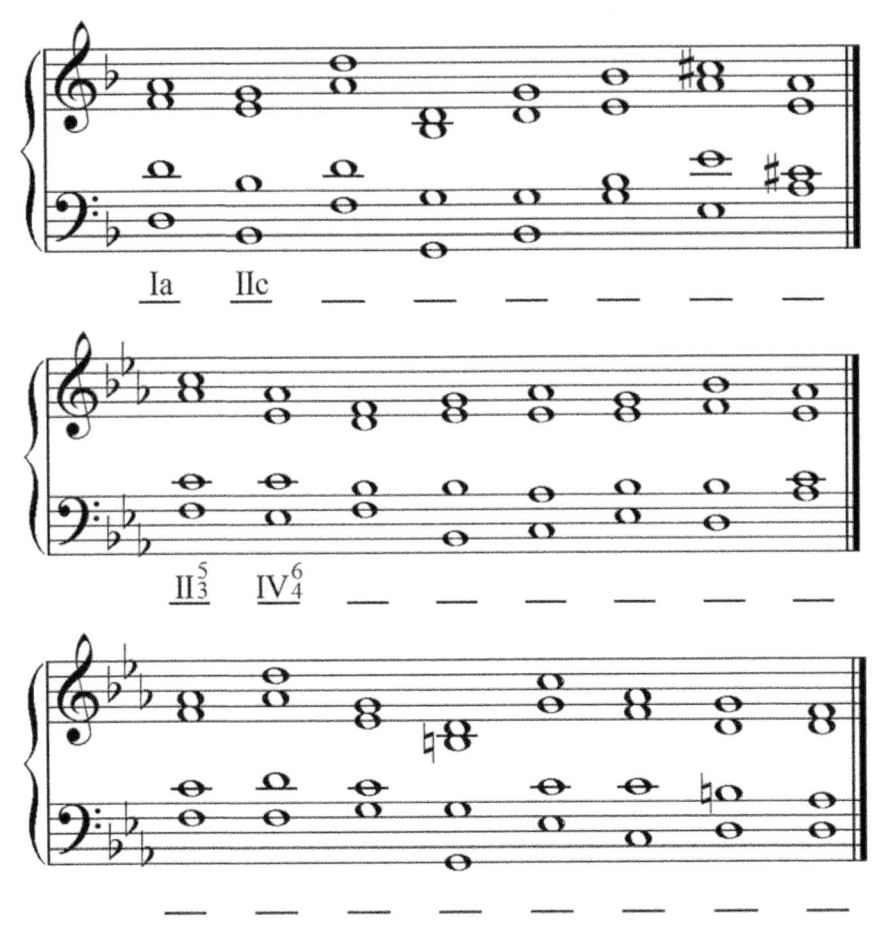

Ia   IIc   __   __   __   __   __   __

II$^5_3$ IV$^6_4$ __   __   __   __   __   __

__   __   __   __   __   __   __   __

How many did get right? /20

Book 5 page 44

COMPOSITION

At this level you will be required to compose a short melody of not more than eight bars in length. Adopt a positive attitude towards this exercise and enjoy being a composer!

There will be a choice. You can compose a melody to fit some given words or you can write a melody for an instrument.

Begin with the rhythm

Begin with the rhythm, whether you choose voice or instrument. It will be useful to read again my comments on four-bar rhythms in Music Theory is Fun Books 2 and 3.

Planning the Rhythm
Plan the rhythm first in rough.
Think of **2** four-bar rhythms.

You could repeat the first four bars.

You could begin each set of four bars differently but end in a similar way.

You might decide to start the second set of four bars in the same way but end differently.

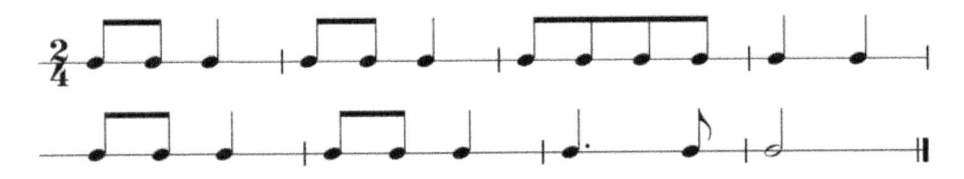

Your turn to write some rhythms.

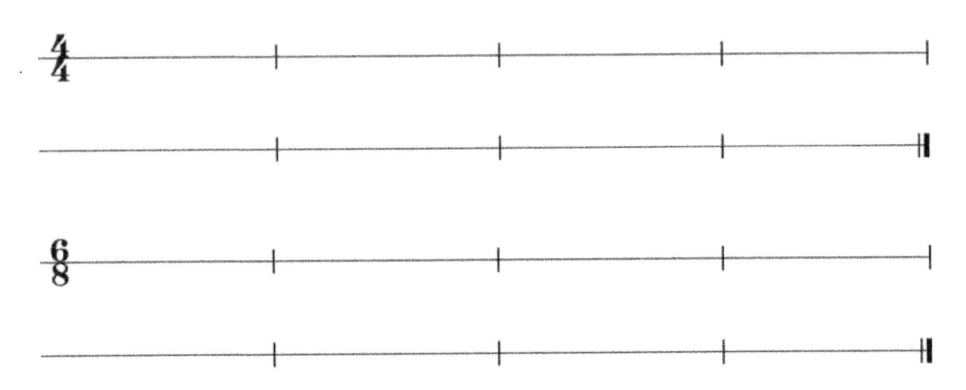

Melody for an instrument

In this exercise you will be given the opening with, where appropriate, a key signature and a time signature. You have to choose one instrument from a given group, e.g. [cello, bassoon, trombone], [violin, flute, oboe], etc., and then write a melody for that instrument.

Guidelines

Try to write exactly eight bars, including the given opening. Give directions of tempo in words (e.g. Andante, Vivace, etc.) or by a metronome setting (e.g. ♩ = 60). Remember to add dynamics (e.g. *p*, *mf*, *ff*, etc.).

Take care with legato slurs. Draw them from head to head if this is possible, or above the notes if there is a mixture of stems up and down. Staccato dots and ties come inside a slur or below - never above.

Give the melody a shape. Try to make the first four bars move upwards using small ascents and descents. When you reach the highest note in your melody, gradually move downwards until you reach the end.

The highest note is usually a note from the dominant chord and the final note is often the tonic. Lead towards the tonic. Avoid awkward intervals. Keep to scale and broken chord movement.

End on a strong beat.

Read these guidelines again and again, follow them step by step and practise. You will soon be a successful composer - of eight bar melodies!

Highest and lowest
You will need to know the lower and upper limits of the instrument you choose.

Strings
A good player has a range of about 3 octaves above the given note.

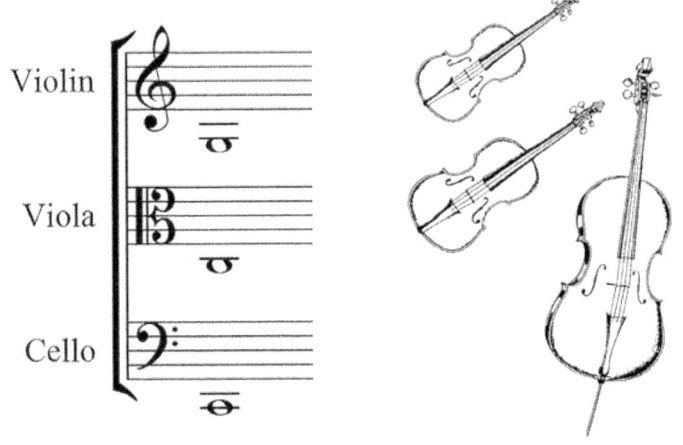

Recorders
The range is 2 octaves plus a tone above the given note.

Descant   Treble   Tenor   Bass
Soprano   Alto   Tenor   Bass

Woodwind

The range is approximately 2½ - 3 octaves above the given note depending upon the skill of the player.

- Flute
- Clarinet in B♭
- Cor anglais *English horn*
- Oboe
- Bassoon

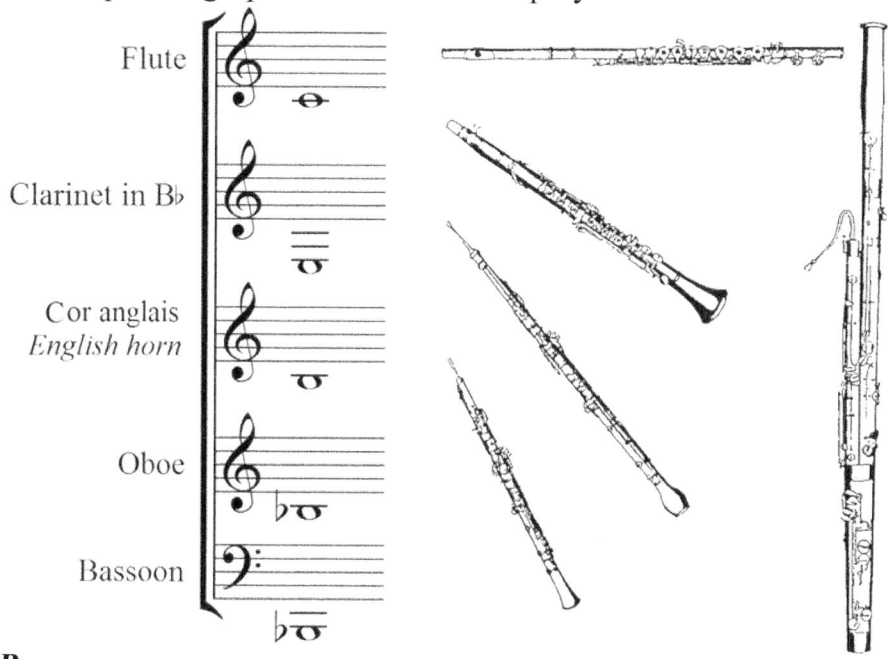

Brass

The range is approximately 2½ - 3 octaves above the given note depending upon the skill of the player.

- Trumpet in B♭
- Tenor Trombone
- Horn in F
- Tuba

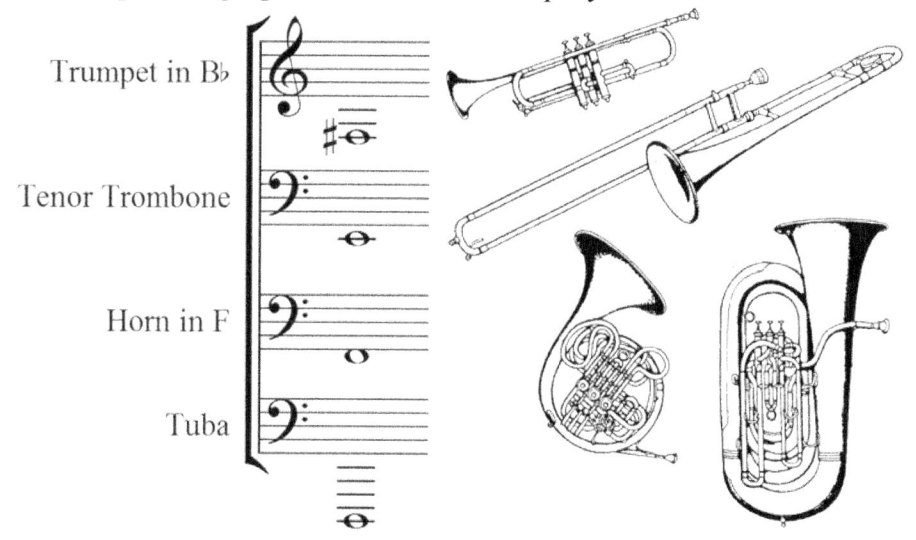

Test yourself

Write a melody of not more than 8 bars for an instrument of your choice. Add marks of expression plus appropriate performance directions. Use the given opening.

Instrument for which the melody is written: _____

Follow the instructions for the previous exercise but write an 8 bar melody for cello or bassoon.

Instrument for which the melody is written: _____

Melody for voice

Here there is no given opening - the choice is yours. Instead you are given a set of words to put to music.

If the theme of the words is cheerful, the melody must be cheerful, the speed brisk, etc. If the words suggest another mood, then it must be reflected in the melody.

All my suggestions for the writing of an eight-bar melody for an instrument are relevant to writing for voice. In addition you must be sure that the melody fits the words and that you stress the important words.

The time signature appears only once, at the beginning. The clef and key signature appear at the beginning of each new stave.

Test yourself

Compose melodies for the following words. Write each syllable under the note or notes to which it is to be sung.

The waves beside them danced, but they
Out-did the sparkling waves in glee.

The kitten sleeps upon the hearth,
The crickets long have ceased their mirth.

March roars in as a raging lion,
'Til April appears as a gentle lamb.

Book 5 page 52

CADENCES

In Music Theory Is Fun Book 3 where I dealt with phrases, you learnt that as you come to the end of each phrase you need to take a 'breathing space'.

It is important to choose the correct chords for these 'resting places'.

A cadence consists of two chords.

At this level you will be asked to choose chords for a passage. The tonic, supertonic, subdominant and dominant chords only will be needed.

When you reach the end of a piece you need a very 'final feeling' so that everyone realises it is the end! For that reason, pieces often end on the tonic chord. Cadences which finish on the tonic chord can end a piece or can provide a substantial resting place.

The perfect cadence

Use this cadence to end a piece. It consists of the dominant chord followed by the tonic chord.

Perfect Cadence = V → I

The dominant chord contains the leading note. The leading note leads to the tonic. The leading note can be in the middle or at the top of the dominant chord. If you put it at the top, then the ending on the tonic will have a much more final feel.

The perfect cadence in two easy steps:-

    1. In the treble / at the top: leading note → tonic
    2. In the bass / at the bottom: dominant → tonic

Here are two examples in C Major.

Here are two other examples of a perfect cadence, this time in D Major.

Write two examples with key signature of a perfect cadence in G Major.

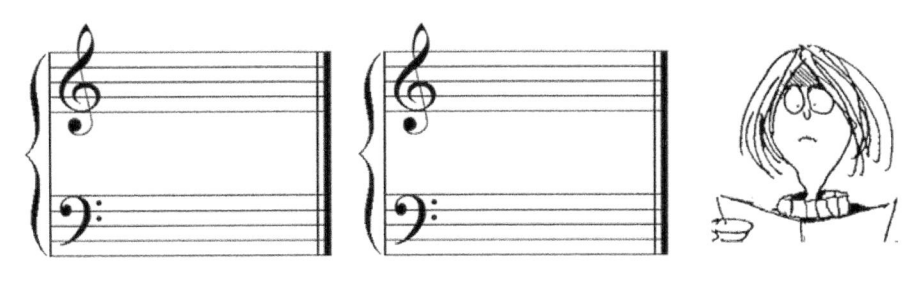

Book 5 page 54

You will probably have noticed, when dealing with cadences, that chords can be written as three notes in the treble and one in the bass **or** as two in the treble and two in the bass. Chords can contain more than four notes but you will not be expected to go beyond four at this level.

Write with key signature two perfect cadences for F Major.

You now have examples of perfect cadences in all the keys you need at this level.

The plagal cadence

This combination of chords does not give as effective an ending as the perfect cadence. It consists of the subdominant chord followed by the tonic chord.

IV   I

Plagal Cadence = IV → I

The Imperfect Cadence

We use this cadence to create an impression of rest at a point where the piece does not end but where a 'breath' is needed. You can think of the imperfect cadence like a comma and the perfect cadence like a full stop.
To write an imperfect cadence any chord can be used in front of the dominant. At this level therefore:

Imperfect Cadence = I → V or II → V or IV → V

Rules to remember

When you are writing chords:

1. Do not double a 3rd.
2. There should be no consecutive 5ths.
3. There should be no consecutive octaves. 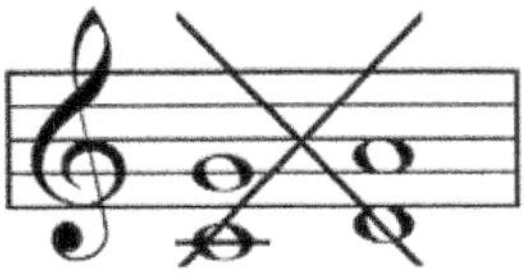
4. Do not leave more than an octave between the tenor and alto parts.
5. Never have all four parts moving in the same direction. Move at least one part in a different way or keep one part on the same note.

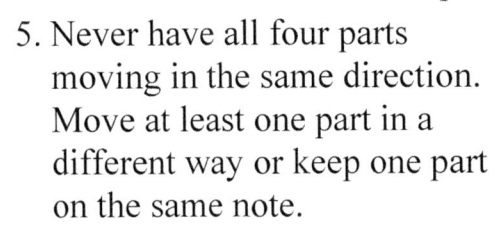

Book 5 page 56

Test yourself

Fill in the missing words.

A perfect cadence is the _____ chord followed by the _____ chord.

In a perfect cadence the _____ note leads to the _____ .

The subdominant chord plus the tonic chord is a _____ cadence.

I → V, II → V and IV → V are all ways of writing an _____ cadence.

Put I, II, IV or V to complete the following:

A plagal cadence = ____ → ____.

A perfect cadence = ____ → ____.

An imperfect cadence = ____ , ____ or ____ → ____.

Although a test question may not actually use the word 'cadence', you will probably have to complete chords in a given passage. This may possibly include the writing of a chord which is in front of the two cadence chords. Write suitable chords for the last three notes of the following passage.

CODA

Repetition of rests

The ornament signs, discussed in depth in my Book 4, are useful in that they avoid the need to write out numerous notes. The method for showing the number of bars rest is also economical. Imagine some percussion parts if there was no such method!

This is how you should indicate a rest of 9 bars. You can use this method with any number of bars.

Repetition of notes

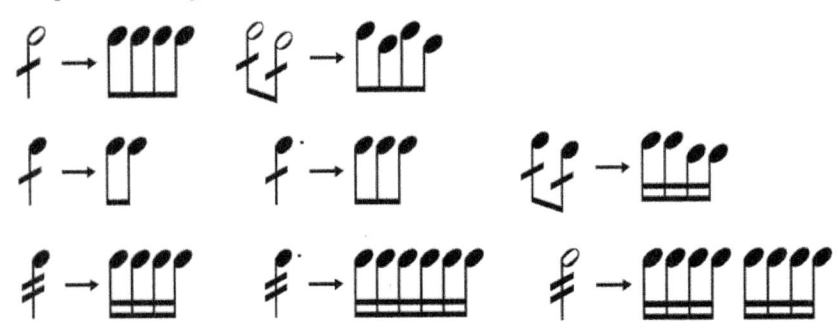

Repetition of identical chords in the same bar

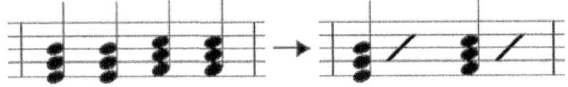

Repetition of a one-bar pattern

Repetition of a two-bar pattern

Book 5 page 58

PUZZLES

QUIZZES

TESTS

Book 5 page 59

Fun page 1

Add the missing clefs, flats and sharps to show all seven accidentals.

Fun page 2

Tie the balloons to the correct chords in C major.

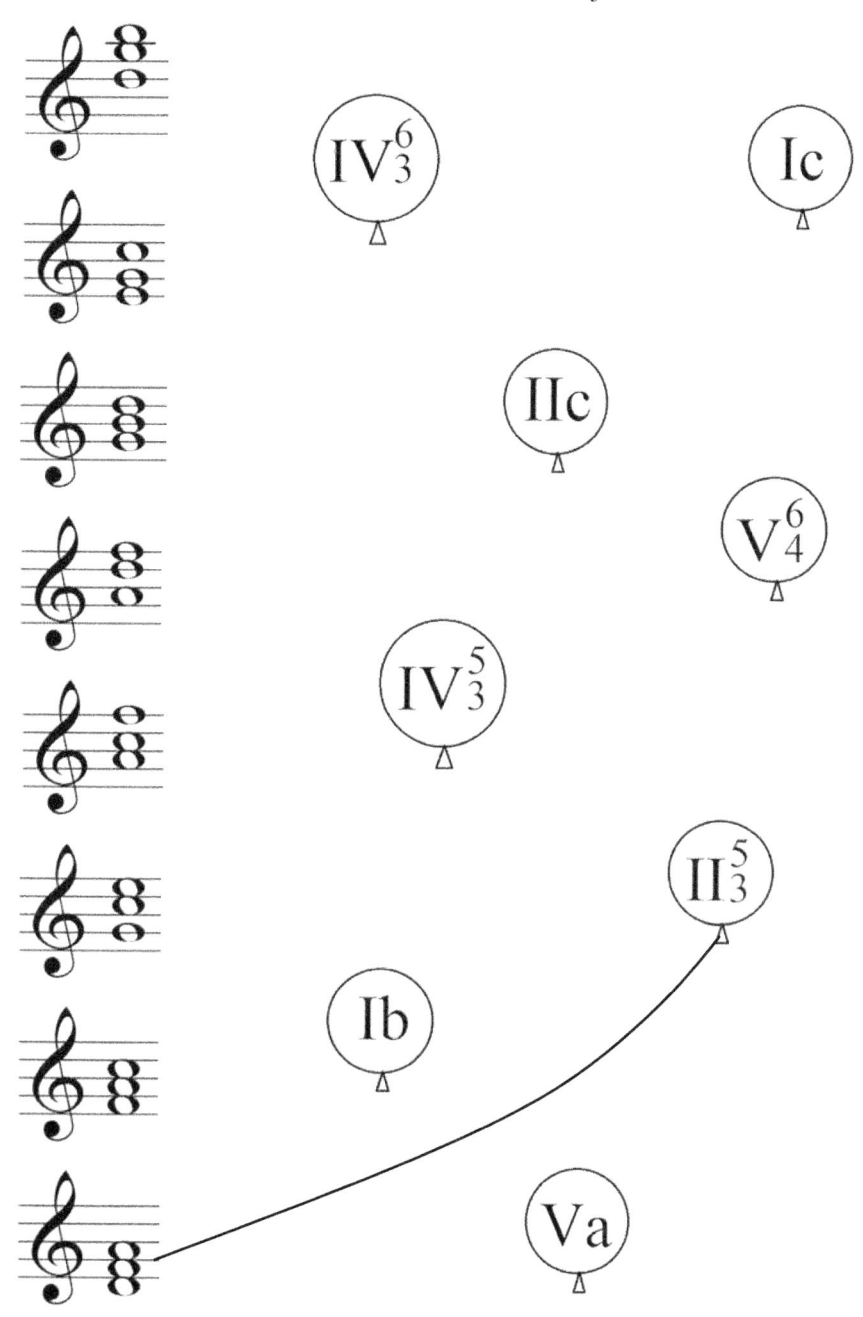

Crossword

Clues

Across

2 diminished 7th interval in A minor
4 time
6 stringed instrument with range below violin and above cello
9 woodwind with double reed
10 without

11 note twice the length of a whole note
12 tender, delicate
17 enough, sufficiently
18 woodwind blown across the edge of the hole
19 perfect 5th interval in D major

Down

1 voice below soprano and above tenor
3 full
5 chord 1b in F major
6 turn the page quickly
7 at a moderate speed
8 at a moderate speed
13 clef used for tuba
14 lively
15 unpitched percussion instrument
16 with a strong accent

Book 5 page 63

Musical terms word search

P	A	M	Y	S	O	P	R	A	W
O	P	D	E	C	I	S	I	O	E
S	S	J	A	Q	U	A	S	I	N
S	A	S	O	G	I	N	N	H	I
I	M	M	E	R	I	F	T	N	G
B	A	O	O	A	A	O	U	Y	A
I	B	D	S	C	R	O	T	P	O
L	I	O	H	O	G	Z	T	T	E
E	L	E	F	R	O	T	I	G	O
H	E	A	L	L	A	E	S	I	U

Meaning   **Musical term**

in the style of   alla

slow, leisurely   _____

amiable, pleasant   _____

with determination   _____

simple   _____

always   _____

possible   _____

as if, resembling   _____

above   _____

all   _____

little   _____

Anagrams

pemfercit acneced

Clue: Produced by any chord in front of the dominant.

gallap

Clue: Cadence produced by chord IV followed by chord I.

osnobas

Clue: Woodwind that uses a double reed.

frits rosenvini

Clue: Chords such as Ib, IIb, IVb and Vb.

netombro

Clue: Music for this instrument can use tenor or bass clef.

oorspan

Clue: In a short score the part for this voice is on the upper stave.

Quiz 1

Put a tick / *check mark* in the correct box.

1. **sospirando**

☐ sighing

☐ gradually faster

☐ gradually slower

☐ in a speaking manner

2. **at a moderate speed**

☐ mässig

☐ ruhig

☐ traurig

☐ wenig

3. **inverted turn**

☐ 〰

☐ ∽

☐ 〰

☐ ↝

4. **with**

☐ ohne

☐ sans

☐ senza

☐ avec

5. **sempre**

☐ above

☐ always

☐ simple

☐ below

6. **staccatissimo**

☐ (note with line above)

☐ (note with dot above)

☐ (note with wedge above)

☐ (notes with dots below)

Book 5 page 66

Quiz 2

Do you know your orchestral instruments?

Which one has the most strings?
_____

Which one is struck with a mallet?
_____

Which brass instrument has no valves?
_____

Which woodwind plays the highest note?
_____

Which woodwind plays the lowest note?
_____

Which single reed instrument is found mainly in jazz bands?
_____

Which is the smallest percussion instrument that is struck and shaken?
_____

Which percussion instrument has two sets of wooden bars arranged like piano keys?
_____

/8

Book 5 page 67

Handy hints for tests

This section is for you to practise the different types of questions you could have in a test or an exam.

The questions could be on any topic covered in this book and in Music Theory is Fun Books 1 2, 3 and 4.

Revise each topic in this book thoroughly.

Don't forget to study musical terms and signs – they are **always** included.

Practice makes perfect!

Practice makes perfect!

If you have worked through this book carefully and understood each topic, this will be an easy task for you.

> Before you begin any test, write out your key signature charts (see page 7). Always refer to the charts when tackling questions that require you to know a key signature.

Test 1

1. Name these notes

   F ☐   D ☐   E ☐

   E♭ ☐   B♭ ☐   A ☐

2. Which is the correct time signature?

   6/8 ☐   3/4 ☐   3/8 ☐

3. Which rest or rests should complete the bar?

   𝄾𝄾 ☐   𝄽 ☐   𝄾· ☐

4. Which note is the dominant of the minor key shown by this key signature?

   C♯ ☐   E ☐   D♯ ☐

5. Which note is the subdominant of the minor key shown by this key signature?

   E♭ ☐   C ☐   B♭ ☐

6. Which Roman numeral fits below this dominant chord?

   Vb ☐   V ☐   Vc ☐

Book 5 page 69

Test 2

1. Write a one octave C♯ melodic minor scale ascending in minims / *half notes* with key signature in the bass clef.

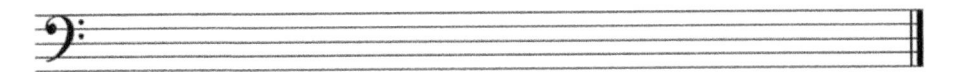

2. Write a one octave E♭ harmonic minor scale in semibreves / *whole notes* descending in the tenor clef without key signature.

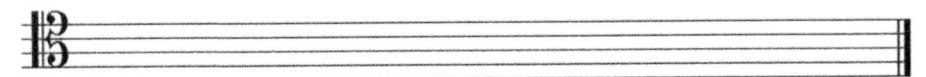

3. Write a one octave chromatic scale of D major with key signature ascending in crotchets / *quarter notes* using the treble clef. Remember to put in the accidentals.

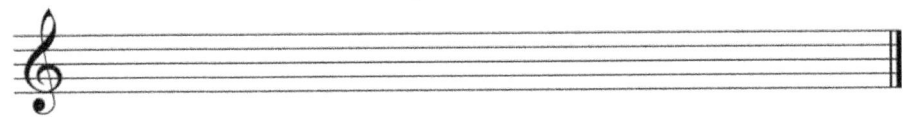

4. Write a rhythm to fit the following words from William Wordsworth's poem *Daffodils*. Give the time signature.

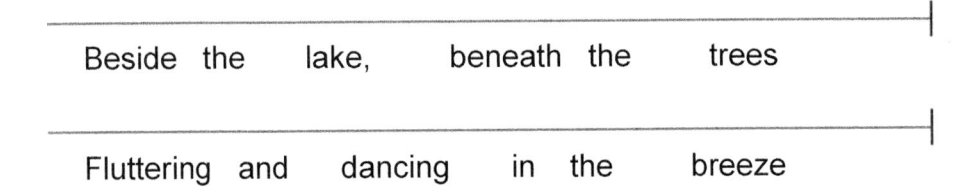

   Beside the lake, beneath the trees

   Fluttering and dancing in the breeze

5. Write a note above the given note to produce the interval.

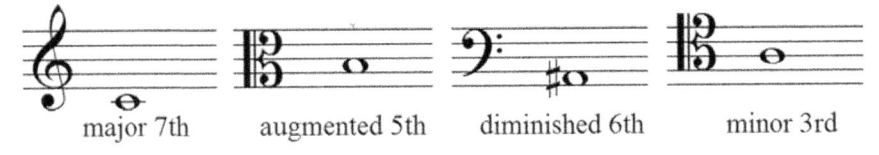

   major 7th   augmented 5th   diminished 6th   minor 3rd

Book 5 page 70

Test 3

1. Write the key signature of 4 flats and one octave ascending of the harmonic minor scale with that key signature. Use semibreves / *whole notes*.

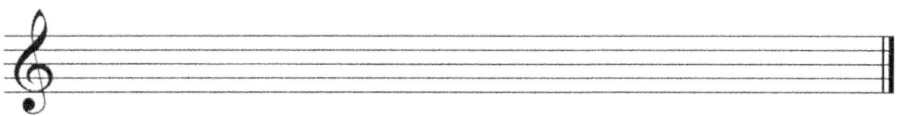

2. Write the scale of E major descending without key signature in semibreves / *whole notes*. Put accidentals in front of the notes as needed.

3. Write the tonic, supertonic and dominant triads of C major in root position. Add their Roman numerals.

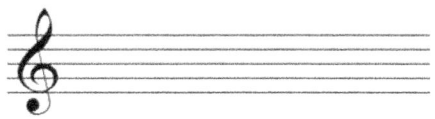

4. Write the tonic, subdominant and dominant triads of D major in their second inversions with the key signature. Add their Roman numerals.

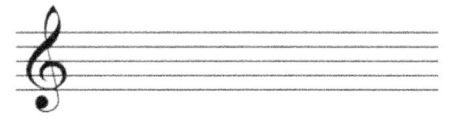

5. Write the supertonic, subdominant and dominant triads of F major in their first inversions without key signature. Add their Roman numerals and any necessary accidentals.

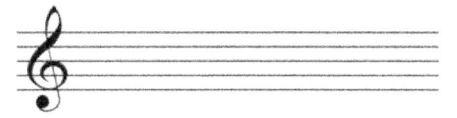

Book 5 page 71

Test 4

1. Write the following notes at the same pitch but using the given clef.

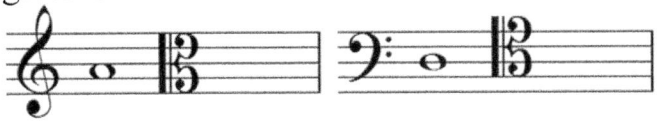

2. Transpose this melody up a perfect 5th in each of these clefs.

3. Using semibreves / *whole notes*, write out 4-part chords for SATB in short score using the chords shown by the Roman numerals.

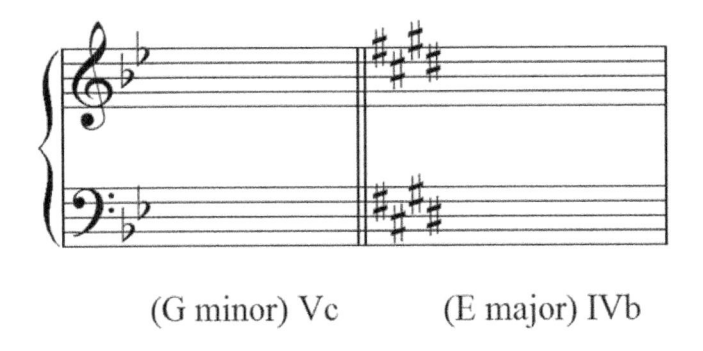

   (G minor) Vc   (E major) IVb

Book 5 page 72

Test 5

1. Write this melody a perfect 5th **lower** in each of the given clefs. Include the time signature and new key signature.

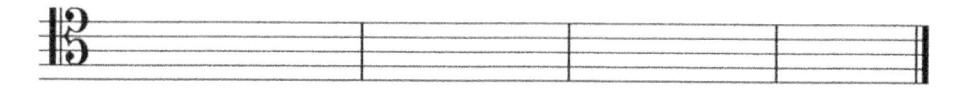

2. Write the following notes at the same pitch but using the given clef.

3. Using semibreves / *whole notes*, write out 4-part chords for SATB in short score using the chords shown by the Roman numerals.

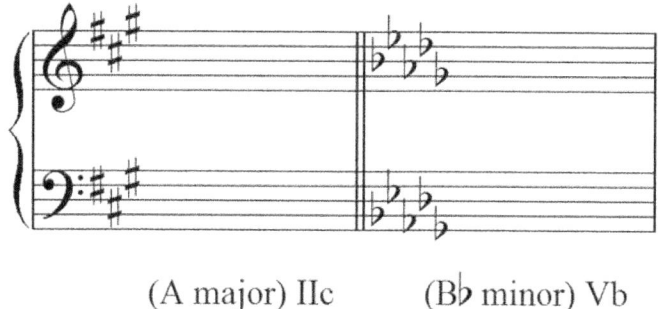

(A major) IIc   (B♭ minor) Vb

Book 5 page 73

Test 6

1. Put a time signature for each bar / *measure* of notes.

2. Rewrite this passage, doubling the time values. Add the new time signature.

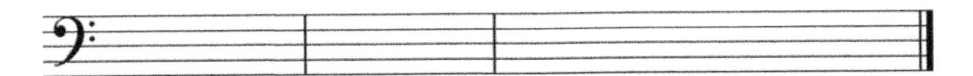

3. Write one bar / *measure* in quavers / *8th notes* using the given time signature. Place the notes on the line or in the space for E.

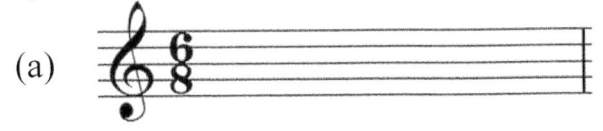

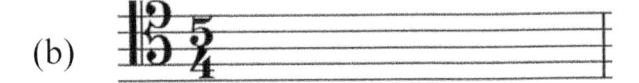

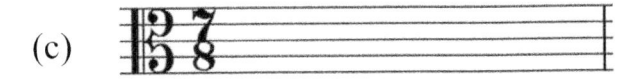

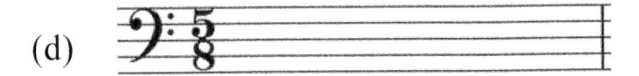

(a)

(b)

(c)

(d)

Book 5 page 74

Test 7

1. Describe fully each of these melodic intervals, e.g. minor 3rd, perfect 4th.

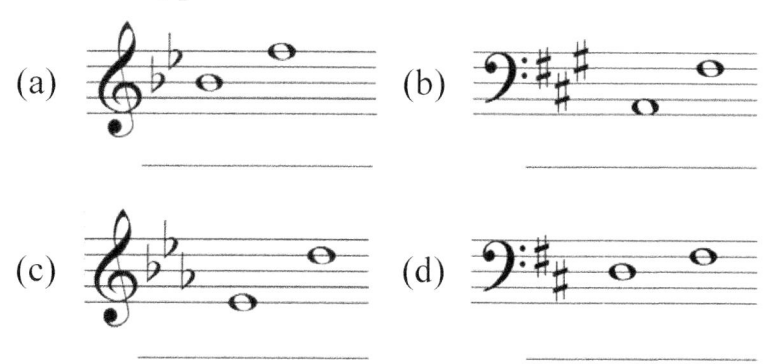

   (a)   (b)

   (c)   (d)

2. Write a higher note to form the named melodic interval with the given note.

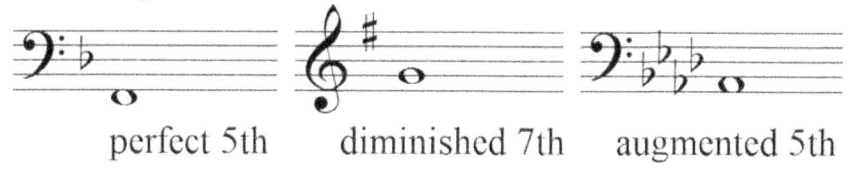

   perfect 5th   diminished 7th   augmented 5th

3. Rewrite this passage in the alto clef.

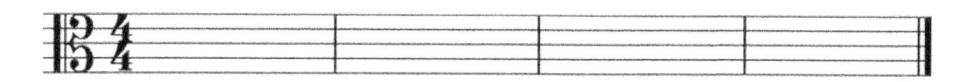

4. Give the letter names of the strings of the viola.

Book 5 page 75

Test 8

1. This rhythm begins on the first beat of the bar. Put in the missing bar lines.

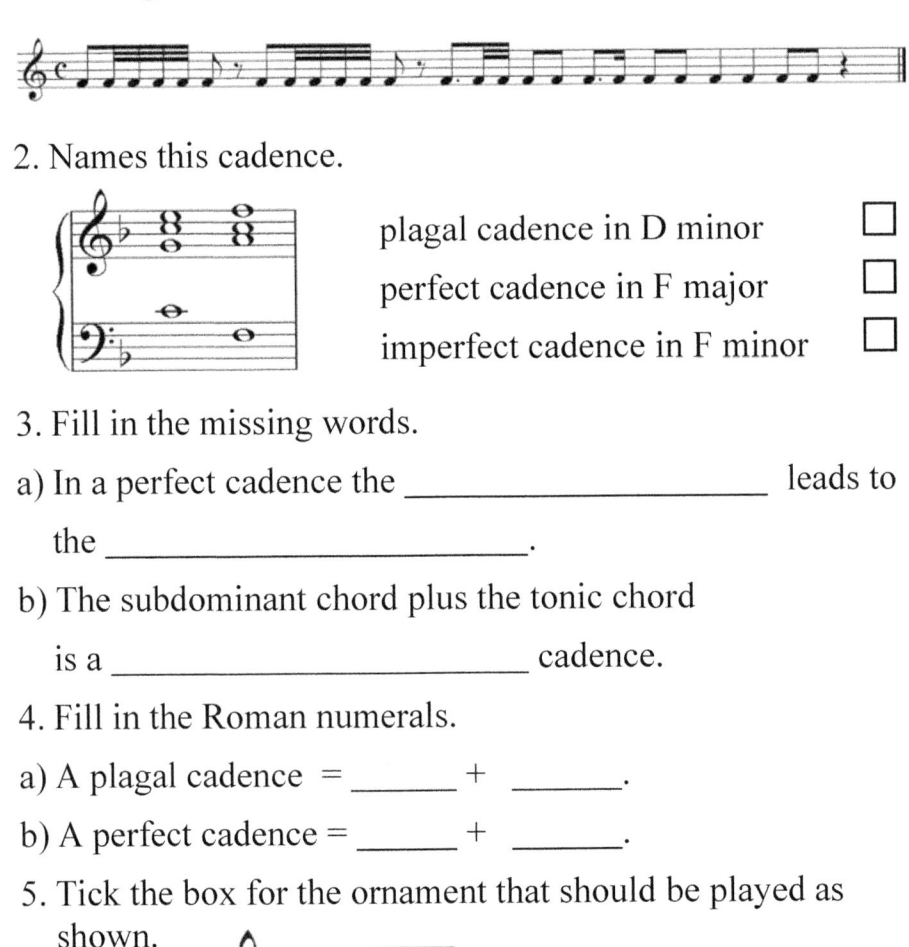

2. Names this cadence.

   plagal cadence in D minor ☐
   perfect cadence in F major ☐
   imperfect cadence in F minor ☐

3. Fill in the missing words.

a) In a perfect cadence the _____ leads to the _____.

b) The subdominant chord plus the tonic chord is a _____ cadence.

4. Fill in the Roman numerals.

a) A plagal cadence = _____ + _____.

b) A perfect cadence = _____ + _____.

5. Tick the box for the ornament that should be played as shown.

   tr ~~~ ☐   ☐   ☐

Book 5 page 76

Test 9

After looking at this extract, answer the questions below.

1. Name the ornament (♪) in bar 2. _____

2. Name the ornament (𝄽) in bar 4. _____

3. Give the meaning of Leggiero.
_____

4. How should you play the notes of the 3rd beat in bar 1?
_____

5. What does the sign mean over the note in bar 5?
_____

6. Give the meaning of *pp*.
_____

7. Complete bar 6 with a rest or rests.

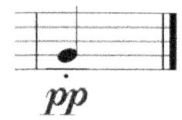

8. Name all the notes in bar 4 in order.
____   ____   ____   ____   ____   ____

9. Give the meaning of
   (a) *mp* _____
   (b) ⟨cresc.⟩ _____

Book 5 page 77

Test 10

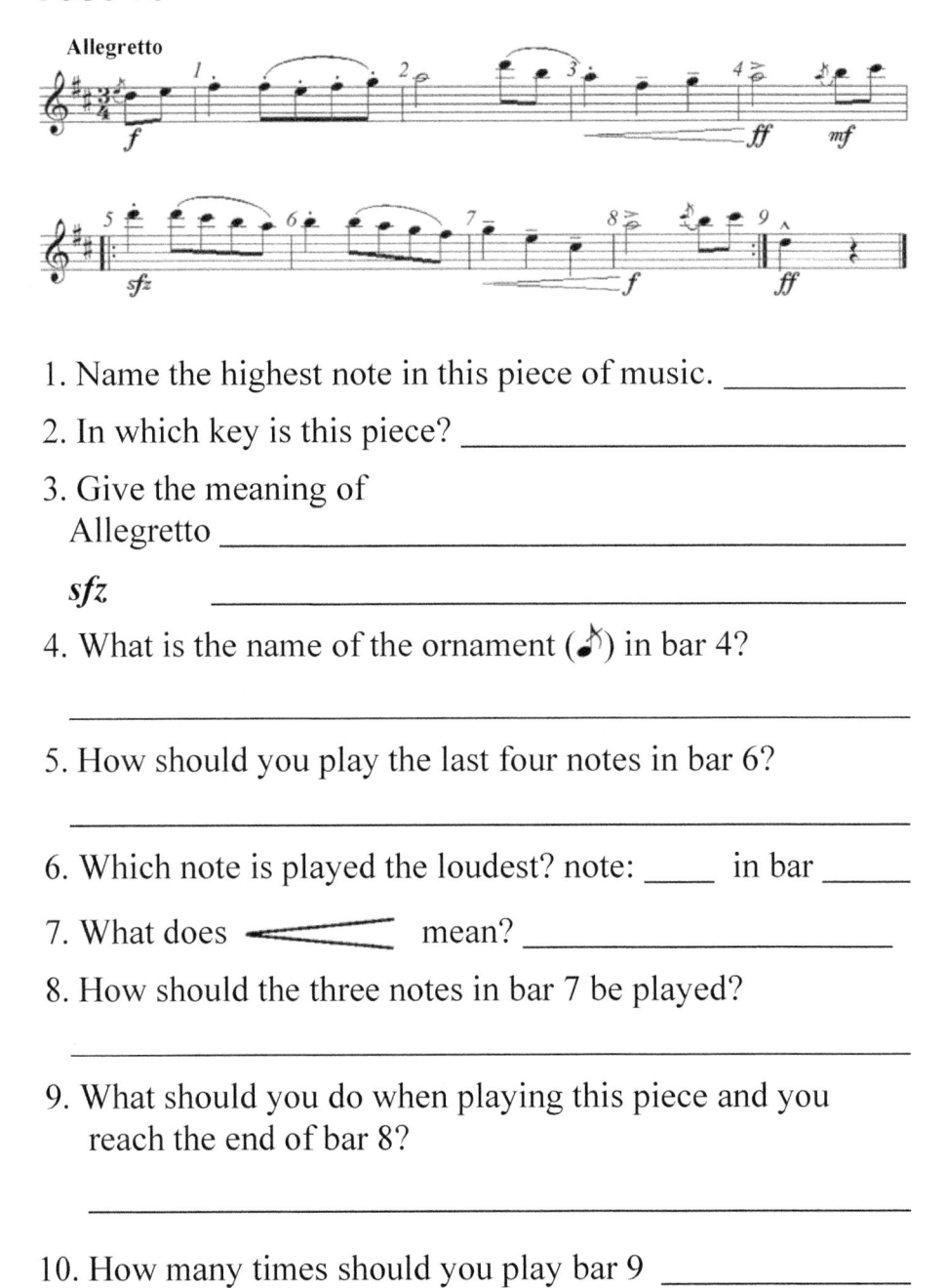

1. Name the highest note in this piece of music. _____

2. In which key is this piece? _____

3. Give the meaning of
   Allegretto _____

   sfz   _____

4. What is the name of the ornament (♪) in bar 4?

   _____

5. How should you play the last four notes in bar 6?

   _____

6. Which note is played the loudest? note: _____ in bar _____

7. What does ⟨ mean? _____

8. How should the three notes in bar 7 be played?

   _____

9. What should you do when playing this piece and you reach the end of bar 8?

   _____

10. How many times should you play bar 9 _____

Book 5 page 78

MUSICAL TERMS AND SIGNS

Musical terms

A (à) - at, to, by, for, in the style of
Aber - but
Accelerando - becoming gradually faster
Adagietto - rather slow
Adagio - slow, leisurely
Adagissimo - very slow
Affetuoso - tenderly
Affrettando - hurrying
Agitato - agitated
Alla - in the style of
    Alla marcia - in the style of a march
    Alla polacca - in the style of a Polonaise
Allargando - broadening out
Allegretto - slightly slower than allegro
Allegro - lively, reasonably fast
    Allegro assai - very quick
Amabile - amiable, pleasant
Andante - at a walking pace
Andantino - a little slower or a little faster than andante
Animato - lively, animated
Animé - animated, lively
Appassionata - with passion
Assai - very
Assez - enough, sufficiently
Attacca - go on immediately
A tempo - resume the normal speed
Ausdruck - expression
Avec - with
Bewegt - with movement. agitated
Bravura - with boldness and spirit
Breit - broad, expansive

Brillante - sparkling, brilliant
Cantabile - in a singing style
Cantando - in a singing style
Cédez - yield, relax the speed
Coda - a passage, at the end, to round off a piece of music
Col; Con - with
    Con anima - with deep feeling - soul
    Con brio - with vigour
    Con moto - with movement
    Con spirito - with spirit, life, energy
Crescendo [cresc.] - gradually louder
Da capo [D.C.] - from the beginning
Dal segno [D.S.] - repeat from the sign
Deciso - with determination
Decrescendo [decresc.] - gradually softer
Delicato - delicately
Diminuendo [dim.] - gradually softer
Dolce - sweetly
Dolcissimo - very sweetly
Dolente - sadly
Dolore - grief, sorrow
Doppio - double
    Doppio movimento - double the speed
Douce - sweet
Ein - a, one
Einfach - simple
En dehors - prominent
Energico - with energy
Espressione - expression
Espressivo [Espress., Espr.] – with expression, feeling
Et - and
Etwas - somewhat, rather
Facile – easy

Fortepiano [*fp*] - loud, then immediately soft
Fine - the end
Forte [*f*] - loud
Fortissimo [*ff*] - very loud
Forza - force, power
Forzando [*fz*] - with a strong accent
Fröhlich - cheerful, joyful
Fuoco - fire
Furioso - furiously
Giocoso - merry
Giusto - exact, proper
Grandioso - in a grand manner
Grave - very slow
Grazioso - gracefully
Immer - always
Lacrimoso - tearfully
Langsam - slow
Largamente - in a broad style
Larghetto - faster than largo
Largo - slow & stately, broad
Lebhaft - lively
Legatissimo - as smoothly as possible
Legato - smoothly
Légèrement - lightly
Leggiero - lightly
Lent - slow
Lento - slowly
L'Istesso - the same
Ma - but
    Ma non troppo - but not too much
Maestoso - majestically
Mais - but
Marcato - strong accent

Martellato - hammered out
Marziale - in a military style
Mässig - at a moderate speed
Meno - less
    Meno mosso - less movement
Mesto - sadly
Mezzo forte [*mf*] - moderately loud
Mezzo piano [*mp*] - moderately soft
Misterioso - mysteriously
Mit - with
Moderato - at a moderate pace
Modéré - at a moderate speed
Moins - less
Molto - much
Morendo - dying away
Mosso - movement
Moto - movement
Movimento - movement
Nicht - not
Niente - nothing
Nobilmente - nobly
Non - not
    Non tanto - not so much
    Non troppo - not too much
Ohne - without
Parlando - in a speaking manner
Parlante - in a speaking manner
Pastorale - in a pastoral style
Patetico - with feeling
Perdendosi - dying away
Pesante - heavily
Peu - little
Pianissimo [*pp*] - very soft
Piano [*p*] – soft

Piu - more
Pizzicato [pizz.] - plucked
Plus - more
Poco a poco - little by little
Possibile - possible
    Presto possibile - as fast as possible
Presser - hurry
    En pressant - hurrying on
Prestissimo - as fast as possible
Presto - very quick
Quasi - as if, resembling
Ralentir - slow down
Rallentando [rall.] - becoming gradually slower
Retenu - held back
    En retenant - holding back
Risoluto - boldly
Ritardando [ritard. rit.] - gradually slower
Ritenuto [riten. rit.] - hold back, slower at once
Ritmico - rhythmically
Ruhig - peaceful
Sans - without
Scherzando - playfully
Scherzo - a joke
Schnell - fast
Semplice - simple
Sempre - always
Senza - without
Sforzando [*sf*, *sfz*] - with a sudden accent
Simile [Sim.] - in the same way
Slargando - gradually slower
Slentando - gradually slower
Smorzando - dying away
Sonoro - with rich tone

Sopra - above
Sospirando - sighing
Sostenuto - sustained
Sotto - below
    Sotto voce - in an undertone
Spiritoso - lively, animated
Staccatissimo - very detached
Staccato - short, detached
Stringendo - gradually faster
Subito - suddenly
Süss - sweet
Tanto - so much
Tempo - speed, time
    Tempo comodo - at a comfortable speed
    Tempo primo - resume the original speed
    Tempo rubato - with some freedom of time
Tenuto - held on
Tranquillo - quietly
Traurig - sad
Très - very
Triste, Tristamente - sad, sorrowful
Troppo - too much
Tutti - all
Und - and
Veloce - swift
Vibrato - vibrating
Vif - lively
Vite - quick
Vivace, Vivo - lively, quick
Vivacissimo - very lively
Voce - voice
Voll – full

Volta - time
   Prima volta - first time
   Seconda volta - second time
Volti subito [V.S.] - turn the page quickly
Wenig - little
Wieder - again
Zart - tender, delicate
Zu - to, too

Common Alternative Terms

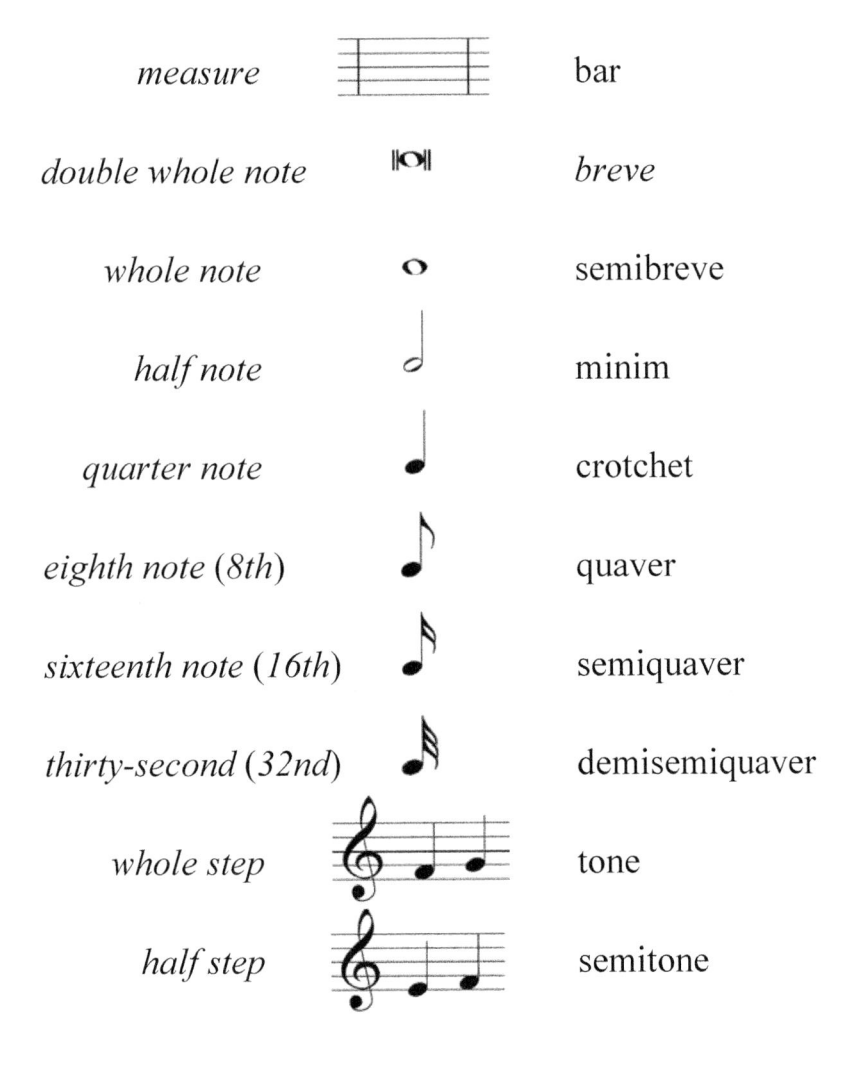

measure		bar
double whole note		breve
whole note		semibreve
half note		minim
quarter note		crotchet
eighth note (8th)		quaver
sixteenth note (16th)		semiquaver
thirty-second (32nd)		demisemiquaver
whole step		tone
half step		semitone

Musical signs and symbols

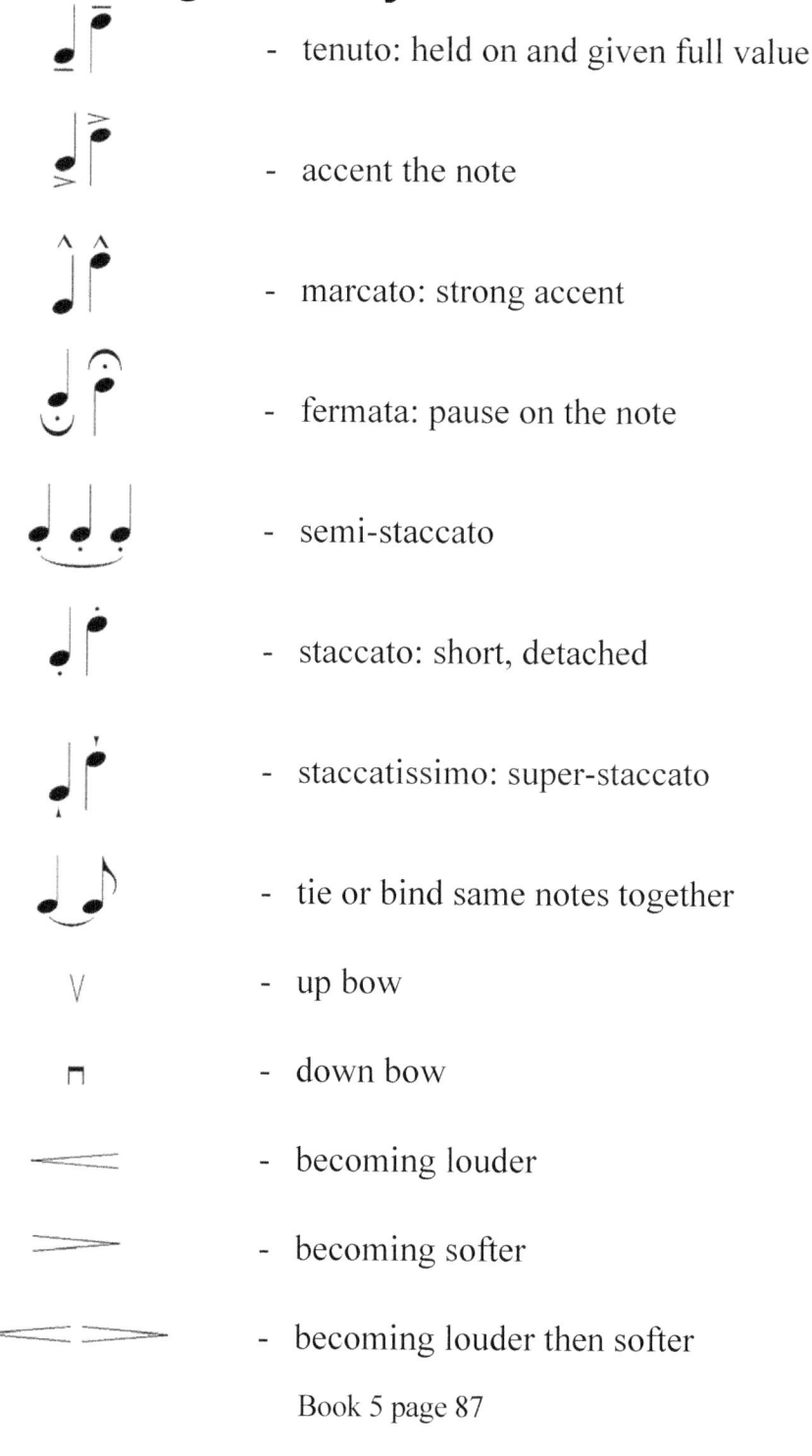

- tenuto: held on and given full value
- accent the note
- marcato: strong accent
- fermata: pause on the note
- semi-staccato
- staccato: short, detached
- staccatissimo: super-staccato
- tie or bind same notes together
- up bow
- down bow
- becoming louder
- becoming softer
- becoming louder then softer

Book 5 page 87

- start repeat and end repeat

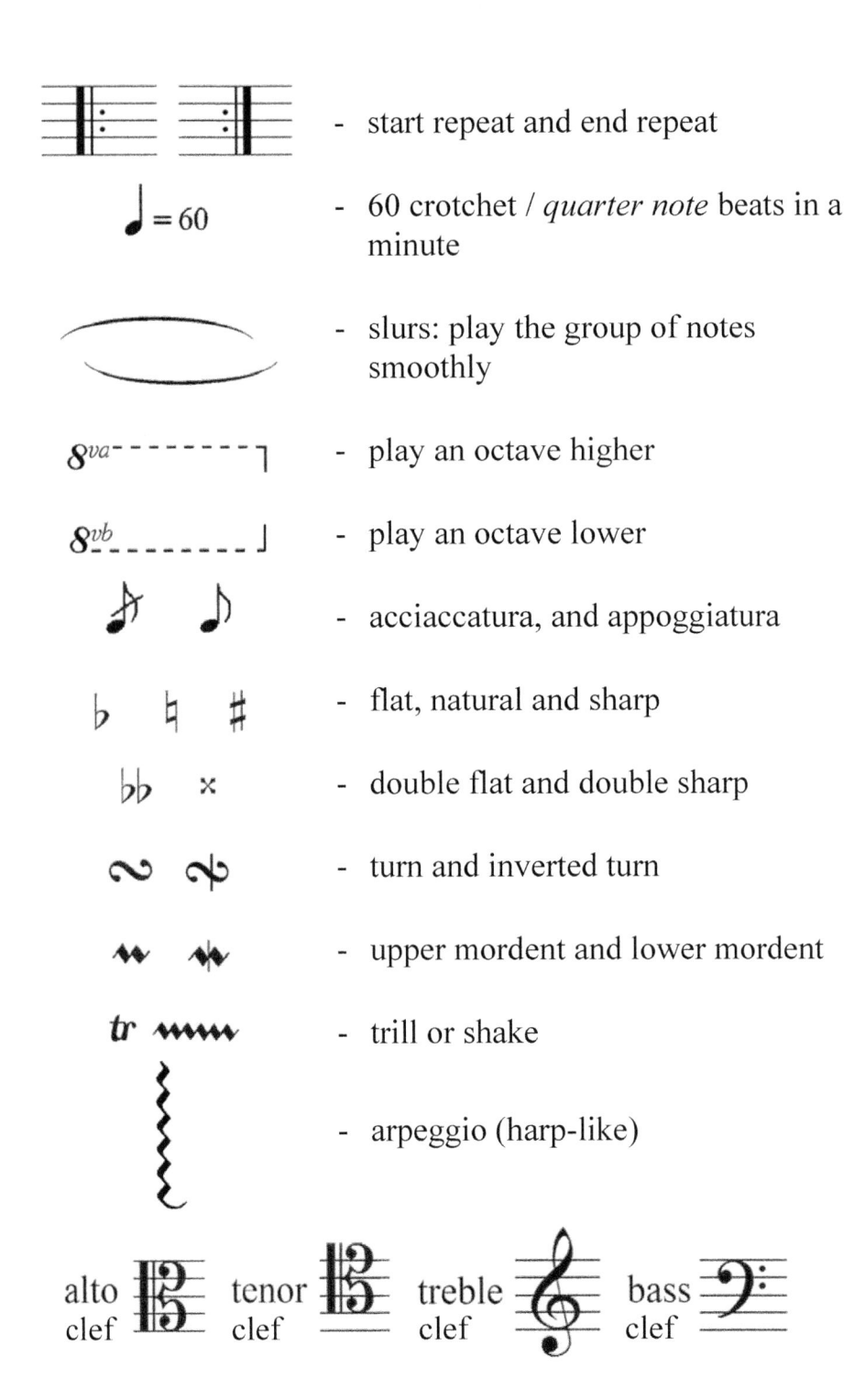

- 60 crotchet / *quarter note* beats in a minute

- slurs: play the group of notes smoothly

- play an octave higher

- play an octave lower

- acciaccatura, and appoggiatura

- flat, natural and sharp

- double flat and double sharp

- turn and inverted turn

- upper mordent and lower mordent

- trill or shake

- arpeggio (harp-like)

alto clef   tenor clef   treble clef   bass clef